Living Devotion *and the* Whole Desire of God

Living Devotion *and the* Whole Desire of God

ROBERT JOHN SPRIDDELL

RESOURCE *Publications* · Eugene, Oregon

LIVING DEVOTION AND THE WHOLE DESIRE OF GOD

Copyright © 2025 Robert John Spriddell. All rights reserved. Except for brief quotations in critical publications or reviews, no part of this book may be reproduced in any manner without prior written permission from the publisher. Write: Permissions, Wipf and Stock Publishers, 199 W. 8th Ave., Suite 3, Eugene, OR 97401.

Resource Publications
An Imprint of Wipf and Stock Publishers
199 W. 8th Ave., Suite 3
Eugene, OR 97401

www.wipfandstock.com

PAPERBACK ISBN: 979-8-3852-4872-8
HARDCOVER ISBN: 979-8-3852-4873-5
EBOOK ISBN: 979-8-3852-4874-2
VERSION NUMBER 06/03/25

All Scripture references are taken from the NEW KING JAMES VERSION (NKJV): Scripture taken from the NEW KING JAMES VERSION®. Copyright© 1982 by Thomas Nelson, Inc. Used by permission. All rights reserved.

This book is dedicated to my wife and daughter, Michelle and Georgina, to whom I am extremely grateful for all their time in listening to me deliberating on these subjects for years.

Psalm 118:19
Open to me the gates of righteousness;
I will go through them, And I will praise the L<small>ORD</small>.

Contents

About the Author | ix
Preface and Structure | xi

Part 1: The Whole Desire of God
"One Thing Is Needed" | 3
The Whole Desire of God | 15
The Pearl of Our Devotion | 35
Positional Identity and Positional Blessings | 48
Positional Responsibility | 80
The Privacy of Devotion | 94

Part 2: The Precious Gates of Devotion
The Heart Attitude of the Devotionist | 103
The Precious Gates of Devotion | 117

Part 3: The Participation of Devotion
The Precious Gift of Positional Devotion | 141
Positional Devotion and the Reading of Scripture | 151
Devotional Reading | 160
The Immersive Reading of Scripture and the
    Precious Gates of Devotion | 166

Devotional Reading Methods | 186

Method 1: Nurturing Our Souls Through Devotional "Lectio Divina" | 189

Method 2: Nurturing Our Souls Through Speaking Scripture and Reflective Reading | 196

Method 3: The Personal Examination Method of Devotional Reading and Contemplation | 199

Post-Reading: Waiting in the Outer Courts of His Presence | 206

Personal Study for Great Gain | 209

Positional Devotional Prayer | 213

The Precious Gates of Devotion in Private Prayer | 228

Part 4: Living Devotion

The Exit Gate: The Precious Gate of Received Peace | 249

Living Devotion | 259

Conclusion: The Glorious Tapestry of Living Devotion | 283

Appendix: The Blessed Positional Blessings: Passages for Reflective Reading, Lectio Divina, and Private Prayer | 287

Bibliography | 301

About the Author

Since becoming a Christian in 2000, Robert developed a deep personal interest in theology, doctrine, hermeneutics, church history, and monastic writings. He has taught home Bible studies over many years and has also been invited to teach and preach at various churches as a lay visitor. He has a BA(hons) and MPhil from Birmingham and Reading Universities, England, and works in property and business advisory. He lives in Cambridge, England, with his wife and daughter.

Disclaimer

The opinions expressed in this book are personal, as is much of the thinking that formulated the book in the first place. This book has been written with the perspectives of ordinary Christians in mind and is addressed to them, to help nurture and edify. I believe the opinions expressed to be entirely biblical and to have been nurtured over many years of reading and contemplating the issues involved. My hope is that the reader will be blessed by what is discussed and how the ideas and concepts are presented and, through it all, that Jesus will be further glorified.

Robert John Spriddell, 2025

Preface and Structure

THIS BOOK HAS BEEN created for the ordinary Christian believer living day-to-day in the reality of the real world and addresses some of the biblical and practical issues involved in our devotion. We will explore the real imperatives of God and His expectations and requirements as they relate to the believer's spiritual life—which are not necessarily what we think they are. The book is designed to edify, enrich, and encourage by exposing the only matter that God is ultimately interested in when it comes to the individual Christian believer: our hearts and our devotion.

The approach that has been taken within this book is neither purely academic nor strictly theological. While the contents are centered on the Bible, I have endeavored to address the subjects in a way that I hope is interesting, edifying, and accessible to all believers.

The particular focus is on what are known in some circles as positional truths—though in this book I have chosen to prefer to refer to, or rather refine the definition of, them as "Positional Blessings"—and how these can be used augment our approach to, and practice of, devotion. This then helps posit and explore various methods to engender and strengthen the most precious of responsibilities: the nurturing of our souls through what we term "Living Devotion." In order to develop this into a manageable format that I hope the believer will be able to use to foster their times of devotion, I have developed the metaphor of passing through "Precious Gates of Devotion" into the presence of God. I develop this metaphor of passing through these Precious Gates as a practical and spiritual methodology that can be utilized and adapted, or simply considered as a means of edification and spiritual engagement.

When gathering my thoughts around the content of this book, I felt that it needed to address some of the biblical theological issues around devotion, while wanting it not to be purely dry theology, but also that it should help point to methods and ways that a believer might be able to use to augment their own devotion. At the same time, self-help or instructive guides err on the side of being subjective and legalistic at the same time and are obviously very culturally specific in their acceptance and applicability. And yet, to write a book on devotion that merely concentrates on the *why* of theology without at least exploring some questions like "How can I put this into practice?" would probably be deeply unsatisfying for the ordinary Christian reader and would, in the end, prove to have little or no impact on the believer's devotional or spiritual life. It would, in other words, completely miss the purpose of writing it in the first place. Thus, to present a book that is neither a full-on theological study nor a self-help guide but which attempts to straddle the *why* with the *how* is what this book attempts to do. Accordingly, I have adopted a few oblique references in the Bible and metaphorically adapted them as a bridge or conduit between the theory and practice of devotion while simultaneously enhancing and stimulating spiritual development.

The book has been divided into four parts that demonstrate the flow from theology to practice, to draw the ordinary believer forward in engaging with God in a manner that conforms with both biblical practices and the practical restrictions of everyday life.

Part 1 examines the theme of devotion through the Scriptures by taking the perspective of what is required of the believer by God. It examines how devotion is a missing aspect of how we assess the activities of normal believers throughout the Bible and begins to center on one of the major themes that run through the course of the book: how the believer's faith and devotion can be dramatically enhanced and developed with an understanding and appropriation of "Positional Blessings."

Part 2 introduces the concept of the "Precious Gates of Devotion" as a metaphor that is expounded upon and utilized as a means of conveying the journey that believers take when seeking to enter into the presence of God during their times of devotion. We have chosen this metaphor from the beautiful imagery conjured by King David in Ps 118:19 and have given these gates names based the biblical precedent as described in Acts

3:2. We expound upon how the Scriptures describe our engagement with our souls and their desire to be in the presence of God, and by developing the concept of passing through the Gates of Devotion, we explore how the believer can establish a mindset and framework for the preparation and participation in devotion.

Part 3 exhorts the believer to fully consider the beauty of how our position and status in the household of God affects our approach to and practice of devotion. By way of assisting in this, we develop various methods to engender and strengthen the most precious of responsibilities: the nurturing of our souls through the personal reading of Scripture and through private prayer. This is both practical and theological but is not meant to be seen as either a comprehensive guide or blueprint to foster devotion, but rather as means to open the believer's heart and mind to means of entering into the presence of God.

In part 4 we explore the beauty of Living Devotion within the overall context of the Precious Gates and specifically through consideration of the exit gate, called the Precious Gate of Received Peace This is the Gate that is taken as believers leave the presence of God in their times of devotional acts of reading and private prayer. The focus is on living in and with the peace of God so that our lives become filled with His presence and devotion itself becomes a living part of everything we do and are—it is termed "Living Devotion." We explore what this concept means for us and how it transforms everything to the glory and honor of God.

Appendix: "The Blessed Positional Blessings." The appendix seeks to serve as a resource that believers can use for their own private prayer, reflective reading, and contemplation through Lectio Divina. Accordingly, it provides a breakdown of the primary Scripture texts relating to what is discussed in the book as being the Positional Blessings and Positional Identity in Christ as they relate to every believer. These are designed as a tool for the reader to use, much like what is discussed in the form of Lectio Divina.

Bibliography: I have put forward a list of books and resources that have been inspirational and informative to the thinking behind what is posited and discussed throughout the book. It is my hope that these will encourage further research and act as a point of reference for the reader.

PART 1

The Whole Desire of God

"One Thing Is Needed"

> O my God, since Thou art with me, and I must now, in obedience to Thy commands, apply my mind to these outward things, I beseech Thee to grant me the grace to continue in Thy presence; and to this end do Thou prosper me with Thy assistance, receive all my works, and possess all my affections.
>
> Brother Lawrence, *The Practice of the Presence of God*

If we are honest, I suspect that many of us have asked the question "What is the purpose of being a Christian?" or perhaps the deeper one of "What does the Lord actually want from me?" I am sure that many of us who consider ourselves to be ordinary, everyday Christians have felt at times a little disenfranchised in our Christian life, compared with what we are taught, and are led to believe, it "should" look like. Many are unsure where they stand regarding their salvation and are insecure in their relationship with Christ. Many feel second-rate and unsure about the commitment to their faith as they look at the seeming proficiency of their fellow Christians around them—feelings that are exacerbated when, if they are being honest with themselves, all they feel really is disconnected from God and their faith on a day-to-day basis, not owing to any lack of willingness but fundamentally due to the realities of everyday life.

As ordinary Christians, we can sometimes feel deflated in our walk with God, especially when even our church life is lackluster and enfeebled. Even when this is not the case, conversely this, too, can eventually result in feelings of condemnation, guilt, and even apprehension as we feel that in reality our personal lives do not seem to measure up to what is apparently required of us by those who live lives that for the most part are totally disconnected from the realities and pressures of our own everyday lives—mounting more pressure and greater senses of inadequacy and alienation in our faith. This, to be clear, is not owing to any lack of willingness or concern on our part; it's just that "life" happens, and then we start to feel even more condemned as we fail to live up to what we are told is to be expected of us. But why is this?

Over the years, I have come to refer to this inevitability as the "Monday Morning Syndrome," where what is learned or experienced on a Sunday at church or during fellowship virtually evaporates as soon as Monday morning comes with all the pressures of everyday life: be it school runs, journey to work, work itself, and the pressures and grind of real life. For years, I have wrestled with the question of where my faith and walk with God fits into this and how I learn to "be" and function as a Christian in this environment when there is no guidance or teachings that seemingly address these very real issues that most ordinary Christians have and have always had. It seems that we so quickly become reabsorbed into what we call the "real world" and soon put our faith to one side as we focus on the practical needs of daily life. If we reflect at all on this, and are totally honest, then perhaps for most of us, this "Christian" aspect of our lives becomes simply something which is performed and participated in at the time out of perfunctory obedience or a skewed sense of obligation. And yet, we also know that our faith in God demands otherwise and that deep down, we feel that something is missing and yearn for a more profound spiritual relationship with Him. While we are unsure of what that necessarily entails, we suspect that it has much to do with the fact that God deserves more from us, and we instinctively know that this deeper spirituality has little to do with mere knowledge and more to do with living and being in fellowship with Him. There becomes a divide between what we come to think, and are taught, about what our Christian lives should be and the demands of our normal, daily lives. But is this meant to be the case? Is there something we are missing or are not being taught? My contention is that we have been looking in the wrong direction—for surely the right questions to ask here are, "What does God, not man, actually require from us?" and "What are His real expectations of me in my day-to-day life?" The exploration of the answers to these questions permeates the rationale for all that follows in this book.

Throughout the Bible it has always been clear that what God expects and requires from us is that He, and our relationship with Him, is to be our primary concern. Our priority is meant to be to God and our own relationship with Him first—all else stems and flows from this, and all else is secondary to this. If this is not right, then all else is mere showmanship bordering on hypocrisy. Of course, God understands that our practical daily obligations are real and existential in the real world—they matter to us and therefore they matter to Him. However, perhaps we have been taught to place too much importance and emphasis on works and activities (as spiritual as they may seem), to the detriment of our own personal relationship with Jesus. In other words we neglect, to our utter detriment, our devotion to God.

Do not get me wrong; I am totally convinced of the complete inerrancy of the Bible, that it is the very word of God Himself, and that all it says is truth in its entirety (Ps 119:160). God is in complete control of all things, including the future. His word is consistent in telling us that what He has said will happen, will happen—and thus there is both nothing that one can do to alter the fact and, therefore, no point in obsessing about matters beyond our own control or sphere of influence. This is not meant to diminish in any way our concerns and worries that we naturally have about the future given the state of the world and events of the recent past, not to mention future upheavals. Indeed, one of the main motivations for writing this book has come from a deep consideration and contemplation of what my response should be as an ordinary Christian to these tensions. The fact that the Bible predicts all these things is both comforting at one level and challenging at another, as we wrestle with the impact of these events and phenomena not just at the macrolevel but how they affect our own personal lives in the here and now in the very difficult real world of physical, emotional, financial, and spiritual stresses and strains. Oft-given biblical platitudes of "Be anxious for nothing" and "Seek the Kingdom of God first," though well-intentioned, can appear to be demeaning not only to the giver of such phrases but also to the contemporary recipients of them whose lives are being stretched, often to breaking point. Indeed, even faithful Christians of all ages struggle to remain true in this onslaught, on the one hand, and resistant against apathy and weariness, on the other. There comes a point when, as the real world imposes itself so fully on oneself and upon loved ones, one must reflect on what is necessary and spiritually satisfying individually, but also on what is of practical spiritual benefit to the very real needs of fellow Christians who require above all else security and assurance of peace with God. And so, one starts to ask questions.

The goal of our faith, in this life, is the strengthening and enjoyment of our relationship with God—and perhaps even more importantly, being able to impart hope, comfort, and the love of God to those whom we care most about and to the world around us. While reflecting on my own inadequacies in this area, I have begun to reexamine the Scriptures and devotional writings in search of a more profoundly encompassing relationship with Christ whereby His presence is more real, and through that my spirit and soul are nurtured. As such, I have come to realize that the more biblical, reverential, faithful, and spiritual attitude or response to God is learning to focus on what He actually requires us to focus on— being secure in the knowledge of His sovereign control and, even more importantly, at peace with this knowledge. At some point, though, we all should ask the question, "What does God really want from us?" Put simply the answer is as follows: all God wants—and all He has ever wanted—is willing, dedicated devotion and for us to experience and enjoy His presence. This book is in part an attempt to expound and expand upon this answer, and I hope that it brings the reader comfort. In an age when all, including most Christians, are living through times of huge upheaval in their everyday lives, we are all in need of certainty and consistency. We need to draw closer to God and to know that it is this that sustains us and that it this that is required of us: to love Him and to be devoted to him.

The One Interconnected Commandment

There is, and only ever has been, one interconnected commandment of God, and it should be the only thing that concerns any believer. It is the commandment that God gave to the Israelites and upon which the rest of the law of Moses hung, and it is the one and only interconnected commandment that Jesus gave to the disciples to take out into the world, and hence it is the one commandment upon which the foundation of the church hung: *to love the Lord your God with all your heart and to love your neighbor as yourself* (Deut 6:1; Lev 19:18; Matt 22:36–40). And all He wants—all He has ever wanted—in return is willing, dedicated devotion.

It is interesting that there is no consolidated theology around this, and yet it is so utterly vital to all of us. This being perhaps even more so for those who live "everyday lives" in the "real world." Sometimes it feels that we ordinary Christians are expected to just automatically know how we are to live as Christians in this world around us and that simply by following various instructions to read our Bibles, we should just absorb this knowledge. We are told that we need to have personal relationships with God but receive little or no actual guidance as to what that is or involves. So, when we do ask natural questions—"How then do we live as Christians within this world, not just when we are among other believers but during the course of our daily lives?"—we seem to be given just vague instructions or blank expressions. The only adequate response to this is found not in others but deep within us and in the acknowledgment that we hunger for something that only God Himself can satisfy—His presence. As we will discuss, this hunger comes from the Holy Spirit within us who believe. It is the hunger of our souls yearning to be in the presence of God.

It is here then that we see the other great truth within the Bible: our own responsibility. In our consumerist age, we have become lulled as Christians into believing that our own growth and the deepening of our faith is something that "happens" to us, that we somehow absorb it from others through some strange form of spiritual osmosis or are content to be merely spoon fed from the pulpit or screen. The Bible, though, says that the opposite is true. Within the doctrine of the sovereignty of God, it has always been that it is His responsibility to reveal His word and instruct us; but it is our own responsibility to ask God, it is our responsibility to act upon what is instructed, and it is our responsibility to seek the Lord.

The Reality of God

The entire revelation of God, through nature and through His word, leads to the indisputable contention of the "Reality of God." What is meant by this phrase, the Reality of God, is that if God is real, and if all that is revealed in nature and in the Bible is true, including with regard to His sovereignty, ways, and characteristics, then our only reasonable response to this "Reality" is to respond accordingly—not in terms of token gestures or acknowledgments but in a way that permeates all that we are. The practice and pursuit of the Reality of God is not only living and breathing His sovereignty (1 Chr 29:10–13) but is participatory in that our lives become intertwined into the kingdom of God, such that our perspectives and God's are inseparable. As we pivot ever closer to God and He draws closer to us in response (Jas 4:8), the Reality of God becomes the paradigm that affects and shapes everything that we do and everything that we are as Christians—from our worship of Him through to how we interact with others, how we perceive ourselves down to our very thought processes (Col 3:17, Phil 4:8–9). This "Reality" includes a greater realization, appropriation, and appreciation of His Providence, attributes, and direct personal involvement; in other words we see His presence continually and that we are never away from it and can never leave it, for as the psalmist says, "Where can I go from Your Spirit? Or where can I flee from Your presence?" (Ps 139:7). The composite reality of this Reality, so to speak, is a divine infusion that we cannot separate or divorce ourselves from. And if we try to do so, then our whole understanding of God is diminished, which to some extent has been the great tragedy of our modern mindset. This mindset manifests not only as a new perspective but a different psychology within the believer. It is a transformation itself that translates into a whole new psyche that reflects the renewing of our minds by the Holy Spirit (Rom 12:2). For once we are transformed by and into the Reality of God, we cannot but live by it and within it—to do otherwise not only seems dishonoring to God but even becomes irrational to the believer. We see this so clearly in the lives of those in the Bible, such as King David and the apostles of course, and throughout the ages through so many men and women of God as well. But it is not a mindset that is the prerogative of, and can only be possessed by, the few and the super godly, but is available to all who believe. It is the distinguishing distinctive that we see in the likes of the psalmists who have what we refer to later on as hearts that are aligned with God. Heart and mind alignment in the Spirit of God, though, is not just a trait for the "super-worthy" but categorically available to all, and every bit part and parcel of the gifts that all who believe in Christ are given by Him. As we absorb the Reality of God into our lives, so our devotion is shaped toward Him and becomes entirely encompassing and deeply profound. The entire revelation of God makes it abundantly clear that devotion per se is not only our only reasonable response to His grace and mercy, nor does it just reveal that it is His expectation of all who believe, but that most surprisingly devotion is integral to our very beings, and we are only complete when in His presence.

The Bible is not the ultimate purpose of the Bible—God is. At one extreme, the Bible is not just a form of literature to be studied, dissected, and analyzed, but neither is it to be virtually worshiped, for it is the created not the Creator. At the other end, we could see the reading of the Bible as mere legalism and obligation, even as an exercise to be undertaken out of guilt and compulsion. In order to progress from this conundrum, we need to retreat a little and ask the question, "Why did God inspire the Bible?" What was His intention for the original readers of it then as it was written and read, as it was gradually collated, and for readers ever since, including us now? With all the time that has passed, as the readers and hearers of it had come originally from the Middle East and have expanded to various cultures in various times throughout the world (which was clearly in God's mind when He inspired the writings and even the original recorded dialogues and events), there can only be one possible answer to this question of why, and it is of utmost importance for the everyday believer to know and understand the answer to that question. The answer can only be quite simply this: to inspire and inform devotion to God.

We shall see that throughout the Bible what God has always simply wanted is a "people unto Himself"—which effectively means our heart belonging and being dedicated to Him. God has gone to unparalleled and extreme lengths to demonstrate Himself to us as being worthy, and to have a devoted relationship with us. It is how we respond to this that matters.

What Then Is Devotion for the Christian?

I wonder what people generally think of, or what images they conjure up, when they use the word "devotion"—private times of study, private prayer, journaling, scriptural study? All these are very valid devotional activities, but because these themselves can become legalistic, monotonous, and undertaken under compulsion, we need to go deeper to discover what "devotion" is. My contention herein is that devotion is a heart attitude, first and foremost. It is not about works or doing or activities (though of course these can be how it manifests), but it is about immersion, absorption of the Reality of God, and our response to that Reality. Put simply, devotion is the only reasonable and required response of the believer to the Reality of God in our lives.

Devotion is, in a manner speaking, the projection of our hearts unto God through the influence and guidance of the Holy Spirit. Devotion is directed to God and to God alone. "The Devotionist" is a term and title I have deployed in this series to describe one who understands the presence of God by receiving and appropriating the "spirit of devotion" from the Holy Spirit. In this manner, devotion is not just about understanding or head-knowledge, and it is also not just the activity people regard it as or associate with it. For devotion not only comes from the heart, but it is also the heart of the believer. It is not about "doing," it is ultimately about being and identification. It is not works, for even the "activity" of devotion is not devotion. Devotion is all-encompassing, all-absorbing, and ever-present within the believer. As we will discuss later on, the position of the believer in the family of God is one of a Devotionist. Just as all believers are indwelled by the Holy Spirit, so all believers are Devotionists. What is missing from all biblical theology is that this is what God actually wants us primarily to be and what, reverentially, is actually all that is required of us.

We must correct this single misconception right from the start: devotion is not a legalistic "works activity." Devotion is not about what we do, how often, or where we do it; it is much, much more than that. It is in fact all-pervasive. In order for devotion as a concept to comply with the precepts of God, it has to glorify God alone and not us. Acts of devotion only glorify God, and are therefore only accepted by God, when they come from a believer's heart. And because true devotion comes from the heart and is honoring God, it is therefore all He requires and ever required from those who love Him. What is meant by this is that devotion or the desire for it can only come from deep within us. It is the expression of the Holy Spirit engaging with our souls.

Paradoxically, the Bible also declares that God is not limited to His word. As such, devotion should not be limited and restricted to mere Bible readings, study, or even to prayer—as important as these are. Our devotion with God is all-encompassing and directed at Him in every way through the means that He values. What this means practically is that our devotion, and our personal dedication to that devotion, becomes our most willing sacrifice to our most worthy and most wonderful God.

From the very start though, it is important to make sure that we realize that "there is no condemnation for those who are in Christ Jesus" (Rom 8:1). If one feels lacking in thinking about devotion it is because we have been taught to think of it again as something which has to be performed or "done." This is a works mindset and is unbiblical, un-Christian even in the true sense, as we will show. But we need to understand now that devotion is more than a mindset or even a set of performed activities that reflect that mindset; it is so much deeper than that, for it is our position and it is our identity. Devotion is the way we think, not what we do, and it comes from the Holy Spirit. It is honoring God because of who He is and what He has done; it is letting Him be all-pervasive in our lives because that is what He is.

The Spirit of Devotion

During the course of this book, we will see how dedication and devotion weaves their way through the Bible—but where does the desire for devotion come from first? This desire does not come to us naturally, for it is a good desire, and hence because it is good and pertains to the spiritual, so it must come from God, for "every good gift and every perfect gift is from above, and comes down from the Father of lights, with whom there is no variation or shadow of turning." (Jas 1:17) However, it is true that in many Christian circles, devotion is probably a concept that is known of but considered secondary at best, treated with derision by some and even with a hint of suspicion by many.

The Bible teaches us that the natural man cannot see the spiritual things of God (1 Cor 2). Therefore, the actual desire to engage in devotion is a sign of the Holy Spirit being within the believer (or upon the person, in the Old Testament). This then, in doctrinal terms as we'll discuss below, becomes an aspect of the believer's position in the household of God, for the Lord "has blessed us with every spiritual blessing in the heavenly places in Christ" (Eph 1:3). A more meaningful and profound relationship with God through devotion is, without doubt, both a good gift and a spiritual blessing. Further on we will consider the beauty of this and its irreversible implications as we delve into what we term our "Positional Blessings." Through these we will also learn that this good gift is available to, and can be received by, all if only we ask—for as Jesus said, ask and you shall receive that which is already yours (Matt 7:7–8)

We see this spirit of devotion flow and permeate throughout the Bible, and it is important to realize that it manifested through individuals not just in the New Testament but also in the Old, within those who had what we call an aligned heart, those who are referred to as "the righteous." Throughout this book we will refer to those in both Testaments who have this spirit of devotion as Devotionists.

A Function of the Holy Spirit Within Us

As the Helper, the Holy Spirit assists us in conforming us and guiding us to Jesus; as the Councilor, the Holy Spirit assists us as we seek to nurture our souls, and so devotion is the means by which the Holy Spirit expresses our hearts back to God. Devotion comes from within us and is love, wonder, awe, appreciation, and gratitude directed to God and to God alone. It is contemplation of the divine and involvement of the divine in every aspect of what we do. As God is ever-present, all-knowing, and omnipresent, so our devotion to Him is simply living consciously aware of these facts by involving Him and thereby honoring Him in the process—this is the way of the Devotionist.

Finally, because, as we said, the spirit of devotion is a spiritual blessing that every believer already has and is available to all, all we need to do is ask for it and we will receive—ask and let the Holy Spirit work this good work within us as devotion draws us closer to God and into His presence. We are not to feel condemned if we have not had this type of relationship with Him before, or to feel condemned by not spending enough time reading the Bible or in prayer, for if undertaken without a devotionist mindset, these are works and condemnation comes from a works mindset. The spirit of devotion comes from the same Spirit who makes us free, and hence we are simply to come before the throne of grace, boldly, and receive what is already ours.

A most beautiful doctrine that is little taught and its implications little considered within most churches and by most commentators is that which is termed by some as positional truths or as "our position in Christ." These are the Positional Blessings that collectively form the gift of "Positional Identity" that is given to every believer. The influence and ramifications of these blessings and gifts upon the believer should not be underestimated and should, probably, in fact be one of the first doctrinal summaries that are taught to young-in-faith Christians, for they are nothing short of transformative. In short, the Bible is very clear that upon salvation a number of blessings are poured out upon the new believer, who is recreated and transitioned into being considered a member of the household of God. The Holy Spirit indwells the believer and thereby enables the believer to appropriate and participate in the blessings of God, which are multiple, wonderful, and utterly transformative. Once grasped, these are fundamental to achieving a personal relationship with Christ that is constant, close, secure, mature, and full of hope, peace, and joy.

Living Devotion: "One Thing Is Needed"

In the famous passage in Luke 10 where Mary and Martha, the friends of Jesus, are visited by Him and the disciples, Jesus describes Mary's action of sitting at His feet and enjoying His presence as compared to Martha's activities around them as follows:

> And Jesus answered and said to her, "Martha, Martha, you are worried and troubled about many things. But one thing is needed, and Mary has chosen that good part, which will not be taken away from her." (Luke 10:41–42)

The "one thing" that is needed by all Christians is to rest in the presence of Jesus; to do so is the "good part" that no one can take away from us, for it comes from within the heart and that to experience His presence should be sought above all else. It is interesting that elsewhere we see this same thing; for example, the immediate response of the demoniac (the famous "Legion"). Having been miraculously healed by Jesus, his first response is to sit at His feet (Luke 8:35)—he too immediately understood that "one thing is needed," and he too chose "that good part" of sitting in the presence of Christ. And so too, with us, the "one thing" that is needed is for us to be in His presence, to seek and relish in it, to be replenished and refreshed by it. This is the peace and beauty that our souls hunger and thirst for, and it can only be satisfied by the presence of God.

Even Mary's action of sitting at the feet of Jesus is the manifestation of devotion that in itself is both an immediate, natural response and also one that demonstrates that her heart was already "aligned" with God's. This is an Old Testament phrase which, when applied to Mary here, means that she expresses her devotion in the only way possible in her thinking. It is inferred in the passage that for Mary to sit in His presence and at His feet is not only the most natural thing for her to do, but even more than this, not to do so does not even occur to her. It is not that she is normally a bad a host or inconsiderate of her sister; it's just that nothing else matters to her more than being in the presence of Jesus and all else merely fades into the background. Such is the heart of the Devotionist— one who chooses the "good part."

When we look at the other sister, Martha, in the passage, we see also the heart of one who wishes to serve, and it is in the serving that she finds her identity. Of course there is absolutely nothing wrong at all in this, as is proven in the gentle and loving response of Jesus to her. His response, though, points to a deeper need from Him, to a need which, perhaps in her activities, Martha herself does not give the time to recognize. For we see from Jesus that His need and greatest desire is to be in the presence of His loved ones, and this is what He desires and needs. For God does not need our activities and services; He wants our relationship first and foremost—He wants us to choose the "good part." And He wants us to make this our priority when other matters can wait. We should, however, in no way read Jesus's comments to Martha as being a reprimand. He clearly sees her heart too in wanting to do things for Him, and He clearly appreciates her love and the sacrificial heart of the hostess, but He wants her to see that His presence is to be enjoyed and participated in without distraction or concern for other transient matters. The question, though, that we will seek to explore is whether we too can participate in such a way and, if so, how?

To do so, we would argue, starts with a transformed heart and a hunger that comes from the Holy Spirit within us and hence is available to all believers. With the help of the Helper, we too can choose "that good part," and this choosing is part of what is explored in what follows as "Living Devotion." For devotion to be real, it is not about performances or doing certain actions or rituals, and it is also not just about the undertaking of the ephemeral. Living Devotion is participation in the permanent presence of Jesus. It is, to put it another way and in the phraseology of Jesus, "abiding in Him" (John 15:1–10). It is, to be clear, not something that is only available to the super-spiritual or "ultra-Christians" but is available to all believers by the very fact that all believers are indwelled by the Holy Spirit. And as Living Devotion is a manifestation of the Holy Spirit, so it conforms with the traits of the fruit of the Spirit and, as such, is always controlled, sincere, and never haughty or brash. It is reverential and yet it is also mutual and participatory. It is dedicated but not pious or legalistic. It is engaged in willingly, without compulsion. It is having peace with God. It brings beauty and meaning. It is identity and belonging as members of the household of God.

The Whole Desire of God

If we are to take seriously what the Bible says about itself, we must conclude that it is not just a book—it is a divine message. From this message we are to learn of the heart of God, who He is and what He is like. Most importantly, it is a message written to humankind that reveals that what He desires most, and what He pursues so extraordinarily and remarkably, is a people who will be dedicated to Him, freely and willingly:

> I will take you as My people, and I will be your God. Then you shall know that I am the Lord your God who brings you out from under the burdens of the Egyptians. (Exod 6:7)

> I will walk among you and be your God, and you shall be My people. (Lev 26:12)

> But this is what I commanded them, saying, "Obey My voice, and I will be your God, and you shall be My people. And walk in all the ways that I have commanded you, that it may be well with you. (Jer 7:23)

> But you are a chosen generation, a royal priesthood, a holy nation, His own special people, that you may proclaim the praises of Him who called you out of darkness into His marvelous light; who once were not a people but are now the people of God, who had not obtained mercy but now have obtained mercy. (1 Pet 2:9–10)

In essence, these verses encapsulate that which can be termed the "whole desire of God," as it is now and as it has always been. This desire can be summarized as follows: "I am the Only True God and am all-powerful, all-knowing, all-seeing, and will never, can never, do anything against my own attributes—will you be My people? I am Almighty and will do extreme things for you to prove to you who I am; despite everything you do, have done, and will do, I will love you and I want a permanent relationship with you—forever. My terms? They are simple because I am God and will not give My glory to another: all you have to do is believe in Me with your whole heart. All you have to do thereafter is believe in Me with your whole heart, for I am God and I am in control of all things—past, present, and future. All you have to do is *be* with Me."

It is important that we think about the actual word "people" in these contexts. For God is not just referring to the Levitical priesthood or the religious elite or rulers, or even just the odd great, faithful person that we hear so much of throughout the Bible—no, He also includes the ordinary, everyday person, the great and the small, the rich and the poor. This becomes even more interesting when we start to consider what God actually desires and what He requires from us as His people, for the majority of His "people" have always lived ordinary lives, for thousands of years now. Therefore, perhaps we need to consider what these requirements and expectations are if we are to really understand His desires for all His people, not just a select few.

Exodus 19:1–8 records the incredible events of the Lord descending with power and wonder onto Mount Sinai to declare to the Israelites what can be summarized as follows: "I have brought you out of Egypt through mighty wonders and now after having all done this for you, without asking anything in return thus far, I am asking now if you would willingly become My people—and if you do so, I will love you and bless you and keep you because I love you and always will." It is God who instigates this. He has performed all the miracles and signs and wonders of His own volition, and it is only at this point He asks the question, *Now will you be My people?* This is, of course, a pattern that is repeated throughout the Scriptures as prophecy is fulfilled and miracles performed, reaching ultimate fulfillment in the miracles of Jesus during His lifetime, His death, resurrection and ascension, and of course culminating in the magnificence and awe of His second coming—all unilateral demonstrations of power and wonder to draw us to Himself.

The Requirements of God

Exodus 19:8 shows us that the people accept God's offer without knowing what God's requirements will entail. This leads, then, to the most obvious questions to ask after this: *How then shall we now live and what does the Lord require of us?* The answer given to these natural questions is as revealing in its simplicity as it is in its implications, as they are told what is now expected or required of them. The instructions were simple, brief, and were for all, great and small, ruler, priest, and layperson alike:

> Hear, O Israel: The Lord our God, the Lord is one! You shall love the Lord your God with all your heart, with all your soul, and with all your strength. (Deut 6:4–5)

> And now, Israel, what does the Lord your God require of you, but to fear the Lord your God, to walk in all His ways and to love Him, to serve the Lord your God with all your heart and with all your soul, and to keep the commandments of the Lord and His statutes which I command you today for your good? (Deut 10:12–14)

> You shall love your neighbor as yourself. (Lev 19:18)

These then are pivotal in terms of the simplicity of the instructions to the people—they are the core to the whole of the law of Moses. They are beautifully simple because from these foundational instructions, a people could build their lives. From these they knew where they stood when they embarked on the new life of living under God. They were the points of referral as to how they were to be as His people before they knew and had revealed the other commandments which all came from these. And hence, we see this too setting a pattern with Jesus and as the first apostles were sent out, for the message to the new Christians was simple again because it had to be, before they had access to the remainder of the New Testament in its entirety some several hundred years later. The message was the same in its beautiful simplicity for those who believed, the great and the small, the rich and the poor: love the Lord Your God with all your heart and your neighbor as yourself. This is always what God has required from us, and it is all He has ever required from us as His people.

Three Intertwined and Inseparable Themes

From these pivotal passages, we see unfold three intertwined and inseparable themes that assist us in understanding the requirements upon the righteous under the old covenant and their impact on the Devotionist in the new.

1. **Worthiness:** God is worthy because He is both sovereign and familial.
2. **Dedication:** He is to be honored externally through the keeping of His commandments.
3. **Devotion:** He is to be honored internally within ourselves.

Worthiness

God is worthy. This seems like such a basic statement to make and yet its implications are so ill-considered by most. All He has ever done is seek to prove His worthiness and desire for us to recognize this worthiness through respect and reverence for who He is. We forget that God did not have to do anything and yet He chose to create, He chose to offer us perfection in the garden of Eden, and after the fall He chose to implement the divine plan of ultimate redemption for all humankind. He chose to demonstrate His love and power by leading the Hebrews out of Egypt; He chose to demonstrate His holiness through the law of Moses; He chose to send His Son to die on a cross and be resurrected; He chooses to offer us eternal life through simple belief in Him. This demonstrates His love, His utter worthiness, and all He has ever said is, "Look at my worthiness and what I do for you; love Me in return. All I want and require is your devotion, as everything else is under My control."

It has ever been the case that if believers want to go deeper with their relationship with God, then the best place to start is to understand His attributes and His characteristics. Without this understanding of the sovereignty of God, we are unable to be either fully dedicated to Him in terms of undertaking His commandments or to be fully devoted to Him in our hearts, for both require that we fully acknowledge His sovereignty in all things. Both require the internalization of the understanding of the attributes and characteristics of God.

Without an understanding of God's attributes and characteristics in how they apply to both dedication and devotion, devotion itself becomes, so to speak, a house built on sand. For true devotion is based on, and toward, God. Hence it must be founded on God; otherwise, it becomes devoid devotion—devoid of purpose and meaning and function.

For God to be God, He must have all the divine attributes of being all-powerful, all-knowing, all-seeing, and immutable—and it is these that surround and envelop His holy characteristics. He is divinely perfect, He is constant, He is consistent, He is good, He is holy, He is love and loving, He is glorious and magnificent, He is beauty, and He is unchanging, unchangeable, and trustworthy. He alone is to be trusted because He alone is powerful enough to be utterly trustworthy. And for our purposes, when we consider our devotion to Him and His devotion to us, it is vital that we know that these characteristics enshrine His attributes of constancy and immutability. He will not waiver, and because He is all-powerful, when He says He will do something, He will. When He makes a promise, it is kept by His limitless, infinite power.

> Indeed I have spoken it;
> I will also bring it to pass.
> I have purposed it;
> I will also do it.
> (Isa 46:11)

Indeed most importantly, as we continue to examine the requirements for dedication and devotion, it is essential that we, once and for all, settle in our hearts that God will never do, and can never do, anything that will contradict any of His attributes or characteristics. And as this includes the fact that He is utterly sovereign and in control of all things, so we can simply rest in this knowledge and trust Him in that what He promises to us is true. We are not to be fearful of the future, for He has ordained that what will happen, will happen—but at the same time, we are to live in sure and certain knowledge that all He requires from us, all He is interested in from us, is a deepening and strengthening bond of trust, love, and above all devotion to Him through fellowship and being with Him. To think otherwise and to do otherwise is actually beyond our remit as His children, and it is, in fact, contrary to His instructions and desires of us.

The revelation to us of the attributes and characteristics of God are designed to reflect our own selves. As we were created in the image of God, so when we hold up these characteristics as a mirror to ourselves, it reveals His beauty and our failings. His utter worthiness is not to be contrasted and compared with our utter unworthiness but is meant to point us to the fact that through Him, and Him alone, we are not utterly and irredeemably lost in an eternity of meaninglessness, emptiness, and ultimately irrelevance.

Of course, in order to gain the required perspective, we must understand that despite these awesome and majestic attributes and characteristics, our God is not remote and unapproachable. He is personable and wants fellowship and relationship with all who believe—there is no partiality with Him as, in His opinion, we are all equal because we all are His. A devoted heart knows this; but more than that, a devoted heart embraces this without fear or compulsion. God offers—and the righteous have always been able to enjoy—the exquisite beauty of both familial and intimate relationship with Him. Consider the depth of trust and strength of closeness that is behind the words of Ps 23 for instance. And in terms of the familial aspect, this is behind the opening of the Lord's Prayer in Matt 6: "Our Father." It is familial and it is possessive in its character. He is "our Father" and no one else's.

Dedication

The law of Moses contained 613 commandments that encompassed virtually every aspect of people's lives and instigated a whole system of ceremonies, celebrations, directions on life and wellbeing, and the overall requirements expected by a holy God to live under His auspices and even protection. The Israelites in the wilderness chose to accept the terms put forward by God, and the rest, as they say, is history.

From the distance that we are now at from this period, it is too easy to miss or even to be dismissive of the actual purpose of the Law of Moses and the commandments. For as we said, God chose to implement the commandments, and so we must look to why and what they tell us of Himself and His heart for His people. As with all things from God, the commandments not only reflected His sovereign attributes but also His divine characteristics of love, grace, mercy, justice, and constancy. The whole theocratic system was established to present a framework under which the Israelites would be able to live while all the while having continual and ever-present reminders of who their God is, whom they worship, and why. These reminders then are what can be defined as external—the temple itself, the sacrificial system, the life-living commands (dietary, agricultural, business, etc.)—and they were all designed to be not static monuments, as it were, but a living means for the people to absorb the requirements of God into their very beings.

In this way we see that the external does and did matter, not least because it was ordained and commanded by God. The external matters because it helps to draw the person in to remind them of the Lord's attributes and to reveal His heart, His all-encompassing care, love, and compassion for them as His people. Hence, we see that God ordains and uses multisensory stimuli to draw the Israelites to Himself and to act as perpetual ever-present reminders of His presence and divinity in their midst, that He is their God and that they are His people. Consider for example the magnificence and awe-inspiring beauty of the temple and all its multisensory services (artistry, music, prayer, smells, and sacrifices), the presence of the priests and their divinely ordained garments and mandated ceremonies, the watchmen, and the very nature of a theocratic kingdom under God all instigated to display and commemorate the fact that the Israelites not only belong to the Lord, but that He is also the God of creation, creativity, and beauty—and that their own ability to appreciate these comes from our senses is proof of our having been created in His image (Gen 1:26–27). Just as the aromas of the burning oil candles and the incense in the temple would have infiltrated all the air around, so the message of God, being invisible yet present, would have permeated everything in society.

From the perspective of the everyday, ordinary Israelite, the presence of God was felt and conveyed through these multisensory stimuli which were ordained to not only inspire worship but, more than that, to generate and impart understanding of the Lord through experiential participation. Thus, the sharing through oral tradition and ceremonial participation, the expectation of protection, and the deliverance from sin all engendered inclusion in the sense of belonging to the community of God. But even more than this, there was no discontinuity between the divine and mundane, as what was in heaven was meant to be on earth. The mysteries and miracles of God interfaced and interacted within the very fabric and structure of society so that there was there was no disconnect with the presence of God in history, culture, and community. It is here that we see the instructions for everyday living as perpetual reminders to being part of this community. Indeed, it is the personal, individual instructions that reveal God's heart for the ordinary people most. For again, we miss the purpose of them if we consider them as being only relevant to the priests and leaders and ignore the wider reason for their implementation, which was to demonstrate and be a point of reference for all that His whole desire is to have a personal relationship with each person and for each person to feel part of the overall identity within His kingdom. These were designed, out of love, to present to each person a perpetual reminder that the Lord is omnipresent and so must be involved and consist in everything that we do. When we truly comprehend both the omniscience and omnipresence of God, it becomes obvious that consideration of Him must permeate everything we do, everywhere we go, at all times. This is the purpose of such commands as,

> And these words which I command you today shall be in your heart. You shall teach them diligently to your children, and shall talk of them when you sit in your house, when you walk by the way, when you lie down, and when you rise up. You shall bind them as a sign on your hand, and they shall be as frontlets between your eyes. You shall write them on the doorposts of your house and on your gates. (Deut 6:6–9)

These constant reminders are both relationally symbolic and possessive. They are external in that they are actions but become what can be defined as externalism when they become merely ritualistic, legalistic, or ostentatious. An example of how these very commandments became removed from their original purpose is how the prayer shawls and the ringlets became ever longer and larger, thereby making them more visible, conspicuous, and reflective of the inestimable piety of the wearer. Hence this false piety becomes projected to those around, to seek the approval and respect of others—impressing God not one jot. This externalism was exposed by Jesus on numerous occasions for being the false piety and hypocrisy that it is. But this does not negate the original heart and purpose behind the instructions but reveals how legalism and this externalism always comes from a heart within that is corrupted, at worst, or misguided, at best.

The Acceptable Sacrifice to God

While it is abundantly clear from the history of Israel that there was great rebellion and apostasy against God and His ways, we would also be naive to conclude that this was true of all the people at these times, for there were always those who remained true to the calling of God. And while corruption frequently occurred at the top, within the ruling establishment, we are given glimpses of the fidelity of the ordinary people through the likes of David while he was a mere shepherd boy, or indeed a thousand years later through the shepherds outside of Bethlehem on the night of Jesus's birth: ordinary people loving the Lord despite everything. If we read Scripture properly, we see this juxtaposition between the faithful and the faithless throughout. But it is wrong to conclude that the faithful were merely confined to those few that are mentioned. For, as always, there were many who did not subscribe to the zeitgeist, who were excluded from the temptations of metropolitan life, and who exercised a simple faith, dedicated to the Lord, and accepted by Him in their simplicity of faith.

Indeed, that this was always the intention of God is abundantly clear from the following passages that make explicit that what God requires, and has always required, from His people is to be loved with a pure heart. Scripture is perfectly clear in that while He instigated the Law of Moses with its 613 regulations, these were always only ever meant to be undertaken because of love, not to earn it or to earn favor. Consider the following verses.

> For You do not desire sacrifice, or else I would give it;
> You do not delight in burnt offering.
> The sacrifices of God are a broken spirit,
> A broken and a contrite heart—
> These, O God, You will not despise.
> (Ps 51:16–17)

> To what purpose is the multitude of your sacrifices to Me? (Isa 1:11)

> To do righteousness and justice is more acceptable to the Lord than sacrifice. (Prov 21:3)

Providence and Devotion

The purpose of these external observances was that they were to serve as constant reminders both of God's Providence and of His omnipresence in their daily lives. For God knows that if He is not seen to be involved in our lives, then He becomes removed from them. We start to think that He is not interested in us, and as He becomes more remote, the more we feel isolated.

This is where the loving-kindness of God in the pursuit of our devotion becomes clear—for the instigation of such personal instructions served as visual and physical reminders of God's ever-present love for His people. In an age where trips to the temple would have happened once a year, visual reminders become vital in maintaining the connection between the individual and God. Of course, this too was about identity and being part of the community bond. But the instructions to speak of His works and talk about them were conceived of to strengthen their bond with God throughout the course of their daily lives—to remind each other of "God in their lives" and reestablish the heart connection between the individual and God.

As such, we see that it is thus that Providence comes to be visually celebrated. All of the gorgeous decorations, carvings, and even the architectural layout of the temple itself were deliberately designed to be reflective of the fact that beauty itself is from God, but also reflective of God's Providence in the lives of all those who dwelled in Israel. It also absolutely shows that beauty in design, music, and the arts when dedicated is more than acceptable, for it shows God's mind is beautiful, as He truly loves beauty. As God is a multisensory Creator, and as we are designed in His image, so He uses multisensory stimuli (smell, taste, color, and beauty as expressed through creation, the arts, music, and the written word) to captivate us, to draw us toward Him so we experience Him in all His glory. Hence, the wonderful words of the Devotionist King David: "Oh, taste and see that the Lord is good" (Ps 34:8).

As with Providence, so too with God's attribute of omnipresence: as we too little consider its significance, so we easily drift into indifference, lethargy, and remoteness from Him. For reminders of God that are everywhere, all around us, do just that—namely, bring to our realization that God is everywhere. And when we are never far from His presence, then our devotion becomes that much easier. Hence, physical and visual reminders of Him were meant to be constant reminders to the individual and the community of this. As David says in Ps 139:7, "Where can I go from Your Spirit? Or where can I flee from Your presence?"

The Application for the Everyday Israelite

But so much for these grandiose statements. What, in the meantime, of the myriads of normal Israelites who loved the Lord and obeyed the commandments as best they could within the difficulties of life? What about them? They were not priests, Levites, prophets, or even Nazirites, but merely the sheep of Israel—ordinary people, going about their everyday lives. The majority of individual Israelites did not have daily access to the Torah in order to be able to study it and to learn the ways of God, but this ignores the whole concept of cultural assimilation that is implicit with the influence of living under a theocratic regime—namely, the absorption was thus made much easier, thereby creating the cultural opportunity and space for devotion to flourish. Which, of course, was God's intention all along.

It is this omnipresent characteristic of God's that serves to be a constant behavioral influence upon the people, for if God is both all-seeing and all-knowing, then there is literally nowhere to hide or behave badly in secret. This is why throughout the Bible, from Genesis to Revelation, it is abundantly clear that there should be no separation between what can be called our times of labor and our times of worship, our times of activity and our times of rest. All are to be undertaken in the light of God's revelation and His expectations as to how we live. Behavioral guidance was given through the Law, the Prophets, and particularly through the wisdom literature as to the expectations of human conduct under God—integrity, honesty, care for the weak and poor, justice, and mercy. Emphatically, we are told that these are more important to God than even sacrifice is, as they show the true heart of the individual living under God's universal jurisdiction. This covered every aspect of an individual's life within the community, whether at home or in business. All was to be undertaken under the auspices of God, under the sure and certain knowledge of His inescapable presence and ability to see the motives as well as the actions of everyone, everywhere.

I suspect that if we are honest, we look back at these times in history with pity and sympathy for those who had to endure living under such a regulatory framework. This, however, is again not what we see in either history or in Scripture. For we see times of great celebration and community bonding around their common culture, and we also see it in the form of spontaneous expressions of devotion and love toward God. Consider, for example, the fact that the Lord in His grace made provision in the law for just such expressions. This was the whole function of the very little appreciated peace offering set out in Lev 7. For to be true to the heart and intentions of God, we must consider what it meant and signified, not just as a cold perfunctory theological instruction but as what it represented for the people: to the layperson the peace offering represented a means of expressing their heart and gratitude and their total conviction that all that is good comes from God. It was a means of showing heartfelt appreciation to God for good events (such as the birth of a child) and, more to the point, was often undertaken simply for no other reason than that of wanting to express thanksgiving to the Lord for the covenant relationship between the individual and their God. This cannot be ignored or brushed over, for it is where we see the expression of the individual love of the individual believer within the community. It was the sacrifice to God as a love-expression. It represented the complete pervasiveness of God within their lives and His active involvement in every aspect of their lives. The peace offering was a voluntary, spontaneous offering reflecting God's goodness and all that is good, for only God is good, as Jesus said, and hence all that is good must come from Him.

But individual thanksgiving itself stems from a culture understanding this as part of daily life. The psalmists continually exhort us to give thanks to Him and for His works. Yes, there are the mighty works of God that we are to consider in terms of the exodus and creation itself, but the works of God are also in the detail of life itself. The habit of thanking the Lord, though, is the act of internalizing the external. It is taking events and applying them to our own walk with God. But it goes further than this, for it shows that there is an aspect of the realization of the nature and workings of our Lord that generates a spontaneous response that signifies His sovereignty and our own subservience to this—put simply, gratitude. Thus, we see that the true motivation and instigation behind acts of devotion come not from compulsion but from this most glorious of responses from created to Creator—gratitude and appreciation. This is, of course, exactly the same thinking we see from the former Pharisee Paul the apostle in Phil 4:6–9, transposed into a Christian context, using the same techniques of exhortation of example through the passing on of oral tradition:

> Be anxious for nothing, but in everything by prayer and supplication, with thanksgiving, let your requests be made known to God; and the peace of God, which surpasses all understanding, will guard your hearts and minds through Christ Jesus. Finally, brethren, whatever things are true, whatever things are noble,

whatever things are just, whatever things are pure, whatever things are lovely, whatever things are of good report, if there is any virtue and if there is anything praiseworthy—meditate on these things. The things which you learned and received and heard and saw in me, these do, and the God of peace will be with you. (Phil 4:6–9)

Devotion

It seems, on first examination, a strange and even counterintuitive thing to do—to command love, let alone the all-encompassing, all-consuming, unconditional love that is clearly implied. But we forget that from God's perspective this is only in effect asking us to love Him the way He loves us as believers—though this goes even further in that it is simultaneously unilateral, ubiquitous, unlimited, and unconditional. For He loved us first. Is it so strange, then, to be expectant of love in return for such love like this? We would do well to be grateful that it is reciprocated love that is "commanded" and not just blind, robotic, loveless obedience—for God knows more than anyone that for love to be reciprocated, the one wanting to be loved needs to be worthy of that love. And this, one can say, is precisely what God does throughout Scripture and ever since. He has undertaken such extreme acts to demonstrate His unconditional love for us, culminating in the sacrifice on the cross of Himself, that we should all look upon such love in awe and wonder. Not least because it was all undertaken despite us, despite the way we are, despite the way we have always treated Him. This is the unconditional love that is delivered without hypocrisy that we can only aspire to (Rom 12:9). Perhaps the better way to look at this is that such unilateral, unconditional, all-consuming love from the Creator of all things, who has all power and wonder, all beauty and majesty, all grace and mercy, and yet who loves us in this way, should produce nothing but reciprocated love and respect from those who truly believe in Him. The love of God is the Hebrew and Christian distinctive—for love means relationship, care, compassion, and daily involvement in the reality of life; to be otherwise would not be love. This is the message of the Bible and the story of God's engagement with His creation from before creation itself; and of course, this then fits perfectly with the type of love described by the apostle Paul in 1 Cor 13.

The Aligned Heart

Such love, though, is meant to produce a response from the loved; it is meant to be reciprocated and is meant to find expression. The external manifestation of what has been internalized is meant to emanate from the heart, for what has been inwardly absorbed produces expression from the internal outwards—in this case in the form of deeply committed, mutually reciprocated love. This is what we can describe as being the "aligned heart," and it is to be found in those whom we can describe as "Devotionists."

These were the people who loved the Lord with all their heart. They constituted the everyday Israelite who found wonder in their faith and who sought to obey the Lord as best they could from the position of heart-felt love, trust, and faith. These were the people who, as we discussed earlier, would undertake the peace and freewill offerings, who would attend the festivals and ceremonies not from compulsion and tradition but from the position of Devotionists. They would wonder in awe at the beauty of the temple and the objects within it, not as externalists (only recognizing the physical and material with no consideration of the divine) but as Devotionists—giving God the glory for inspiring the craftsmen and seeing in the beauty of these artifacts the beauty of God and of His own awesome creativity. For as objects may be beautiful, how much more beautiful must be the One who inspired such beauty? The making of such connections and considerations distinguishes the aligned heart of the Devotionist.

Indeed, we see from Exod 35 that the gifting of the original artifacts for the tabernacle were given by the ordinary people in a spirit of love as "freewill" offerings, from those who were of "willing heart," and to such an extent that eventually Moses had to instruct them to stop bringing them(Exod 36:3). Thus, we see that there always was this internalist spirit within the community that found devotionist expression in the peace and freewill offerings which were spontaneous and "heart-aligned." And it was not just material offerings but also those of skill, as those who were skilled craftsmen offered their services as freewill offerings and as joyous gifts back to God. The design of the tabernacle itself came to represent the act of creation itself in that after all was done, the craftsmen were told to rest and Moses looked upon what was done as an offering to the Lord, saw it as good, and blessed it (Exod 39:43). And through this, we see the golden thread of devotion weave its way through the Scriptures to when the Second Temple is rededicated back to God in Ezra 8:28, and the artifacts are given again as freewill offerings to the Lord.

The Devotionist has always understood that first and foremost it is the heart that God is interested in. But the Devotionist has always known the heart can be deceptive, is prone to deceit, and that sin will arise. Even after probably one of the most sinful acts one can imagine, the Devotionist King David did not speak of repenting through dramatic externalist means of elaborate performances of contrition or multiple sacrifices or declaring His sin in open public displays. No, he knew that this is not the way of God, as Ps 51 so beautifully and poignantly shows.

From Cain and Abel onwards, we are shown that the only acceptable sacrifices to God were always behavioral and can only come from a position of righteousness first—meaning that the whole function of the Law of Moses was never that it would, in itself, satisfy God but was only ever acceptable when undertaken with a heart that was already aligned with God. The aligned heart then was the position of the Devotionist before Pentecost; it is the position of the believer before and after coming to faith in God. It always has been. Thus, we see from Jesus Himself in the Beatitudes (namely, before His resurrection) that it is this aligned heart that is needed to enter into the kingdom of God, and it always has been (Matt 5:3–10).

Forgiveness

It is little appreciated but extremely important for our purposes in following the thread of devotion that we comprehend that for the ordinary, everyday Israelite, as far as they were concerned, God did forgive their sins when they offered the sacrifices that were required. This was not just the national forgiveness at the Day of Atonement but the regular daily sacrifices for sin. It was, as we have seen, only acceptable when performed by one with a preexisting state of an aligned heart toward God. It was the state of contrition in the aligned heart that was the actual "sacrificial state" that God required from the believer, more than the sacrifice itself. The Devotionist King David explains it better:

> For You do not desire sacrifice, or else I would give it;
> You do not delight in burnt offering.
> The sacrifices of God are a broken spirit,
> A broken and a contrite heart—
> These, O God, You will not despise.
> (Ps 51:16–17)

That the individual was forgiven when they came before the Lord, though, must be appreciated; it must have been appropriate, otherwise the whole validity and purpose of the system would have withered or collapsed. The individual had to know that—even if only temporarily—their sins were forgiven. For if there was no concept of actual forgiveness, then the act of sin itself would have become nullified and dulled; the holiness of God without the actual ability to restore fellowship would have made a mockery of the whole concept of the intimacy He required from His people individually. The believer had to know that if they sinned, then there could be restoration, otherwise the whole edifice of the Mosaic system would have crumbled. The aligned heart had to know there was the means to achieve restored fellowship. The importance of this for the Devotionist could not be made clearer. It is the same then as it is for us today, as the apostle John would later say, "If we confess our sins, He is faithful and just to forgive us our sins and to cleanse us from all unrighteousness" (1 John 1:9).

It was ever thus, as they say. If this were not the case, then it would make utterly meaningless, at best, or deceiving, at worst, such wonderful lines from King David in the psalms:

> Bless the Lord, O my soul;
> And all that is within me, bless His holy name!
> Bless the Lord, O my soul,
> And forget not all His benefits:
> Who forgives all your iniquities. . . .
> He has not dealt with us according to our sins,
> Nor punished us according to our iniquities.
> For as the heavens are high above the earth,
> So great is His mercy toward those who fear Him;
> As far as the east is from the west,
> So far has He removed our transgressions from us.
> (Ps 103:1–3, 10–12)

The problem, though, was that the sinful nature of humankind was still there—as the writer of the Hebrews would explain—and the continual daily sacrifices and the continual daily struggle of the believer with their own troublesome heart only served to point to the fact that the believer could not always do or behave as they wanted to for God. Just as we see in the New Testament believers struggling with the flesh, so in the Old Testament we see them contesting the vagaries of the heart. Hence, we see in the call of David in Ps 51:10, "Create in me a clean heart, O God," as He sees that it will require God Himself to intervene into His own sinful nature. As we are incapable of resolving this ourselves, so the faithful began to look to the only one who could: God Himself. As our sinful nature is within us, only an external intervention can be the solution. Hence, as prophetic revelation developed so the faithful realized that this intervention would come from God through the Messiah and that He would intervene to not only create new hearts that would be permanently realigned with the eternally devoted to God, but that finally sin would be permanently forgiven:

> Behold, the days are coming, says the Lord, when I will make a new covenant with the house of Israel and with the house of Judah—not according to the covenant that I made with their fathers in the day that I took them by the hand to lead them out of the land of Egypt, My covenant which they broke, though I was a husband to them, says the Lord. But this is the covenant that I will make with the house of Israel after those days, says the Lord: I will put My law in their minds, and write it on their hearts; and I will be their God, and they shall be My people. No more shall every man teach His neighbor, and every man His brother, saying, "Know the Lord," for they all shall know Me, from the least of them to the greatest of them, says the Lord. For I will forgive their iniquity, and their sin I will remember no more. (Jer 31:31–35)

Full Circle—The Righteous

Thus, we come full circle back to the people of God. It is true that while we see, within the retrospective context of biblical history, the seeming abject failure of the nation of Israel to obey the Lord as He required, this is perhaps not seeing the trees for the wood, so to speak. Or rather, not seeing the individuals within the nation. For the Old Testament is replete with references to the faithful, the remnant, and those who are spoken of in the psalms and elsewhere as "the righteous," which became an Old Testament term that encapsulates those who truly believe and obey to their best of their ability. Importantly, nowhere is this term used solely concerning the religious or ruling elite but is a generalism applying to all who still remain true to God and seek to love Him with all their heart, while honoring His commands as best they can. So, while the nation sinned as a whole, there were always those who simply got on with their lives, living within the framework of their simple, sincere, and faithful love of God, the vast majority of whom would have been normal, everyday believers—Devotionists, every one of them, whom the Lord loves and holds in special regard among His people.

Psalm 34:15—The eyes of the Lord are on the righteous.

Psalm 37:17—The Lord upholds the righteous.

Psalm 146:7—The Lord loves the righteous.

But who actually are the righteous? We see from Prov 10, with all its references to the righteous, that it is the righteous who are a blessing to those who are around them and are set in contrast to the wicked and the unrighteous. Interestingly, there seems here to be no "halfway house," for one is either one or the other in God's eyes (paralleled in the New Testament in much the same way, of course, as one is either a Christian or not). This means at the very least that what is being described is not a cultural, class, or ethnic distinctive between the two, but something much deeper and more esoteric—namely, that the distinction comes from within, from the heart. What is also implied—and this is vitally important to absorb—is that to be included among the righteous is not an exclusive club but is open to everyone who holds to the values of God as set before them. And of course, everyone means everyone—men and women, the young and the old, the rich and the poor, all who believe in Him in sincerity of heart. Hence, we see on numerous occasions that it is the women who are commended for how closely they hold to the precepts of God. Consider Rachel, Hannah, Ruth, Esther, Mary the mother of Jesus, Anna the prophetess, Mary and Martha, Joanna, Timothy's mother, and the countless other ordinary faithful women down through the centuries who just loved the Lord in truth and in simplicity, longing for His will to be done on earth as it is in heaven. And ordinary is again the right word; for most of these, they were in generally lowly positions and would have had no inkling at all that they would come to be mentioned in Scripture and remembered for their fortitude and faith for millennia. And yet what is most striking is that their actions clearly must have come from hearts that were already aligned and devoted to the Lord, and hence their actions were manifestations or outworkings of principle inherent from the righteous being "doers as well as hearers" (Jas 1:22). Or more poignantly, they are the physical examples of the biblical truth pertaining to the righteous that the goodness of God is received by them to enjoy personally so that God is glorified and others are drawn to Him through their actions and very demeanor:

> I have not hidden Your righteousness within my heart;
> I have declared Your faithfulness and Your salvation;
> I have not concealed Your lovingkindness and Your truth
> From the great assembly.
> (Ps 40:10)

> Let your light so shine before men, that they may see your good works and glorify your Father in heaven. (Matt 5:16)

The righteous are those, then, who are in a position of fellowship and security in the Lord. While righteousness comes from the Lord and is imputed to those who are righteous, it is also the response of the individual to the Lord. In other words, it is a reciprocal relationship encompassing the sovereignty of God in its imputation and the responsibility of the individual to respond to the open invitation to righteousness from the Lord. This is clearly a precursor to the new covenant relationship between the believer and the Holy Spirit, with righteousness presented by grace from God and responded to through faith by the individual, not through works, lest the recipient boast of their own achievements (Eph 2:8–9). The distinction being that in the Old Testament the righteous person, while clearly having a relationship with the Holy Spirit, is not indwelled by Him and hence is aware that this relationship might, depending on the circumstances, be removed (though that circumstance would need to be extreme and could be interceded against, as David shows us in Ps 51:11). Reference to Ps 51:11 is an interesting one here for the purposes of our discussion on the righteous, for the focus in the verse is always traditionally on David pleading with God not to remove the Holy Spirit from him; but David also asks not to be cast away from the Lord's presence. Now, clearly David is not meaning just the times when he may have gone to the tabernacle to be with God and so is in fear of not being allowed to go there anymore, but that this presence is a more encompassing, even ever-present, phenomenon in his relationship with the Lord which he does not wish to lose. Thus we see this, for those who are the righteous share in this peculiarity of the ever-present presence of the Lord, for He lives, or tabernacles, in their hearts and engages with their souls, as we'll discuss in detail in later chapters.

We see from the generic references to the righteous that they include not just the elite but comprise ordinary people who love the Lord and are dedicated to Him—they are treated and regarded, as we have said, differently by the Lord than those who are unrighteous or wicked. Thus, we can say for certain that despite the atrocious actions of apostasy committed by multiple kings and religious rulers over the course of at least fifteen hundred years, there was always those who remained true to the Lord—remaining true despite the odds and because God has always been personable to the individual. Consider, for example, the scene in 1 Kgs 19 where Elijah complains to the Lord that he is alone in his anguish for Him, and the Lord corrects him by pointing out that there are actually seven thousand others like him. But the Lord did not mean that there were seven thousand other prophets, or even Levites or priests, who felt the same; what is implied is that these would have included every day, ordinary people who also felt this anguish because they knew God's heart and could see His pain too. These are the righteous, our Devotionists of old from across all sections of the Israelite community. Yes, the history of Israel was one of absolute apostasy and downright evil at times, but that does not mean to say that this thread of devotion was broken by such evil. There were always those who were simply, faithfully, following the Lord—devotionally obeying His voice and commandments, devotionally seeking forgiveness for their sins, devotionally going to the ceremonies and festivals, devotionally performing peace sacrifices, and devotionally awaiting the Messiah who would create in them a new heart and bring rest to those who labor and struggle.

The requirements of God are simple and are threaded throughout Scripture—namely, that it is the heart and only the heart that God has ever been interested in. We show this both externally and internally: externally by following His instructions and heeding His voice, and internally through what might be termed our "aligned heart attitude." Scripture is very clear that the only acceptable external actions are those that come from the heart that is aligned with God. They are undertaken because of our love for the Lord, not to gain or earn that love. If we do this, then His love is so clear, for He has always loved us first. And this is what the history of His people throughout the Old Testament shows us: life and love come from God. And He gives them freely and without compulsion. He loved us first and all He requires is reciprocation. This then has always been His only ultimate desire—a people unto Himself participating in reciprocated love.

The Pearl of Our Devotion

The Drama of the Gospels

IN ORDER TO UNDERSTAND the Gospels, one should consider them not only as history but as culturally, theologically, and prophetically interwoven dramatic accounts. Only in this way can one understand why certain events happen and why certain people do or say what they do—whether that's the crowds, the disciples, the religious leaders, or Jesus Himself. This drama is set within the melting pot of a profound cultural awareness, pervasive religion, and intense religious expectation. These are what we might call the metanarratives of the culture of the time, and they are the factors that shaped everything in everybody's lives, all the time, in first-century Israel. When we read the Gospels, we have a tendency, as with much of Scripture, to read them in some form of vacuum. But in fact, this shouldn't be further from the truth for it is impossible to appreciate the nuances and events within the Gospels without an understanding of the interplay between many of these grand themes or metanarratives.

Theological Interpretation Versus the People

It is outside the scope of this chapter to speak in detail of these metanarratives or grand themes of theological interpretation that we see dramatically revealed in the Gospels. These being such themes as the

"Oneness of God," apostasy, blasphemy, and the nature of the Messiah and the Messianic kingdom. However, for our purposes within this section, there are some other factors which I believe are important to grasp that would help us.

First and foremost, we tend to forget that this drama was played out in real life, with real people, experiencing real events and prophetic fulfillments being played out before their eyes. While cultures vary both within history and geographically, people at their core through the ages have seldom differed in their cares, struggles, and motivations. This is why we can read of such events and the reactions of the people within them after two thousand years and still empathize without looking into them as if into an alien universe. And yet within the Gospels we see two worlds collide as the kingdom of God manifests among the people in the form of Jesus of Nazareth and exposes the hearts and minds of all those He encounters. In order to explore this collision further and understand the reactions of people to Him, we need to delve a little into how we might be able to define some the characteristic traits of people in perhaps a very generalist manner, but which nevertheless helps us to categorize behavioral attitudes and responses. Simplistically speaking though, we see within the Gospels the reactions of people to Jesus who fall within two main characteristic camps that we can describe as being externalist and internalist. An externalist, put simply, is mainly concerned with the tangible, the material, and the visible; they are motivated by material possessions, social status, power, and wealth. In religious contexts, this externalism translates into rigidity, legalism, judgmentalism, pride, and a lack of compassion. Internalists are those who, while not necessarily diametrically opposite (for people have always been a mixture of both), share an attitude to life and people around them that is deeper spiritually and are more experiential in their appreciation of beauty and the intangible. One might, at this point, quite rightly ask how these really apply to those whom we see in the Gospels who formed the majority of the population of Israel at the time, who lived hand-to-mouth in daily survival mode whether in towns or in the country. The truth, though, is that no matter who we are or where we are, it is our hearts that reveal our true selves, and it is our hearts that Jesus came to address, challenge, and restore, for it is our hearts that God has always been most interested in. And it is our hearts that either accept or reject Him, no matter our personal circumstances.

To comprehend the drama of the Gospels, we need to understand that, for all intents and purposes, the Israel at the time of Jesus, despite being under occupation by the Romans, operated as a theocracy where everyday life was controlled absolutely by adherence to the Law of Moses under the ultimate control and guidance of the religious leaders in Jerusalem. Culturally, the children were taught only the Scriptures at school and every town had a synagogue.[1] This led naturally to the fact that all the people had a degree of education up to a certain age, and everyone was taught the Scriptures on the Sabbath. Everything was seen through the eyes of religious practice. Between the time of the Testaments, from the return from Babylonian exile to the birth of Jesus, the religious elite had themselves formed into numerous factions—these included the Sadducees, Pharisees, and scribes, as well as breakaway movements based on the expectation of a messiah, such as the Essenes and Zealots.[2] By the time of the Gospels, these factions had developed their own traditions and differing interpretations, leading to a mass of confusion between themselves and (more importantly for our purposes) for the ordinary Israelites as well. Nuances and discrepancies of doctrine and interpretation were (and are) literally manna for intellectual elites who loved to dispute and debate—but for most people they simply served to distract, confuse, and ultimately cause disinterest. This, of course, is as empirically true today as it always has been.

Such is bad enough in any situation of faith. But ideas have consequences, and this proved absolutely devastating when it came to the acceptance of Jesus as the Messiah, as the people were told by the authorities that, despite Jesus fulfilling every single aspect of what both the Scriptures and their rabbis (especially the Pharisees) had told them the Messiah would be and what only the Messiah could do, He was not in fact the Messiah (see Matt 12).[3] But it is into this mess and mass of confusion that Jesus brings unparalleled clarity and radicalism as He challenged orthodoxy and authority on behalf of those whom He saw had become the victims of deception, hypocrisy, and deliberate distortions of truth.

To Jesus, the people were the lost sheep of Israel who had, through no fault of their own, been driven to go their own way. He expounded for them that He alone was the Good Shepherd promised in the Scriptures,

---

1. Wilson, *Our Father Abraham*, 278–319 (a chapter titled "A Life of Learning: The Heart of Jewish Heritage").

2. Balla, *Four Centuries*.

3. Fruchtenbaum, *Three Messianic Miracles*.

and the religious elite were the false shepherds that Scripture also warned against. His compassion for the ordinary people is set starkly against the false piety and false legalism of their religious elite. With His Sermon on the Mount, His public ministry effectively starts with Himself taking authority over the Law of Moses on behalf of the people and removing that authority from the religious elite. Jesus exhorts and encourages individual responsibility for faith and actions as He expounds for them the practical outworking of the two greatest commandments: to love the Lord and to love one's neighbor. At no point does He refer to the religious rulers except in exposing their interpretative errors and hypocrisy. It is this emphasis upon the individual actually applying the heart of God's law to their lives, without telling them to consult their rabbi or other religious leaders, that is so truly revolutionary—it is this that truly riles the elite. There is nothing new under the sun, for it does not take much of a leap of thought processes to see how true this is today too. For personal devotion and taking personal responsibility for one's faith, study, learning, and walk with God immediately challenges the need for, and role of, elite control and authority.

An Examination of Mark 12:28–34

In order to demonstrate this and to explore how this has a direct impact on devotion, I want to spend some time by exploring a fascinating scene that occurs at the end of Jesus's ministry during one of His last encounters with the religious elite in Jerusalem:

> Then one of the scribes came, and having heard them reasoning together, perceiving that He had answered them well, asked Him, "Which is the first commandment of all?"
>
> Jesus answered him, "The first of all the commandments is: 'Hear, O Israel, the Lord our God, the Lord is one. And you shall love the Lord your God with all your heart, with all your soul, with all your mind, and with all your strength.' This is the first commandment. And the second, like it, is this: 'You shall love your neighbor as yourself.' There is no other commandment greater than these."
>
> So the scribe said to Him, "Well said, Teacher. You have spoken the truth, for there is one God, and there is no other but He. And to love Him with all the heart, with all the understanding, with all the soul, and with all the strength, and to love one's

neighbor as oneself, is more than all the whole burnt offerings and sacrifices."

Now when Jesus saw that He answered wisely, He said to him, "You are not far from the kingdom of God." (Mark 12:28–34)

Background to the Scene in Question

During this exchange, we are drawn into what was probably the last of many encounters between Jesus and the religious ruling factions at the time and, through this, the culmination of one of the fundamental issues that faced Jesus during His "ministry years"—namely, the constant collision between two irreconcilable worldviews.

The fact that the scribe asks this question and considers it to be a test that Jesus will either fail or trip over is in itself incredibly revealing. For in their way of thinking, they have become so embroiled in the nuances and minutia of the Law that they cannot see the wood for the trees, so to speak. Their whole internal culture and cultic mindset had become showmanship, typified with endless debates and disagreements—hence, the very thought of being able to condense all 613 commandments into a single defining one would seem utterly preposterous to them. It also reveals just how far they had gone in terms of missing the whole purpose of the Law and how their own teachings had only served to tie the people in endless restrictions that only ever kept them further from God, rather than drawing them closer to Him. It is implied that their God had become the law, not the giver of the law.

We see therefore within this scene how the worldviews or mindsets of externalism and internalism collide. The legalism and misinterpretation within the externalism of the religious elite metamorphoses into what can be defined as "socio-theocracy," whereby the version of religion as defined by them alone considers the people within the community as a single entity and, thereby, themselves as being the sole arbiters of the religious continuity and functioning of the community itself within this theocratic state. Given the occupation by Rome, the religious rulers of Israel knew that while they didn't have actual legal control over the country, they had absolute moral control contorted through religious and cultural hegemony. Within this mode of thinking, for the religious class the whole nation of people is formed into one body under their own moral, social, and religious jurisdiction. Thus, their only concern for the individual is in relation to how that individual conforms or otherwise to this socio-theocratic system devised by themselves to serve their own purposes of control and power preservation. This is to be contrasted with that of Jesus as He regularly adopts what we can define as the "kingdom community" mindset when engaging with the various factions of the religious ruling class. Within this kingdom community mindset, concern for the individual emanates from the concept of familial identification within the community where all belong and all are valued members, while society functions for them through their position within the household—in this case, the household of the God of Israel. Most importantly, within this mindset or framework, the Law is for the people not the people for the Law, which is the very antithesis of the elitist mindset and hence the collision.

In this wonderful scene we see the collision between the interpretation of the meaning of the Law and the expectations of God as applied by the Pharisees in the socio-theocratic sense, against those applied by Jesus in the kingdom community mindset. We see this elsewhere in their encounters, such as where the simple question of paying taxes comes from the perspective of those who think in terms of the theocratic, whereas Jesus's penetrating response is from the perspective of the kingdom community—which is why to the Pharisees His response borders on the incomprehensible. They were speaking the same language but had entirely different perspectives—or as we would say in contemporary terminology, two entirely different worldviews. Hence their confusion when in another context they ask of Jesus, "Who is my neighbor?" (Luke 10:29). Jesus responds to these questions from the kingdom community perspective, whereas the questions are all posed from that of the socio-theocratic; when we see these scenes in this manner, we start to understand why they found Him just so perplexing and ultimately a threat to their world order.

For Jesus there is always the difference between the theology or political positions that individuals or sects represent and the individuals themselves within those sects. This is clear in this passage as Jesus immediately turns from the theological to the particular and personal, as it affects the individual—in this instance He sees the scribe as an individual person, not as a scribe or a member of the religious elite. This was (if I can perhaps border on the irreverent to make my point) Jesus's genius in what He shows us here: that compassion and concern for the individual always outweighs any theological disputes. The stakes are really high—and this is exactly what Jesus is saying to the scribe.

In order to understand just what a threat this was, one only needs to consider what Jesus thought Himself, not of the individuals but of their theology and how that theology outworked into their function as the religious leaders of Israel. This scene exposes the fact that the so-called teachers of the Law were not even in agreement, and so how could we expect the normal people to be anything other than confused too? This is what frustrated Jesus so much, which is why His methods to reach the ordinary people were seen to be so unorthodox and so literally incomprehensible to the religious rulers of the time. But it is even more profound than that, for following this scene Jesus then goes on to condemn in no uncertain terms the religious elite for their role in keeping the people from accepting Him as their Messiah.

Jesus, the internalist, exposes the externalism of the religious rulers for what it is: hierarchical, legalistic, restrictive, unmeritorious, egotistical, elitist, and their actions as hypocritical, myopic, grandiose, arrogant, self-centered, unworthy, and corrupt. For the externalist, appearance matters over intentions and substance, and religious rulers exemplify this perfectly. Consequently, we see ultimately that while this question is posed from the perspective of an externalist, Jesus replies as an internalist. Note how He does this as He distills what was regarded by the religious elite as the epitome of their self-justification—the Shema from Deut 6:3—and immediately personalizes it with the command to love one another. For the Pharisees, the second would have been utterly diminutive to the first, for religious orthodoxy would always outweigh the personal or societal. But for Jesus, the two are inseparable—two sides of the same coin, as it were. For to Him you cannot do one without the other. This, of course, reflects the same themes that are expounded upon in the book of James concerning faith and works and in the writings of the apostle John concerning love of God and love of the brethren.

Thus, we see the continuation of the golden thread of devotion weaving its way through the drama of the Gospels. To Jesus, the whole of the Law as it applies to everyone could be condensed to the single, wondrous pinnacle: to love the Lord your God and to love others as yourself. But the truly radical implication behind this for those who seek is the emphasis upon not only the individual but individual responsibility to align your own heart with God. And this leads us to the real point to be made—namely, what Jesus was interested in from the individual was one's heart and devotion. And the truly radical impact of taking responsibility includes being accountable not just within the community but, perhaps even more importantly, also in private, where it's just you and the Lord. Throughout His teachings, Jesus always advocated the imperative of taking personal, direct responsibility for one's actions whether in worship, relationships, or especially in relation to one's spiritual growth and faith. For Jesus, this could never be assumed as being coopted within corporate and social structures, or even through tradition, but had to be embraced from the position of an aligned heart attitude—or more simply, as He said, "in spirit and truth" (John 4:4). But note what He says to the woman at the well regarding how this starts now, not just in the future (John 4:23–24).

Radical Clarity for Those Who Need It Most

It is where the words and actions of Jesus come into seeming conflict with the Law of Moses that He receives most condemnation from the religious leaders. For it is these areas where the control of the people is paramount, and the standing of the religious elite is most threatened. His teaching went against their own self-righteousness and self-aggrandizement in the community—it is ever thus with any and all who seek to claim extra-revelation and impose legalism on their congregations and communities. Hence we see the utter outrage of the statements like, "The Sabbath was made for man, and not man for the Sabbath" (Mark 2:27); it's "not what goes into the mouth defiles a man; but what comes out of the mouth, this defiles a man" (Matt 15:11); that you should "render therefore to Caesar the things that are Caesar's, and to God the things that are God's" (Matt 22:21). These statements are the equivalent of cultural sledgehammers and are directed at the ordinary people, for His message to them is one of hope outside of the strictures and confinements of unnecessary religiosity.

But among this, the truly radical message of Jesus came to those who least expected it. With the assumption that the Messiah would come in glory to overthrow the Romans, most would have expected Him to have come and declared Himself in the temple at least and to have been from the Pharisaic sect. But no, Jesus's mission right from the start was directed at something much more profound. Even while declaring that the kingdom of God was at hand, He meant it not as the majority expected but in a much more radical way—from the inside. And He directed His message from the very beginning not to the religious leaders but to the ordinary people: the poor, the sick, the downtrodden, the sinful, and the believing families. He came to bring hope through a new type of cleansing, from the inside out—a cleansing of the heart not the exterior.

His message started with the heart of the matter. The Sermon on the Mount is the most beautiful exposition on how the people had been taught erroneously about the nature and holiness of God. Rather, to understand the Law you had to look through it to the Author of the Law and see His heart through it. This leads then to complete realization that one could never measure and live up to the true requirements, which brings you right back to the start of the Beatitudes that says blessed are the poor in spirit for they will see the kingdom of God. In the Sermon on the Mount, we see that Jesus addresses and is concerned with individual behavior toward each other and more particularly toward God. In other words, it is His statements concerning the individual's devotion that must have astounded most in how contrary they were to the cultural norms and institutionalized religion of the day. His instructions as addressed to the general populace were that despite the inadequacies of their religious rulers (or perhaps because of them), they were to take personal responsibility for their direct, private relationship with God. This is demonstrated from His revelation to them regarding their privilege of considering themselves as part of the household of God ("our Father") to the imperative expressions of personal and private faith ("when you fast," "when you pray," etc.). This is the language of devotional empowerment as they are being told that they have direct access to the Father and told of their positional, familial, and communal relationship with Him. And indeed, we see this revolutionary principle expand and unfold throughout the Gospels as it affects individuals as they encounter the presence of Jesus. For we see it in the woman at the well, the woman who had been bleeding for twelve years, the poor man filled with the legion of demons—all poor in spirit coming to Jesus as they see that He is only answer to their torment. Read these accounts again in the light of the most beautiful and profound words ever spoken toward the heart of any human being, ever:

> Come to Me, all you who labor and are heavy laden, and I will give you rest. Take My yoke upon you and learn from Me, for I am gentle and lowly in heart, and you will find rest for your souls. For My yoke is easy and My burden is light. (Matt 11:28–30)

Here we have it: the declaration of divinity to the individual heart. To Jesus it is the condition of the heart in this world and the concomitant future of the soul of all people, without exclusion, that matters more than anything else. He constantly implores the people to focus on their souls with an eye firmly fixed on eternity. We see this so emphatically in His emphasis again on eternal life; and we can only ponder that the impact of this on the individual Israelite at the time could not have been more radical. This was a new message, totally different from anything they would have heard before. Think through the impact of the Mosaic law on those living under a society dominated in culture and everyday life with the workings and teachings of Moses and expanded upon by generations of rabbis, and then the Messiah comes to teach simply that this eternal life is available to all, with only one caveat:

> And as Moses lifted up the serpent in the wilderness, even so must the Son of Man be lifted up, that whoever believes in Him should not perish but have eternal life. For God so loved the world that He gave His only begotten Son, that whoever believes in Him should not perish but have everlasting life. . . . He who believes in the Son has everlasting life. (John 3:14–16, 36)

Now this concept of eternal life is not one that is mentioned much in the Old Testament at all, but here it is not only being revealed by the One who has authority over eternity, but it is being offered to all—freely, without works other than belief in Him as the Messiah. The enormity, originality, and simplicity of this would have been (and still is!) outrageous and awe-inspiring, the same we see today with the message of Christ; for to so many it is too simple. So simple, in fact, that even after salvation we have a tendency to want to add to it with regulations and rules and doctrines made by man. But the message from Jesus was simply this: come, sit, rest, and have peace.

Jesus and the Trials of Ordinary Life

When we think about the time of the Gospels and the message to the people, we see Jesus time and time again address the concept of the external to the internal and bring these two concepts together with radical clarity. The most significant factors affecting the average citizen of Israel's relationship with God rested on two interrelated and utterly inseparable factors: God's Providence and His omnipresence. Jesus too is more than aware of the trials of daily life for most. His concern for our daily lives, though, is for them to be more God-centric in that our worries and concerns should be laid at God's feet, for He is in control of all things. His statements about not being worried or concerned about the future are not the ravings of some unrealistic lunatic who understands nothing of what ordinary people go through (or some cultic charlatan who lives solely off other people)—no, they are simply the wisdom of God in our lives that what is of real concern is that God is sovereign and knows the future and that as His children we are part of His household. Jesus never backed away from the fact that life can be and will be difficult for believers—even unto persecution and death—but what He means is that on an everyday basis we are simply called to trust in His goodness and sovereignty. That is all that is required. For Jesus, the onus on the individual person having to deal with daily vagaries of life is simple: store up in heaven treasures that count. "Now what does that mean?" I hear you say. Well, it means that we outwork the greatest commandments in our daily lives. It is living our lives with God included not excluded; for if all things come from the Father, so we are to appreciate them with Him and with each other. We need each other to get through this life, and we need to do so in peace both with God and with our neighbor. This is the beauty of these greatest of commandments and why they are inseparable to living life.

Perhaps it is this whole concept of God's Providence in our world and lives that we have lost through our own sophistication. And it is through this that we see the separation of our worlds, where everyday life becomes separate from God. Providence, as we see, is not just the involvement in the grand design of the universe and outworking of the ultimate plans of God to bring all together in perfection with Him (as utterly beautiful as that is). Providence is so much more than that, as it relates to our own minuscule lives. In the grand scheme of things, we might well say, "What do I matter?" And this is of course the existential crises of existential thought, for if all is meaningless then there is no meaning to purpose. In a time of abject poverty, war, occupation, corruption, and hypocrisy, Jesus cuts through this stupid man-made philosophical thinking by arguing for God's providential care of the individual. For He understands that if God is not seen to care down to the finite details of our individual lives, then He will become abstract and ultimately removed from those lives. Hence, we see from the very start that we are to petition the Lord with anticipated gratitude for our daily bread, and to note from Whom it comes. He is the Provider of His people. But this does not yield to laziness or mad consumerist forms of religion but to a providential relationship between us and God.

Sometimes what I find most revealing in how Jesus deals with the people around Him is what He doesn't say to them, rather than what we (and they) might have expected Him to have said. Indeed, even today, I would say that we think (and are told) that these are the things He is saying to us, when He's not. In all His dealings with individuals or crowds, Jesus never once tells them to go to the temple or synagogue more. He never once tells them to read more Torah or even—and this is even more astounding—to go and make sacrifices to God. And this, when you think about it, is utterly unbelievable. What He does say is personal and addresses the individual's private relationship and status with God. He is as concerned about our earthly circumstances as with our spiritual participation in the heavenlies and the work of our Father—for to Him both are divinely conjoined within His kingdom community mindset. For just as He commands us to sin no more and to examine ourselves as to who is without sin, so He offers forgiveness and, through Him alone, hope in an eternity that starts now, not at some nebulous and tenuous future date; He requires us to take stock of where our hearts are and to store up treasures in heaven, for doing so is the mystical, wonderful key to living our earthly life in all its abundance, joy, wonder, beauty, and humble appreciation of what belief in Jesus Christ truly means.[4] But His teachings were also radically liberating in that He came not to condemn but to give life in all its abundance and to show how we should treat life as the precious gift from God that we are given. It is precious to God and so it is precious to Him that we live it abundantly, through Him (John 10:10).

The Gospel of the Abundant and Abiding Life

The gospel of Jesus is the gospel of life, for He said that He came to give us life in all its fullness. This is not an abstract notion of future hope, but it is the here and now. Life itself is the gift from God—and Jesus takes that one step further to pronounce and announce eternal life through Him. But this eternal life starts now for those who believe. His message is one of peace and rest in Him. This is His only call, that we abide and dwell with Him. That is what is required from us now—and all that is required from us—with a pure heart and one that has been cleansed and purified by the Holy Spirit. This again is the new message and covenant from Christ that through Him we have peace with God. Again, we come back to the

---

4. See Matt 6:19–20; Luke 5:20; John 8:7, 11; 10:10; 17:3.

internalization of this. This is what is meant by Jesus at the ascension when the disciples ask Him again whether He will now set up the messianic kingdom, and His response is basically one of, "You do not need to concern yourselves with the big picture when God will do what He has stated He will do; what is to concern you now is what I have wanted to you to be concerned about all along: your devotion to Me alone."

This thought is ultimately pointing to a time after the resurrection where we would be called to abide in Him as He would abide in us. Note how unbelievably unorthodox such teaching is—nothing about the temple or the institutions or the traditions or the ceremonies. This concept is revealed in Jesus's very last discourse with His disciples in John 14–17. Within this discourse, Jesus sets out how after the resurrection and His ascension, everything will change as what we now call the church age is ushered in. In this discourse Jesus reveals that the church will have a totally new dynamic with Him, the Father, and the Holy Spirit. This is completely revolutionary from all that came before, and it concerns the new privilege that the Christian has in relation to the members of the Trinity in being able to abide with them always; this is not through works but through position. And it is this position that changes everything devotionally as we are literally joined with them. The point that is made throughout this discourse is that this is God finally instigating all that He has ever wanted: a willing people, willingly devoted to Him, abiding together, and above all abiding with Him. And thus, we cannot but stand in awe and wonder at Jesus as our own pearl of great price—the cost paid for by Himself and given freely to all who ask. This is our wonderful God.

Positional Identity and Positional Blessings

Behold what manner of love the Father has bestowed on us, that we should be called children of God!

1 JOHN 3:1

IN THIS MOST BEAUTIFUL and astounding statement, the apostle John starts by drawing our attention to the proclamation that follows "Behold." What follows is not just to be stated but proclaimed in the strongest manner. But it is much more than just a proclamation, it is something that bursts forth from deep within him as he considers all the goodness and utter generosity of God for what He has bestowed upon us who deserve nothing. It is a bursting forth of wonder that comes forth from probably decades of immersing himself in the true implications of what the Lord has given us through his sacrifice on the cross. But it is more than a declaration, for the word "behold" also contains an aspect that what follows needs to be grasped, seen, fully understood, witnessed, and fully registered in belief.

What the apostle is drawing our attention to here is twofold. Firstly, it is the love of God toward those that believe (the "us" of the statement) that is the instigator of the result, which is that those who believe can be called children of God. The result stems from He who loved us first; it is because of this love, and only because of God's love, that this is the case. It is pure grace, and it is utterly unmerited favor. Secondly is the inference in the statement that there is nothing that the believer has undertaken to deserve such a title or position other than belief in Jesus Christ. No wonder the apostle marvels at the generosity of God. From whence, however, comes such confidence in John's identity and comfort in belonging—and is such available to us too? This we shall explore and expound upon, for it has tremendous impact upon all that we are, how we engage with God, and how we live as Christians.

It starts in like manner as with John here, and indeed as with all the apostles: the believer must learn, grasp, fully understand, and immerse oneself within the wonder and miracles that are implicit within all that Jesus achieved and has bestowed upon us who believe in Him. This is all too little taught and applied and we are the poorer for it, for when we do so, we cannot but fail to gaze upon the wonder, majesty, and generosity of our Lord.

Positional Identity: The New Covenant Gift from God

The time has come to address some fundamental precepts that affect all of what we will be discussing subsequently in relation to our devotion. It is here that I have been deeply impacted by the teachings of a number of disparate believers, medieval and modern. Firstly, I have been greatly influenced by the messianic studies of Dr. Arnold Fruchtenbaum and his discourses on the certainty of our status and position in Christ owing to the unconditional promises received upon salvation.[1] This, coupled with C. H. Spurgeon's elucidation of God's promises, has had huge impact in shaping my appreciation of the work of God within every believer, not just in a select few "super-Christians."[2] Indeed, it is the elaboration and expansion of these teachings, when combined with other studies (especially John F. Walvoord on the person and work of the Holy Spirit[3]), that have shaped my thinking on all that follows regarding these precepts and their impact on believers' devotion. My own theology with regard

---

1. Fruchtenbaum, *Messianic Jewish Epistles*; Fruchtenbaum, *Thirty-Three Things*.
2. Spurgeon, *According to Promise*.
3. Walvoord, *Holy Spirit*.

to devotion has been fundamentally inspired and molded through the writings of some from the medieval monastic orders, such as Bernard of Clairvaux (and other Cistercians), Francis of Assisi, Brother Lawrence, Thomas à Kempis, and some earlier mystics (such as Richard Rolle and Walter Hilton), as well as the devotional attitudes held by men such as William Law, John Wesley, John Newton, William Wilberforce, J. C. Ryle, J. N. Darby, John Henry Newman, Dietrich Bonhoeffer, and A. W. Tozer.[4] While for some this may seem like a very eclectic mix, the purpose of naming them like this is to demonstrate a fundamental principle in itself: it is always the Holy Spirit within us who remains the same and does not change, and that devotion is always driven by Him and through Him—always because of, and for, Jesus. The Holy Spirit dwells within each and every believer and God shows no partiality, so while all these may be considered exceptional people (and they were), they had no more special access to God than any ordinary believer has ever had (1 Cor 3:16, Rom 2:11). This thought is fundamental to everything that is discussed below.

As we will see, these precepts, once appreciated and embraced, not only transform our devotion but impact the believer's entire relationship and life with God. These precepts can be amalgamated into a singular term as they form a single, perfect gift from God. It is a singular gift, for while there are individual components taken as a whole, they form a unified entity that can be encapsulated and referred to as a new "Familial and Positional Identity." The nature of this gift is singular in that while there is a plurality of components, they are inseparable as a singular form—in other words, if you have one you have them all. The term "gift" of course implies a giver and a recipient of the gift, it also implies that the gift is given at the sole discretion of the giver acting independently to the recipient in terms of the gift's consistency, function, and motive for the giving. The recipient accordingly has no say in judging either the motives of the giver or the constitution of the gift. Therefore, these basic factors should be taken into consideration here where we discuss the component parts of the gift and also how the Giver looks upon the recipients. For God imparts the gift and makes it available to each and every person who

---

4. Of particular note are Thornton and Varennem, *Honey and Salt*; Matarasso, *Cistercian World*; Vauchez, *Francis of Assisi*; Brother Lawrence, *Practice of the Presence*; Thomas à Kempis, *Imitation of Christ*; Richard Rolle, *Richard Rolle Collection*; Hilton, *Ladder of Perfection*; Law, *Serious Call*; Murray, *Wesley*; Newton, *Collected Letters*; Wilberforce, *Real Christianity*; Murray, *J. C. Ryle*; Newman, *Apologie*; Metaxas, *Bonhoeffer*; Tozer, *Crucified Life*. See the bibliography for further sources.

comes to believe in Jesus as Lord and Savior, God and King. The gift and its component parts come from God and are freely bestowed on all who believe and are only available to those who believe because of how God sees the values of the sacrifice of His Son; hence, how He then sees those who believe has nothing to do with us as individuals and everything to do with Jesus. Taken in their entirety, this gift and its component parts are utterly transformative in nature and as we will see are divine privileges that are beyond compare.

The Gift: A New Familial and Positional Identity

Enmeshed deep within the beauty of salvation is the transformation of the identity of the believer. This gift, this new identity, is fundamentally familial in its constituency. The identity of the believer in Christ is transformed both from the perspective of God and because of how the recipient of the gift is expected to regard themselves. This new identity is bestowed upon the believer as a unilateral gesture formed in love—love based on the sacrifice of Christ alone and the Father's love for His Son. Thus, this gift is given not on our merits but upon the divine merit of Christ. This identity then is the consummation of all the components of the gift. It is encapsulated in the term "belonging," for we now belong to something entirely different to what we did before. With this belonging come privileges and responsibilities. This belonging is inferred within the parallel word "identification," for the gift is given in order that the recipient can be identified as such by the Giver, by themselves internally, and by the outside world externally.

The Recipients of the New Positional Identity

The gift can be referred to as being "new" as both it and its recipients were not revealed in the Old Testament. It goes without saying that the recipients are those who are believers in Jesus Christ, whom we call believers or simply Christians. However, this is too simplistic and misses something much more meaningful—namely, how the Scriptures (and therefore how the Holy Spirit) refers to believers. It is interesting that the term "believer" is not used in Scripture as a name or form of reference by God to those who believe. In fact, almost exclusively the Scriptures show that God prefers to refer to individual Christians in familial terms: members of the household of God, children, heirs, brethren, and of course the bride of Christ. This would seem therefore to be of great importance to God, and yet to grasp its implications and to apply it to our relationship with God is fundamental but too little appreciated by most ordinary Christians. It is the deeply personal nature of this new identity which should not be missed, for these terms imply deep intimacy and belonging, as well as both familial and positional status.

These familial and positional characterizations are not stated lightly and should not be treated as such. For they are how God defines the believer, and therefore how the believer should define themselves, with the all the confidence that such identification infers and imparts. For position implies a standing and status that the believer is identified as having within the kingdom realm of God. This produces privileges, rights, and entitlements that are bestowed upon the believer out of pure love and from pure grace. For ultimately the gift of this "Positional Identity" is a love gift, and it is this that most do not appreciate, in that the motive of giving here is one not just of generosity but of an outpouring of love. This outpouring is not because of any merit or achievement of the recipient but because of the Father's love for His Son and, by divine extension, those who love Him too. This is the distinctive of the gift of this new Positional Identity and its components parts as we'll discuss below. The distinctive pertains to both its inclusivity and its exclusivity—meaning that it is available to every person who believes in Jesus, through which they are indwelled by the Holy Spirit, and only to those who believe. Both these factors should be deeply encouraging to the individual believer, for God shows no partiality between those who believe, while at the same time paying special attention only to those in His care, for "the eyes of the LORD are on the righteous" (Ps 34:15) as the psalmist reassures us.

The Gift's Component Parts: Positional Blessings

Those who are deemed to be "blessed" in biblical terms are those who are in receipt of divine favor that is unmerited and distributed at the sole discretion of God—in short, "blessed" means to be in receipt of grace. While it has component parts, as we said, we can describe this gift in itself as being blessed in that it comes from God and is for those can be termed "the blessed" for being in receipt of the gift. Thus, the gift of Positional Identity is called a blessed gift for that very reason, and it is important that it is regarded as such, for it manifests from God and was divinely ordained. The gift, as we have said, while it forms a single entity is composed of various component parts that I believe can be amalgamated into one frame of reference, and I have called this amalgamation "Positional Blessings"—for they are the blessings that not only are given exclusively to those with the new Positional Identity (all believers) but also are inseparable from each other in their entirety, for the composite forms the whole gift. We start, first of all, by considering why I have termed them Positional Blessings. Quite simply, it is because I have witnessed the deeply emotional and transformative impact that these "truths" have on ordinary believers, when explained to them fully, that they are quite rightly termed Positional Blessings.

As we consider what follows and the Scriptures that are referenced, we will see them as not just truths that applied only to the apostles or even just the early believers. When we examine them together as well as individually and consider to whom they were addressed—namely, to those within the churches, just normal Christians—we can glean from them the most beautiful picture of the unconditional bequeathing of the most monumental blessings ever conceived. So monumental, in fact, that their origin and conception must be divine, for no mortal mind could possibly conceptualize something that is so beautiful, intricate, magisterial, and complex and yet held in such unity of thought and purpose. These Scriptures reveal that these blessings are not just theological constructs but divinely preconceived ordinations and precepts revealed through the apostles by the Holy Spirit. As they largely relate to the work of the Holy Spirit within the believer, they are presented as being available to be appropriated by all upon salvation. Their availabilities and applicability are matters that have already been settled by the Father, available only because of Jesus, and distributed through the Holy Spirit. These are matters that have already been consecrated in the heavens and made available not just to the original recipients but are as available now to all who believe as they were to the very first believers. They are not blessings that will or might occur in the future if certain preconditions are met—no, they have already occurred and are already settled in heaven, so to speak. And because of this they are to be settled in our hearts now and forever. These become the very blessings upon which then we build our current faith and standing, for this was God's intention for them to us. They are the truths and precepts upon which we can rest assured and upon which we can settle our devotion. It is with these that the believer can foster the mindset with which to approach and pass through what we describe later as the "Precious Gates of Devotion." And above all, it is through and because of the truth and veracity of these blessings that we are able and entitled to "come boldly to the throne of grace" (Heb 4:16)—boldly, without fear or trepidation—and it is only because of Jesus.

Just one further point: in order to appreciate, absorb, and appropriate the sheer wonderful enormity of what is stated in all the following passages, it is important for the reader to make note of the verb tenses that are used by the apostles in their discussions. These verb tenses are unequivocal and point to wonderful truths that are already available and apply to the believer upon salvation. The texts couldn't be clearer and, when drawn together, paint the most awe-inspiring picture of what Jesus has achieved and blessed His bride with. In order to fully understand that these blessings are not just the fabrication of wishful thinkers, we need to observe that they are not only interwoven throughout the New Testament but that their impact affects everything and every issue that is addressed in the New Testament—which is why, as we shall see, they are foundational to our devotion and practice thereof.

First and foremost, though, we should consider them to be a manifestation of, and inextricably linked with, the installation of the New Covenant by Jesus. In essence, they could even be considered to be "New Covenant Blessings" on account of them being bestowed in accordance with the logical construct behind the words of the Lord through the prophets Jeremiah and Ezekiel as the New Covenant is announced as being forthcoming and certain:

> I will put My law in their minds, and write it on their hearts; and I will be their God, and they shall be My people. No more shall every man teach His neighbor, and every man his brother, saying, "Know the Lord," for they all shall know Me, from the least of them to the greatest of them, says the Lord. (Jer 31:33–34)

> I will give you a new heart and put a new spirit within you; I will take the heart of stone out of your flesh and give you a heart of flesh. I will put My Spirit within you and cause you to walk in My statutes, and you will keep My judgments and do them. (Ezek 36:26–27)

In the midst of this astounding prophetic promise, we see that something miraculous occurs to those who are now within this New Covenant—namely, God Himself will instigate measures that literally transfigure hearts and minds in order that the New Covenant participant is able to know the Lord and to finally, miraculously, be one of His people. What this transfiguration amounts to fully is only revealed by Jesus and the apostles, but all of these are embellishments and expositions of what it means and what it takes to fulfill this in the New Covenant context. I would argue, though, that technically the whole gambit of Positional Blessings can be divided into those that are familial and those that are positional, or as those that are transfigurative and those that are transformative.

The Transfigurative and Transformative Positional Blessings

As with every single instance of how God embarks on a process of engagement with us, it starts with a miracle as God exercises His divine attributes and makes sure thereby that all that follows is to His glory alone, for He will never, ever give His glory to another (Isa 42:8), which in itself has multiple implications that will be discussed later in subsequent sections. As is implicit within the Jeremiah and Ezekiel passages discussed, this transitional miracle into the new covenant is both transfigurative and transformative. In simplest terms there is a transfiguration and transformation that occurs within every believer in Christ at the very moment of salvation. As we will see, there are numerous passages in Scripture that make it abundantly clear that upon salvation something extraordinary occurs—and it is something that far too few Christians are either aware of or are taught, with the concomitant diminishing and impoverishing of our faith and our devotion to God.

The Transfigurative Positional Blessings

Recreated upon Salvation

It is during Jesus's meeting at night with Nicodemus, as recorded in John 3, that the whole concept of the requirement to be "born again" as a requisite of entering the kingdom of God is first discussed. Nicodemus was a teacher of the Law in the temple at Jerusalem, and Jesus expresses surprise that as a teacher of the Law, he had not already thought this through and did not reason that this would be the case. It therefore could not be a truly new thing that Jesus was revealing—Jesus's surprise at this lack of knowledge from Nicodemus was expressed in manner that suggests that He expected that this rabbi would have at least worked out from the Scriptures that this would be the case, even if it is not fully spelled out within them. The Law of Moses reveals that we can never fulfill the righteous requirements of God through our own efforts because of our inherent sinful nature, hence the need for a complete spiritual re-creation or rather "re-return," so to speak, to how we were created in the first place before sin entered the world. This in effect reveals the fact that since the fall in the garden of Eden, the sin nature of humankind cannot be dealt with through effort alone, that God would have to intervene in some form of miraculous way to basically recreate us so that this sin nature is removed from us in order that the other blessings can follow. For God created Adam and Eve and through them sin entered the world. Thus, in order to resolve this issue while we are still alive, so to speak, we need to be recreated, or regenerated to use the technical parlance, in order to be able to enter this kingdom of God. This is what Nicodemus should have seen in, and reasoned from, Scripture—that God would have to intervene Himself into the human story not just as the restorer of all things but as the redeemer of creation itself, for all of creation was and is affected by the presence of human sin. We explore this in more detail below, but clearly God regards this transfiguration as necessary in order to qualify us, if not literally physically then spiritually, so we can enter into the kingdom of God (John 3:3). To be holy as God is holy is what it would take for us to enter the kingdom of God, and for us in our sinful nature to become holy would entail the miracle of God's intervention—thereby giving Him the glory, not earned through our own efforts. It is perhaps because the method of being born again or regenerated is invisible that we do not appreciate or regard it fully as the miracle that it is. But it is as much a mystery as the virgin birth. It is a miracle and should be treated as such.

In addition to this description of the transfiguration of the believer as being "born again," the apostolic Epistles expound upon this and define it in even more miraculous terms. Through them we discover that this process is not just a spiritual one but one that involves us becoming an actual "new creation": "Therefore, if anyone is in Christ, He is a new creation; old things have passed away; behold, all things have become new" (2 Cor 5:17).

Now this is clearly a miracle of some note, for only the Creator has the authority to recreate. And if we, who are saved or born again, are actually recreated, then this engenders huge implications as to the impact this must have on our lives, our faith, and our devotion to God. To truly embrace the truth of this, we must see it as a necessary step within the believer's eventual complete transfiguration into the very image of Christ. For we will one day be made like Him (1 John 3:2), and one glorious day the Lord will go even further as we are united and unified into God, as we become "one" with Him, not just spiritually but connectively (John 17:20–23). While for the present in this life we are spiritually recreated (which interestingly is of more importance to God than our own physical re-creation), one day our mortal bodies will indeed take on perfection in Christ, for this is our living and most precious hope:

> Behold, I tell you a mystery: We shall not all sleep, but we shall all be changed—in a moment, in the twinkling of an eye, at the last trumpet. For the trumpet will sound, and the dead will be raised incorruptible, and we shall be changed. For this corruptible must put on incorruption, and this mortal must put on immortality. So when this corruptible has put on incorruption, and this mortal has put on immortality, then shall be brought to pass the saying that is written: "Death is swallowed up in victory."(1 Cor 15:51–45)

Three Witnesses

In biblical terms, matters which pertain to the works of God are referred to as witnesses, and miracles are always witnesses to Himself and to His creation. All of God's miracles within our created sphere serve three purposes as "witnesses," and the "re-creation" of every new believer is no different:

1. The very conception, formulation, and execution of the miracle of re-creation exemplifies His sovereignty, power, and other attributes so that no other takes the glory for the miracle itself and for what manifests after the miracle. While the miracle can be seen to be a pure witness of God's majesty (and this in itself would be reason enough for God to undertake it), along with all other miracles, this one to produces two further witnesses not only to the miracle itself but to its purposes and impact, as follows:

2. The miracle is to edify and strengthen the belief in God by those who are already believing in Him and to equip them further with the necessary faith to carry on believing and to live according to

His ways. It serves, in other words, to draw them closer to Him in reverence, gratitude, faith, and love.

3. The miracle serves as a witness to those who are presently "outside" of the family of God, to show them His power, sovereignty, and His worthiness of engendering and generating belief and faith.

Every single miracle as recorded in Scripture has this pattern, and the "re-creation" of all new believers upon salvation is no different. Point 1 is so clearly demonstrated through Eph 2:8–9; point 3 is alluded to and found everywhere in the injunctions of Christ and the apostles and is exemplified by such expressions as found in John 17, where Jesus introduces the very concept of the unification of the believer with the Godhead. From this very introduction it is made clear that this unification is not merely and wonderfully for its own sake, to show the glory of God, or indeed just for the edification of believers, but so "that they [believers] may be made perfect in one, and that the world may know that You have sent Me, and have loved them as You have loved Me" (John 17:23), which in itself is to be a witness in order "that the world may believe that You sent Me" (John 17:21). However, it is point 2 that addresses the subject of concern to us here both in terms of our Positional Blessings and as we will explore in terms of our devotion. We will see how the thread of devotion weaves inextricably through all that becomes possible for every believer as we learn of and appropriate these blessings into the fabric of our life with God.

God, in His infinite wisdom and knowledge of the spiritual weakness of believers in all matters pertaining to God and dealing with the temptations of this world, from the beginning of time knew that He would have to intervene into the very hearts and minds of those who believe in Him in order that we would be both able and willing to love Him fully and to become the people He so desires. His chosen method of doing this defies belief and is beyond comprehension—the very audacity of this as a claim and its own witness of transformed lives is in itself proof not only of the veracity of the Bible but of its authorship too. Only God could claim to be able to do such a thing. God in His mercy knew that He couldn't just recreate us and leave us as empty vessels that have been cleaned but have no "engine" or ability to live as "new creations." What is this thing, this miracle? It is the indwelling of the Holy Spirit within each and every new believer.

Indwelled by the Holy Spirit

> And I will pray the Father, and He will give you another Helper, that He may abide with you forever—the Spirit of truth, whom the world cannot receive, because it neither sees Him nor knows Him; but you know Him, for He dwells with you and will be in you. (John 14:16–17)

> Do you not know that you are the temple of God and that the Spirit of God dwells in you? (1 Cor 3:16)

The passages quoted above tell us that the re-creation of believers includes, as part of this remarkable transfiguration, a further mystery and miracle: upon salvation, the Holy Spirit comes and dwells within each believer. We will discuss the implications of this below, but first of all we need to consider that we are also told that the indwelling of the Holy Spirit is definitive in that it defines who does and who doesn't qualify as a believer and is therefore inextricably linked to the "re-creation miracle" of John 3:3, for Rom 8:9 says in such poignant clarity and almost brutal succinctness, "But you are not in the flesh but in the Spirit, if indeed the Spirit of God dwells in you. Now if anyone does not have the Spirit of Christ, He is not His."

In short, therefore, if we are born again, recreated, then we are also indwelled by the Holy Spirit—it is this that defines who is and who isn't a Christian. The indwelling of the Holy Spirit changes everything in God's eyes for them from this point on; for He no longer regards us as enemies in a fallen, God-hating world, but when He looks upon us, He now sees within us hearts that have been recreated to be realigned toward Him. Even more importantly, what He sees is the Holy Spirit within us and regards us no longer as corrupted but as redeemed, washed, cleansed, and holy. This is the point of inflection that we so little grasp as believers, and it literally changes everything, including our devotion and how we devote ourselves to him.

At this point we need to pause and reflect upon whom we are talking about and what is being discussed and described here. For what we are contemplating is that God Himself in the person of Holy Spirit comes and lives, literally "tabernacles," within us. Man could not conceive of such a suggestion in all honesty, but only God could contemplate such a plan. For God, the Holy Spirit could not, and would not, dwell within something that is corrupt and vile or at enmity with Father or the Son, and so God recreates in order that the Holy Spirit is able to dwell within us. This is the perfect circular argument and closed system that only God can instigate and implement. It is unfathomable as a construct and as a concept; yet it is true. This twofold miracle of re-creation and divine occupation should and does change everything for it is of inestimable value, and yet Christians make far too little of it and rarely connect the two—an unappreciation and disregard bordering on irreverence, which is sadly all too easily explicable given how lightly we treat the miraculous. The concept that God Himself comes to dwell within us should be a factor for awe and wonder every day, and yet most rarely give it a passing thought. Or if they do, they think about it only as it might affect others in its manifestation of the so-called "gifts of the Spirit" and rarely, if ever, as part of the miracle of salvation. By doing so, we diminish the miracle, insult God, and grieve the Holy Spirit, for it is, as we'll discuss, only by having the Holy Spirit within us that we are able to do so much that the Scriptures speak of. But before we do so, we need to look at how this dual miracle of regeneration and indwelling transfigures our status and standing in the eyes of God, for

> when the kindness and the love of God our Savior toward man appeared, not by works of righteousness which we have done, but according to His mercy He saved us, through the washing of regeneration and renewing of the Holy Spirit, whom He poured out on us abundantly through Jesus Christ our Savior, that having been justified by His grace we should become heirs according to the hope of eternal life. (Titus 3:4–7)

Prior to continuing with the further results of this dual miracle of regeneration and indwelling, we must take a step back before we take steps forward, for it is important for the continuing acceptance of the believer of these Positional Blessings that assurance of salvation and its immediate effect is given. This cannot be emphasized enough as we think about this in terms of our devotion. For we must be assured, and convinced, of our consolation in Christ if we are to be able to truly worship Him and if we are to be able to be devoted to Him. Our devotion cannot be "living" if we do not have complete confidence in our salvation. Otherwise, such words from Jesus as "Let not your heart be troubled; you believe in God, believe also in Me" (John 14:1) become meaningless as, if we are not convinced, then we are insecure and apprehensive no matter how brave we are. This is vital for equipping the ordinary believer in the living of daily life in the light of our faith, for if we are not convinced and assured, then we will have no peace—which is the opposite of what we are told we should have. So, to have peace, we must be convinced. And this is why Jesus, and the apostles, are so very clear on this subject, for it really matters that we do know and that we are both convinced and assured. And so, when we examine the following texts, we must do so with an honest understanding of the unconditionality implied and in particular, as we said earlier, noting of the verb tenses as they pertain to the subject matter:

> For God so loved the world that He gave His only begotten Son, that whoever believes in Him should not perish but have everlasting life. (John 3:16)

> He who believes in the Son has everlasting life; and he who does not believe the Son shall not see life, but the wrath of God abides on him. (John 3:36)

> And he brought them out and said, "Sirs, what must I do to be saved?"
> So they said, "Believe on the Lord Jesus Christ, and you will be saved, you and your household." (Acts 16:30–31)

> For by grace you have been saved through faith, and that not of yourselves; it is the gift of God, not of works, lest anyone should boast. (Eph 2:8–9)

It is belief in Jesus Christ and Him alone that saves, nothing more and nothing less. For His sacrifice on the cross was complete, and belief alone in Him is the complete condition that God has ordained for salvation. If you believe then you are saved; it is that simple and, yes, it's that unconditional, for this belief also comes with a promise of eternity and a future filled with unmerited favor and blessings that God has foreordained. The blessings and favors then start upon salvation, as we are transitioned from darkness into His light and from being His enemies to being declared righteous by Him and having been "justified freely by His grace through the redemption that is in Christ Jesus" (Rom 3:24):

> Therefore, as through one man's offense judgment came to all men, resulting in condemnation, even so through one Man's righteous act the free gift came to all men, resulting in justification of life. For as by one man's disobedience many were made

sinners, so also by one Man's obedience many will be made righteous. (Rom 5:18–19)

Yet indeed I also count all things loss for the excellence of the knowledge of Christ Jesus my Lord, for whom I have suffered the loss of all things, and count them as rubbish, that I may gain Christ and be found in Him, not having my own righteousness, which is from the law, but that which is through faith in Christ, the righteousness which is from God by faith. (Phil 3:8–10)

Familial Repositioning

The dual miracle of regeneration and indwelling literally translates us in a twinkling of an eye, the instant we believe, from being considered the enemies of God to being beloved by Him, as we are transported from darkness into His glorious light. But it is to the familial aspect of this change of perspective from God that we again must look upon, in awe and wonder, as we behold what manner of love this is before us. When we learn that whereas once we were strangers and alien to Him, now because of our simple faith in Christ, He has qualified us, unilaterally out of pure grace and love, and identifies us, unconditionally, as intimate family members. The descriptive terms themselves have a composite name—the household of God—and various other terms can be seen to relate to how the believer is seen, relationally, by the members of the Godhead:

- The Bride of Christ

In order to appreciate the beauty of the fullness of our new Positional Identity and its blessings, I want to expand a little on one of the most beautiful and least appreciated images, by ordinary Christians, of how God collectively defines the entirety of those who believe in Jesus. Most are probably broadly familiar with the collective terms "the body of Christ" and "the church," but few are familiar with this term "bride." This may be because it has traditionally been associated with the various eschatological events within the end times and the book of Revelation which, owing to its complexity and the concomitant plethora of different interpretations, most ordinary Christians pay little attention to.[5] However, by doing so with regard to the bride, we miss one of the most reassuring

---

5. Rev 21:2,9–10; 22:17

and important messages that God has given us concerning how He regards our status and position in His household. While, as I said before, it is not my intention to delve into deep theology here, as such, I think it more important for our purposes to concentrate on what the imagery of such descriptions infer for the believer, and hence for our devotion.

What we do learn from the Scripture references is simply that Jesus referred to Himself as being the groom and that the entirety of those who believe in Him are His bride. As believers, we need to restore our identity to ourselves in the possessional once again. To define the blessings without recognizing what they mean in terms of our identity misses their true purpose and value, for we need to be more aware of who we are in Christ and how the Godhead now looks upon us. But even being aware is not enough if we don't truly recognize what this means and what difference it makes to us personally for our lives in the here and now, our every day as ordinary Christians. Theological constructs are all well and good, but they are of little value when it comes to actively pursuing and building real life relationships. Here both identity and certainty really do matter. One can draw a simple analogy in the difference between a couple who are merely dating and when they become engaged. Once engaged, the relationship changes unequivocally from one of uncertainty to one where they can plan for the future and plan their lives around each other, replete in reciprocated love, respect, and belonging. Hence, the same should be, and can be, true for the individual believer. As the engagement of a couple is as much a statement of trust and commitment as it is of love, so too with the believer as Christ's bride. We can trust in our Savior as well as love Him. This difference makes an extraordinary impact on our relationship with Him and makes an utterly transformative difference to our devotion to Him.

We need, as believers, to restore our identity as Christ's bride and see what worth we have as individuals again. This means that we need to learn again to see ourselves as God sees us, for the beauty of the bride in God's eyes, and the power behind this imagery, is ours to behold if we truly look. We need to capture again this essence and grasp what it means to be a Christian from God's perspective, the beauty of which has the most profound impact on our devotion, which is amazingly what God intended all along. He longs to be in our presence and always has done. From the beginning of time, we see it in the most moving question that God has ever asked when, while walking in the garden of Eden immediately after the fall, He called out to Adam, "Where are you?" (Gen 3:9).

This is the same question that He continually asks of us, that it is He who wants to be abide and be with us so that we can abide and be with Him. It is He who initiates, who stands at the door and knocks, who waits for us and longs to be with us, as a groom longs to be with His bride.

The bride comprises, and is composed of, all who believe, and this is all that merits inclusion, participation, in His favor and preference. There is no partiality with God within His household (Eph 6:9), and hence there is no more that we can add ourselves or do to gain more favor with Him. Our devotion then comes from love in response to His love, as has always been the correct pattern. And so, we see again that the only reasonable response of the bride as a whole and as believers individually is dedicated devotion, love, and gratitude expressed in awe and familial acceptance. To reiterate, this is a privilege that is available to all who believe no matter where you are, who you are, or what status or position you have in the secular world or within the "church." In God's eyes, you who believe are blessed, loved, and part of the body and bride of Christ. And in Christ's eyes you are adored, honored, protected, and considered with great beauty that will one day be perfected as He draws us to Himself so that wherever He is, so shall His bride be. This is how our God regards us, and this is surely worth the greatest of devotion.

A further picture here is also worth considering, for as the bride is recognized by the groom's father as a new member of the family, so this is the case within the household of God. For God also refers to us believers in extremely personal terms, such as His children and members of His household. This, again, is a totally new construct within the new covenant, for while God was indeed called Father in the Old Testament, this paternal frame of reference was largely absent until the advent of Jesus.

- Children of God

    But as many as received Him, to them He gave the right to become children of God, to those who believe in His name: who were born, not of blood, nor of the will of the flesh, nor of the will of man, but of God. (John 1:12–13)[6]

- Members of the Household of God

    Now, therefore, you are no longer strangers and foreigners, but fellow citizens with the saints and members of the household of God, having been built on the foundation of the apostles and

6. Cf. 1 John 3:1.

prophets, Jesus Christ Himself being the chief cornerstone, in whom the whole building, being fitted together, grows into a holy temple in the Lord, in whom you also are being built together for a dwelling place of God in the Spirit. (Eph 2:19–22)

The extent that this transformation in status and standing in the eyes of God has on the relationship that the believer has with God—in fact is now entitled to have with God—is explored in considerable detail in the course of the rest of this book, but for now we can only reverently suggest that when appropriated, our very identity and how we consider ourselves becomes transformed too. For our identity is now defined not by what we think of ourselves but by our position as members of the household of the Creator of all things, the One who is all-knowing, all-powerful, and divine to the utmost. And He considers us to be His children and actually wants us to absorb and enjoy all the privileges of relationship and intimacy that a child enjoys. To be defined by such an identity is revealed through the archangel Gabriel who of all creatures could define himself by his own rank, beauty, and glory, but instead sees himself only in relation to his position and standing with God. Consider how he identifies himself to Zacharias in Luke 1:19: "I am Gabriel who stands in the presence of God." What matters to Gabriel, and how he identifies and defines himself, is how God regards him and the privileges that God has bestowed upon him. Perhaps this then is the manner in which all Christians should define ourselves, maybe not as even Christians but as beloved children and members of the household of God—if we were to do so, then certainly the thread of devotion in our lives would grow ever stronger as our identity becomes ever more intertwined with the Positional Blessings of God that He has so freely bestowed upon us.

As believers, we would do well to contemplate and appropriate these blessings more thoroughly into our lives, our relationship with God, and our devotion. When we truly grasp what this truly means not just in our own eyes but through those of God Himself, we see our identity totally differently. How frequently do we really dwell upon the beauty of God in that through Jesus, we are reconciled to God and are above reproach in His sight (Rom 5:10–11, Col 1:21–22)? And how much more we should consider that through this sacrifice, we who believe are now considered to have been redeemed and bought at such a price:

> For if when we were enemies we were reconciled to God through the death of His Son, much more, having been reconciled, we

> shall be saved by His life. And not only that, but we also rejoice in God through our Lord Jesus Christ, through whom we have now received the reconciliation. (Rom 5:10–11)
>
> And you, who once were alienated and enemies in your mind by wicked works, yet now He has reconciled in the body of His flesh through death, to present you holy, and blameless, and above reproach in His sight. (Col 1:21–22)
>
> Or do you not know that your body is the temple of the Holy Spirit who is in you, whom you have from God, and you are not your own? For you were bought at a price; therefore glorify God in your body and in your spirit, which are God's. (1 Cor 6:19–20)
>
> And if you call on the Father, who without partiality judges according to each one's work, conduct yourselves throughout the time of your stay here in fear; knowing that you were not redeemed with corruptible things, like silver or gold, from your aimless conduct received by tradition from your fathers, but with the precious blood of Christ, as of a lamb without blemish and without spot. (1 Pet 1:18–19)

It sounds absurd and paradoxical when first considered, but Jesus was of course correct when He foretold to His disciples that in this life they (and we) would be better off after His ascension, for it would only be then that the Holy Spirit would come to indwell believers (John 16:7). Jesus being God, of course, knew not only that this would occur, but that the benefits to the believer's faith and life would be immense. And this is precisely what we see in Scripture, for when we consider the passages concerning how Christians are to behave and even how we are to engage with God, then without the Holy Spirit within us, these would indeed be so implausible to obtain that even to think so is pure absurdity. Read again Rom 12 and ponder how any one of us could possibly attain to these standards if it were not for the Holy Spirit within us. It is the same point that Jesus was making in the Sermon on the Mount (Matt 5–7), for without the Holy Spirit none of these expectations have ever been possible, but it is now as recreated, indwelled believers that we have the ultimate assistance in the form of God indwelling us.

Of course, this makes a difference to us, for the Holy Spirit's commission is to point us to Jesus, to teach us His ways, and to conform us to His image. Hence, we see this transpire in that it is only because of the Holy Spirit within us that we are able to discern the things of the Spirit and are able to understand Scripture (1 Cor 2:13–16). It is clearly also only through the indwelling of the Holy Spirit that we are able to produce any semblance at all of the fruits of Spirit, which are in all honesty utterly unattainable standards without His help. It is only with the Holy Spirit that we are able to let the peace of God and the word of Christ dwell richly in us. These standards that He assists us to strive for include striving for the mind of Christ with minds that have been transformed and hearts that are realigned to that of God—in short, our very sanctification is dependent upon and conditioned by the indwelling of the Holy Spirit within us. The consideration of God Himself indwelling us becomes all the more poignant when we consider that this indwelling actually marks us out, separates us, and acts as a guarantee of our salvation:

> In Him you also trusted, after you heard the word of truth, the gospel of your salvation; in whom also, having believed, you were sealed with the Holy Spirit of promise, who is the guarantee of our inheritance until the redemption of the purchased possession, to the praise of His glory. (Eph 1:13–14)

Neither our emotions nor our imaginations can fully grasp the immensity of this statement, for by it we see that God has separated us and has given His guarantee that we have eternal life—it is God Himself dwelling within us that is the mark of separation. This means that we are forever included in the plans of God, and this is guaranteed by God Himself, sealed by His power and with His authority. Reverently, we are completely mistaken—and by doing so dishonor God if we treat this too lightly and do not give full weight to what God has performed and instigated here. The apostle Paul in Rom 8:38–39 grasps the full implication of this when he states that because of our position there is nothing that can separate us from the love of Jesus Christ. The reasons for this are clear from what we have just discussed, for God will not "de-create" what He has just "re-created," and He will not remove the Holy Spirit from indwelling within us. Nowhere in Scripture is either of these things discussed or even implied. For to even think thus involves not only a complete misunderstanding of both the attributes of God, nor even just of our own role not just in salvation but thereafter in what is termed sanctification, but actually what it means to be part of the beloved bride of Christ and members of His household and how we are perceived by God because of this.

> For I am persuaded that neither death nor life, nor angels nor principalities nor powers, nor things present nor things to come, nor height nor depth, nor any other created thing, shall be able to separate us from the love of God which is in Christ Jesus our Lord. (Rom 8:38–39)

Collectively speaking, believers are both the body and bride of Christ, as the Scriptures tell us (1 Cor 12:12; Rev 21:9, 22:17), but it is the indwelling of the Holy Spirit that qualifies us to be included in this body and participate in the blessings of the bride. It is this indwelling that qualifies us to be partakers of the fullness of grace and assures us categorically that there is nothing under heaven and earth that can separate us from the love of God, for we are kept by His power so the receipt of our inheritance is guaranteed (Eph 3:16, Phil 1:7, Col 1:12, Rom 8:38–39). And it is because of this indwelling that we can rejoice, secure in the knowledge that "His abundant mercy has begotten us again to a living hope through the resurrection of Jesus Christ from the dead, to an inheritance incorruptible and undefiled and that does not fade away, reserved in heaven for you, who are kept by the power of God through faith for salvation ready to be revealed in the last time" (1 Pet 1:3–5). This then brings great comfort, knowing that our being "sealed" guarantees all this. And as it is guaranteed, then we rest assured knowing that no matter what lies ahead, we have been transfigured, and that the blessings of eternity with Christ have started already. For as Jesus comforted His disciples as He introduced them to what their future life without Him would entail, so the whole concept of the indwelling of the Spirit should bring us all great comfort too: "Let not your heart be troubled, neither let it be afraid" (John 14:27).

All Believers Are Equal in the Eyes of God

> Now you are the body of Christ, and members individually. (1 Cor 12:27)

> For there is no distinction between Jew and Greek, for the same Lord over all is rich to all who call upon Him. (Rom 10:12)

A logical extension to all believers being indwelled by the Holy Spirit and that all are members of the household of God is that there is a natural leveling out of relationship between all who believe and God's perspective of them. It was Jesus's mighty prayer in John 17 that all believers would be one as He and the Father are One, and thus we see this expounded upon and worked out through the Epistles as the marvelous doctrine of Christian equality is developed. Of course, this in itself was (and still is) completely countercultural at the time and totally contrary to Platonic thought processes that held up leaders as superior and to be venerated. Sadly, such Hellenistic thinking immediately penetrated the church but has always been entirely unbiblical. And yet in terms of our devotion and our consideration of ourselves within the body of Christ, it is vital that we realize that this equality applies to every one of us who believes in Jesus:

> For you are all sons of God through faith in Christ Jesus. For as many of you as were baptized into Christ have put on Christ. There is neither Jew nor Greek, there is neither slave nor free, there is neither male nor female; for you are all one in Christ Jesus. (Gal 3:26–28)

> Do not lie to one another, since you have put off the old man with His deeds, and have put on the new man who is renewed in knowledge according to the image of Him who created him, where there is neither Greek nor Jew, circumcised nor uncircumcised, barbarian, Scythian, slave nor free, but Christ is all and in all. (Col 3:9–11)

> For I say, through the grace given to me, to everyone who is among you, not to think of Himself more highly than He ought to think, but to think soberly, as God has dealt to each one a measure of faith. For as we have many members in one body, but all the members do not have the same function, so we, being many, are one body in Christ, and individually members of one another. (Rom 12:3–5)

Citizens of Heaven: Heavenly Status, Identity, and Security

> For our citizenship is in heaven, from which we also eagerly wait for the Savior, the Lord Jesus Christ. (Phil 3:20)

Belonging for the Christian is multidimensional, not only between this life and eternity but also in terms of status, identity, and interestingly even character. For while we are members of God, this too gives us a positional equality of privileges as the people of God. The term "citizenship" used by

Paul here had very different levels of meaning for the original readers of the letter than it does to us today. The term would have been understood only in the framework of what it meant to be living within the Roman Empire and had very distinct connotations associated with being a citizen of Rome. This was a title of great weight and importance, and along with it came great privileges and responsibilities, as well as protective status of the citizen by the state. Along with the concept of citizenship in the Roman Empire came entitlements and privileges accorded to this status. But for the believer, we see that we too have huge entitlements that are given to us not on account of anything we have done, but on account of what Jesus has done.

To be a citizen of Rome was a title of immense privilege that was given to people of merit throughout the empire, and was not associated with any particular nation as it is today. All of this would have been encompassed in the minds of the recipients as they read the phrase "citizenship in heaven." What Paul is doing is transferring this meaning onto the believer's perceived and actual status outside of the confines of this world, into heaven itself. This concept would have been revolutionary to comprehend and appropriate. The original recipients may have been rich or lowly, slave or free, but in God's eyes were now to regard themselves as being elevated to such an incredible position of status in heaven where all are equal and all are free. Whatever the status of the believer on earth, Paul is saying, is not reflected in heaven—for the least on earth are equal with the greatest in the jurisdiction of God. We know this as the phrase is addressed to the corporate "our" by Paul, meaning it was addressed to all the readers of the letter, not just the few. There are no caveats or exceptions of qualifications needed in the expression. Paul is saying to all who believe that all, without exception, are to consider themselves (ourselves) as citizens of heaven. We can see how this then affects the believer's perspective in this life, for we have available to us in the here and now spiritual blessing in heaven (Eph 1:3). Not to be missed, though, is that it is in the here and now, in this life, that we need this assurance and understanding. It is in this life that we need to know how secure we are, that our status is solid and immovable no matter what trials we have to endure. We need to know that our efforts to store up treasures in heaven are not in vain—for otherwise even to suggest that we do so seems disingenuous. Our security in Christ and in His home is secure, in other words. This is the truth and the hope that forms the rock upon which we can build our faith and our lives.

The Transformative Positional Blessings

The Transfigurative Blessings we have discussed above are complemented and completed in many ways by what we can term the concomitant "Transformational Blessings." These Transformational Blessings largely concern the change in the spiritual status of the believer. As we will see, it is this spiritual change that has the most impact on why and how the believer is now able to engage and address God so personally in our devotion, and on the confidence we can have in Christ and in our salvation as a whole. These Transformative Blessings are bestowed upon all believers as soon as they believe and hence are available to be accepted in faith and applied to our general lives with Christ. To fully grasp the truth and the magnitude of these blessings yields such fruit in security and sanctity in our faith and in our appreciation of the unmerited favor and unmitigated love that God has gifted to us through them.

Eternal Life

We start with the one that should matter to us most simply because it matters most to God, for it is why He sent Jesus to die on the cross for us: eternal life. Scripture is very clear that all is required to attain eternal life, as far as God is concerned, is that we believe in His Son, Jesus. And in order to do so, this involves an appreciation of why He had to die—namely, the removal of sin—and that we have to accept this because we "all have sinned and fall short of the glory of God" (Rom 3:23), but that God has provided us a way through Jesus so that "if you confess with your mouth the Lord Jesus and believe in your heart that God has raised Him from the dead, you will be saved" (Rom 10:9).

Please note the verb tenses and the unambiguity associated with the last phrase in Rom 10:9, for this is a factor that is associated with all the texts that we'll be utilizing in our considerations. This is important not only linguistically but also in understanding the clarity that the Holy Spirit wishes to impart through the texts to the believer regarding these sacred truths and blessings which He wishes us to not only believe in our hearts but apply to our faith and our understanding of our new relationship with God. The point being that this so matters to God that sometimes the phraseology and sentence structure seems too simplistic. And this is where, sadly, too many have not taken this at face value and have thought there must be more to add to it, meaning that they approach these texts as externalists, always wanting to legalize and conform them to their own image and prejudices, rather than as Devotionists, who simply regard them in wonder and for the beauty of the messages of hope and love that they convey, and hence to them these texts become sacred and cherished for their lives and devotion. Consider for example the simplicity and unambiguity shown in this passage regarding eternal life:

> Most assuredly, I say to you, He who hears My word and believes in Him who sent Me has everlasting life, and shall not come into judgment, but has passed from death into life. (John 5:24)[7]

From the above, it seems abundantly clear that Jesus wanted to make sure that this whole concept of eternal life was available to all who believe in Him as Messiah, the Christ. This sense of clarity, and urgency to comprehend this clarity, is then passed through to the apostles and hence to us. Consider again the simplicity of message in the following texts, for they are transformative in that if we truly believe them, if we truly accept them and truly live as though they were true, then "transformational" seems almost inadequate as a description. We should never and could never grow weary of contemplating the fact that we have been given this ultimate blessing for so little effort but which came at such a price from the One who is the giver of this promise of eternal life—a life that, as Scripture shows, starts the moment of salvation so that it is irrevocable and assured, for it has already begun:

> And this is the promise that He has promised us—eternal life. (1 John 2:25)

> And this is the testimony: that God has given us eternal life, and this life is in His Son. He who has the Son has life; he who does not have the Son of God does not have life. These things I have written to you who believe in the name of the Son of God, that you may know that you have eternal life, and that you may continue to believe in the name of the Son of God. . . . And we know that the Son of God has come and has given us an understanding, that we may know Him who is true; and we are in Him who is true, in His Son Jesus Christ. This is the true God and eternal life. (1 John 5:11–13, 20)

> And I give them eternal life, and they shall never perish; neither shall anyone snatch them out of My hand. (John 10:28)

---

7. Cf. John 3:14–16, 36.

> And this is eternal life, that they may know You, the only true
> God, and Jesus Christ whom You have sent. (John 17:3)

Of course, to have been given eternal life that actually starts now means that there are aspects of our former lives, before salvation, that must have been addressed at the same moment in order for us to be considered worthy of living this eternal life now. These factors largely stem from how the sacrifice of Jesus fulfilled the righteous requirements of God that are held within the Law of Moses (see the book of Hebrews for the entire exposition of this). Consequently, if Jesus has fulfilled these requirements and all is required of us is belief in Him that He has done so, then these requirements are imputed to us. This imputation then is the gift of the Positional Blessings, for we are made righteous in God's eyes not through our own efforts but for the perfect sacrifice of Jesus on the cross and our belief in Him.

Hence, even a cursory understanding of the requirements of sacrifice under the terms of the Law of Moses makes the vast generosity of God all the clearer. For an ex-Pharisee such as Paul the apostle, the impact of what these mean for the individual must have been utterly extraordinary and completely transformative—which of course they were. One can only imagine what it must have been like for the first set of Jewish believers, being a people who have lived for centuries under the theocratic system of the Mosaic law and especially under the enforced legalistic version it had become, to suddenly be informed that because of Jesus these obligations and requirements had already been met and paid for and that all that was required of them from now on was life in and through the Spirit and not the flesh, to live as His people united in Christ. This then is what the apostles sought to impart to the new gentile believers in the form of the Positional Blessings, and they sought to do so by imparting not only what Christ's sacrifice on the cross achieved in broad terms, but what all this actually means to the individual believer. Hence, such knowledge and explanations were delivered by the Holy Spirit through the apostles so that ordinary new believers could understand where they now stood in relation to their former selves and their new relationship and identity with their new God and Savior. Hence it was (and is) vital that these messages were (and are) conveyed, for they form the very bedrock of our current and future life with Christ, with Him being the foundation and cornerstone of our faith.

The truth that is central to the message that the apostles wished to impart is that there has, through belief in Jesus and consequent salvation, been a fundamental, dramatic alteration in circumstances imparted to the believer on account of this belief. The action of salvation is also termed "justification" in Scripture, and the entire work that was achieved on the cross regarding the salvific state is termed "atonement." Scripture is very clear that salvation, justification, and atonement are "one and only" events—they do not continue, cannot be added to, changed, or altered. Eternal life for the believer, as we said before, starts at this juncture. Of course, it is also at the point of salvation that the Holy Spirit comes to dwell within each and every believer, His role and function is to comfort, teach, and lead to Jesus—the outworking of this during this life of the believer is termed "sanctification," and it is a process that will not be completed until Jesus Himself completes it when we are finally conformed to His likeness, but not before then. Unfortunately, too many confuse the atonement and justification with the sanctification process, whereas they are, of course, inextricably linked and conditional upon each other, they are indeed separate both in function and in form. While the purpose of this series of studies is not to delve too much into deep theology, there are reasons that explanations are needed, not least in this area, for what has been imparted to us through these Positional Blessings by the apostles is of such significance to the believer's ongoing relationship with God that they needed to be set within a theological framework in order to be fully validated as being true.

As we will see, the Positional Blessings are actually set out to comfort and confirm to all believers that their belief has been received, accepted, and produces the following reception from God in response to this belief. Rather than going into detailed explanations on the impact of each of the following on the believer, it is perhaps best to let each one speak for itself and to let the reader absorb what is being said and being implied as to the current status of every single believer through their belief in Jesus. We can only imagine the impact of these for the original recipients and this is the same for all believers as we contemplate their meaning for us personally. But note that there are no "ifs" and no "buts" about these, for they are unconditional and need not be added to or embellished. Jesus has done it all on the cross, and to add to it is to diminish His achievement, which in itself is tantamount to blasphemy. Hence, because of the perfect work of Jesus and our belief in Him, every single believer now has the perfect assurance that all of these Positional Blessings invoke and allude to. Again, they are further components of the perfect gift that constitutes our new Familial and Positional Identity, and the assurance that they bring to our devotion is evidenced when we truly appropriate them within our hearts and souls. The best way to do this is to focus on the unconditionality of the verb tenses as well as the irreversible assurances given and to simply let them sink in until they reach the fertile soil of our awaiting souls and gratefully aligned hearts.

- Redemption Through the Blood of Jesus ("Have Been Forgiven")

    In Him we have redemption through His blood, the forgiveness of sins, according to the riches of His grace. (Eph 1:7)[8]

    And you, being dead in your trespasses and the uncircumcision of your flesh, He has made alive together with Him, having forgiven you all trespasses. (Col 2:13)

- Washed and Cleansed ("Were Sanctified")

    And such were some of you. But you were washed, but you were sanctified, but you were justified in the name of the Lord Jesus and by the Spirit of our God. (1 Cor 6:11)

- Reconciled to God ("Is Above Reproach")

    And you, who once were alienated and enemies in your mind by wicked works, yet now He has reconciled in the body of His flesh through death, to present you holy, and blameless, and above reproach in His sight. (Col 1:21–22)[9]

- Peace with God ("We Have Peace")

    Therefore, having been justified by faith, we have peace with God through our Lord Jesus Christ, through whom also we have access by faith into this grace in which we stand, and rejoice in hope of the glory of God. (Rom 5:1–2)

It is perhaps fitting here to dwell upon a little the implications and sheer profundity of what the simple words expressed by Paul in Rom 5:1 would have meant for him as a former, highly devout Pharisee. It can be without doubt that what he is alluding to here by using the expression

8. Cf. Col 1:14.
9. Cf. Rom 5:10–11.

"peace with God" is the Levitical peace offering as implemented through Lev 7. The peace offering was the final offering made by the righteous individual to God in the series of sin offering, burnt offering, and peace offering. The peace offering signified that the individual had been restored back into right relationship with God. It was a profoundly beautiful and symbolic act of accepted attrition. Thus, for Paul, the single perfect sacrifice of Jesus was the ultimate peace offering of God to Himself, and it was through this offering, and only now through this offering, that the individual can have peace with God on a permanent basis rather than having to go continually before Him. After millennia of sacrifices to God performed by the priesthood, the peace offering itself had its ultimate fulfillment in Christ (as did, of course, the sin and burnt offering too). We cannot but wonder at how Paul must have felt as this beauty and understanding sunk into soul, for its implications resonate to us even today that while we were once His enemies, only through the perfect sinless peace offering of Himself on the cross do we have peace with God. And it is because of this that we rest assured of our ongoing relationship with Him. It is because we have peace *with* God that we are able to "let" the peace *of* God dwell richly in our hearts—for which the only reasonable response is awe, wonder, and utmost gratitude (Col 3:15)!

No Condemnation

> There is therefore now no condemnation to those who are in Christ Jesus, who do not walk according to the flesh, but according to the Spirit. (Rom 8:1)

There is one final blessing that we must consider in the light of having peace with God, for it is a by-product and beautiful counterpart to having peace. For to have peace with God, means that this peace cannot be interrupted by erroneous acts or mistakes, including of course those of not appreciating and taking advantage of the Positional Blessings or our new Positional Identity as a whole. This counterpart is the lack of condemnation from God for the believer when these eventualities inevitably occur—for it would be a strange kind of peace to have if one was continually apprehensive of condemnation or judgement and punishment. Of course, the same is true in terms of ongoing forgiveness where contrition is given, for God is continually willing and able to forgive the believer and to provide comfort in the restoration of the peace relationship. For "if we confess our sins, He is faithful and just to forgive us our sins and to cleanse us from all unrighteousness" (1 John 1:9). Of course, this too points towards what awaits us in the future, for believers do not need to fear the judgment of God but can await the ultimate rewards of our belief in the form of eternity with God and being in His presence forever and ever. For now, though, we know—comfort upon comfort—that Jesus Himself lives to intercede on our behalf with the Father (Heb 7:27).

It is this lack of condemnation that has such vast implications for us as we continue with our discussions on devotion, especially for those of us who are ordinary, everyday Christians. For this blessing means that we have both the freedom and the privilege of knowing that when we fail the Lord or let Him down or miss opportunities to be blessed and participate in His presence, so we know that this can only be temporary. This relationship can be restored, and His blessings can be acquired and appropriated merely by asking for them, and there is never any possible condemnation that could possibly emotionally prevent us from doing so. In terms of our devotion, then, this has immeasurable implications as we seek to enter into His presence with peace and confidence.

As always, though, along with great privileges and immense blessings comes responsibility to act upon them and appropriate them. They were given freely but at such cost to our Savior that we must cherish them with all our heart.

Positional Responsibility

In order to fully appropriate what these verses mean for us and the implications of our relationship with God and the world we live in, we must first comprehend that there is a distinction between our "condition" and our "position." Our ongoing condition is what befalls us as we live in and engage with the fallen world around us—battered, bruised, spiritually downtrodden, still sinning and regretful, feeling inadequate, and feeling a failure in both the eyes of God, in the eyes of others, and also within ourselves. This though is not how God sees us at all—our position is how God Himself views us who are truly saved. These are the glorious truths that apply to all Christians in this life, now and until we are with the Lord. They are fundamental to our relationship with God for they mean that we can change our whole perspective on how we come before God in our times of devotion, in times of prayer. As the letter of Hebrews says, we can come boldly to God now without fear of recrimination or condemnation, not because of anything we have done but because of what Jesus Christ achieved on the cross and because His sacrifice is all sufficient; the requirements of God have been satisfied (Heb 4:16). It is we who believe who are the beneficiaries of this—this is our privilege, and these are our Positional Blessings. This is the position and identity that for a thousand years of sacrifices under the law of Moses an individual could never achieve but is available to us now. And all we need to do is accept these wonderful, irreversible, majestic blessings for what they are and accept our new Positional Identity for the gift from God that it is.

From this position we are all better equipped mentally and spiritually to resist the devil and to stand against His wiles, to grow in our faith, and to strengthen our hearts and souls through our devotion. And this then leads us to the context of sanctification which, as we are told in 1 Thess 4:3, is the will of God. Sanctification is the will of God because this is what matters to God, and it is all that matters to Him regarding us because all else is settled in His providential plan for the future. All He has said will happen, will happen, and there is nothing we can do to either change it or worry about it. Which is why we are exhorted by Paul as follows:

> Be anxious for nothing, but in everything by prayer and supplication, with thanksgiving, let your requests be made known to God; and the peace of God, which surpasses all understanding, will guard your hearts and minds through Christ Jesus. (Phil 4:6–7)

> If then you were raised with Christ, seek those things which are above, where Christ is, sitting at the right hand of God. Set your mind on things above, not on things on the earth. For you died, and your life is hidden with Christ in God. When Christ who is our life appears, then you also will appear with Him in glory. (Col 3:1–3)

Finally, we must pause here to reflect upon the greatness and goodness of God and to whose household we are told that we have now joined. We must also reflect upon the fact that it had not been previously revealed in Scripture that this would take place—it is completely new, unrevealed, and utterly unmerited. But it is in our devotion that we must really see how these blessings are transformative, and it is as we follow this golden thread of devotion that we start to see the beauty of what the Lord has delivered and made available to all who believe in His Son. For when we sit at the feet of Jesus in the full knowledge that these are settled, then our own relationship with the Lord is transformed and thus our only reasonable response to this should be unmitigated adoration and gratitude. If we were to spend the rest of lives doing nothing but praising God and giving thanks for these Positional Blessings, then we would have led lives worth living! For when we consider them as such, thus our devotion becomes alive to the beauty within these blessings and alive to the leading and presence of the Holy Spirit of the Living God—hence, devotion itself becomes living and alive, permanent and perpetual—and thus the term "Living Devotion" is coined.

Positional Responsibility

How Then Shall We Live?

We too easily take for granted the fact that we have the entirety of the Bible at our disposal (whether we choose to invest our time with it is a different matter), as well as having access to more information and guidance on theology and Christian living literally at our fingertips than at any other time in history. What we seem to forget sometimes is that the Bible was written over a long period of time, and even the New Testament was written over a period of sixty years or so (in itself mainly consisting of letters written to a small number of churches which could not have been circulated very widely, even if they were considered worth sharing at that point). The message therefore, in order to spread, had to be a simple one to bring people to the point of salvation and thereafter needed to be a simple one to explain to people the answer to the most obvious, and yet ignored, questions: So what do we do now? How do we now live? What is now expected of us? And we see this immediately after Pentecost itself as the thousands of new believers went back to their towns and cities as far away as Rome. They did not even thereafter have the benefit of being able to learn from Jesus's apostles regarding His teaching and what He would have them do. Quite simply, how did they then know how to live in light of the revelation of Jesus Christ in their hearts?

As I said, the message of Jesus was so simple and yet so perfectly profound in its structure that it did in effect literally change the world: to love the lord your God with all your heart and strength and your neighbor as yourself. It had to be this simple and this profound because to start with, there were no other instructions. This was the disciples' doctrine. There were no other instructions given to the new believers. This was of no fault of their own, but it did not mean that they were any less Christian than we are now. They were as complete in Christ as those who in later years had full access to the New Testament. These Christians did not have fully defined doctrines until they were developed much later. And yet the defining factor in the continuance of the church, its expansion, and the nurturing of the individual believer was the presence of the Holy Spirit dwelling within them. The emphasis has to be here (in case it is missed), on the complete transformational impact and continuing nurture of the individual, individually—for without this it would not, could not, have survived. He became the Instructor and Guide, just as Jesus had predicted He would. Jesus even said that it would be better that He went so that the Holy Spirit would then come (John 16:7).

The instruction of Jesus then is the same as the instruction in the Old Testament, but since Pentecost, there has been the most fundamental difference: the presence of the Holy Spirit dwelling within us. We have the same external instructions, for they have not changed, but with a difference, for we now have God Himself in us, guiding us, convicting but not condemning, and always pointing us to Jesus. This then is and always has been the focus: to become more and more like Christ. The more we love God, the more Christlike we become, for that was the way Jesus was. He and the Father are One, but as He says, the Father loves Him and He loves the Father. The Father honors Him as He honors the Father—and so as we love God more, the more Christlike we become.

This is the process of sanctification, simply becoming more and more Christlike. But, what does this mean and what does it entail? Good questions, but they actually start from the wrong premise. The right first question starts with, "How will You help me to know what this means and what is required?" And so, we see that the external comes from the internal. How do we know what is required? Because it has now been revealed to us through His Spirit. The answers are about "being" and "behavior," and that all-encompassing word "character."

When we consider the great instructional passages of Scripture such as Rom 12, then one sees immediately two things: firstly, that these are about character, and secondly, are utterly impossible to achieve on our own. For example, how can anyone "love without hypocrisy" (Rom 12:9) in our own strength? It is impossible, and yet that is the point. Just as Jesus, in the Sermon on Mount, points out that it is impossible to fulfill the righteous requirements of the Law in our own strength, so the Holy Spirit is pointing out that it is the same here. As with the Sermon on the Mount, these instructions are meant to cause the believer to call to the Holy Spirit for help to be able to do so, and it is the Holy Spirit within us who will cause the believer to even want to do these things and then gives us the strength to do so. Though, of course, we all know that the flesh is weak, and we will never be able to fully do these things until we are finally made perfect in our glorified bodies, which again is the purpose of our struggle now, even in attempting these things, as the very struggle is meant to make us yearn all the more for Christ both in this life and when we are with Him in our glorified bodies. This then is the sanctification process, and it is why this process is both the will of God and is an ongoing one in the life of the believer. However, as we discussed previously this process commences upon salvation—obviously—and therefore is defined by and secured by the position that the believer was bequeathed upon salvation. These cannot be removed, for to do so would be to go against the very attributes of God. Thus, the working out of our own sanctification becomes an enduring process that is undertaken upon these foundations, alongside and with the guidance, support, and power of the Holy Spirit Himself. We too easily forget that it is the Holy Spirit's function and dearest desire within us to assist us in becoming more Christlike. This is, of course, why the fruits of the Spirit are what they are, for these are the same traits that Jesus has.

Positional Responsibility

As with so much in life, along with great privilege comes great responsibility. The same is clearly true that while our Positional Identity is absolutely an unconditional gift, along with it is the expectation from God that the believer will honor the gift and its blessings through living life and honoring Him with a heart that is grateful, from the secure perspective of one who has fully understood and applies the implications of what this identity means.

Previously, we discussed much about the internal and the external, and here again we see the same as we progress towards how we should now live as individual, ordinary Christians. What we do see again is the dual relationship between human responsibility alongside God's sovereignty. We are told to seek first the kingdom of God and His righteousness (Matt 6:33), to cry out for discernment (Prov 2:3), to ask for wisdom (Jas 1:5) and for the enlightenment of our understanding (Eph 1:18), to call on Him to show and teach us His ways (Ps 25:4), to ask the Holy Spirit to sanctify and to guide us (John 16:12), and to hunger and thirst for righteous (Matt 5:6) for He alone "satisfies the longing soul, and fills the hungry soul with goodness" (Ps 107:9). Finally, in the imitable words of Kind David, we join with his heart to plead with the Lord,

> Teach me to do Your will,
> For You are my God;
> Your Spirit is good.
> Lead me in the land of uprightness.
> (Ps 143:10)

As always, none of this is without purpose but is so that we "may walk worthy of the Lord, fully pleasing Him, being fruitful in every good work and increasing in the knowledge of God" (Col 1:10); so that all we do, we do for the glory of God (1 Cor 10:31); and above all else that we may know, grasp, cling to, and truly appropriate "what is the hope of His calling, what are the riches of the glory of His inheritance in the saints, and what is the exceeding greatness of His power toward us who believe" (Eph 1:19). The Holy Spirit is within us and will guide and counsel us, but we need to ask Him to do so. We have to make the effort, and He will respond; but it is our responsibility to do so. Here again, sadly our hearts are so feeble at times that we even need to ask the Holy Spirit to motivate us to ask. Here we touch upon the biggest issue facing the individual believer today in the West: lethargy and general lack of motivation. Hence, we need the Holy Spirit to break us free from this state and to literally set us free.

When we consider such passages for our purposes as Jas 4:8, "Draw near to God and He will draw near to you," I wonder what our reactions are, truthfully. Do we inwardly groan as we know that this is something we should be doing, or do we marvel at the wonder of God that through the awesome sacrifice of His Son, we are able to do so. We are able, as the writer of Hebrews says, to "come boldly to the throne of grace" (Heb 4:16). Perhaps as we said before, if we were to consider more what these statements meant to first-century Jews having been brought up in a culture of endless rules and regulations regarding what is and what isn't permissible to gain approval of and access to God, we would begin to understand just how liberating these new concepts would have been to them. Perhaps if we did, we would take them for granted less and again have more appreciation and gratitude regarding this immense privilege that God has bestowed upon us so freely.

There Is No Condemnation for Those in Christ Jesus!

Before we go any further, though, it is important at this point that we remind ourselves of the matters discussed in the previous section regarding our Positional Blessings, especially the following: we have been washed and cleansed permanently on the inside by the Holy Spirit; we have been forgiven of all our past sins, and when we sin now, Jesus is faithful and just to forgive us again; we now have peace with God because of our belief in His Son; and because of these there is now no condemnation for those in Christ Jesus. God knows that we are not perfect yet. He knows the struggles we have and what we struggle with. He knows that we find it hard in our hearts to make time for Him, to read our Bibles, and to pray for ourselves and for each other. He knows all these things because He knows, too, that we are still in a spiritual battle and that in this life, this will continue. He has, however, given us the means by which we can resist and move on—namely, Himself within us. And the key to this resistance movement is humility in that all we need do is ask.

Condemnation can take many forms for a Christian, but the most common ones are guilt about inadequacy and lack of commitment or even lethargy in our faith. If we are honest, then we would have to admit that we all struggle more frequently than not, I suspect, to spend time with God, to read our Bibles and enjoy doing so, to go to midweek meetings, and even to attend church on Sundays. Jesus said in John 3:17 that "God did not send His Son into the world to condemn the world, but that the world through Him might be saved." And we know from Paul that there is now no condemnation for those in Christ Jesus (Rom 8:1). Therefore, one has to ask, "If we are not to feel condemned, then where does this sense of condemnation come from?" It is true that the Holy Spirit convicts us of sin, but is this really sinning that we are talking about? I do not see it mentioned anywhere in the Bible that this should be considered sin per se. What is sinful though, I would suggest, is to ignore

His commandments to love Him and love our neighbor, as we keep coming back to. My point, though, is what is expected of us by God and what is expected of us by others, including our peer group of Christians, is not necessarily the same thing.

We started this book by discussing this very point—namely, what the requirements of God for the individual Christian are and what His expectations from us are, as part of this relationship. We have drawn out the conclusion that it is our heart and only our heart that He is interested in, for all else is in His control, and to think otherwise actually is contrary to an understanding of His attributes and His overall sovereignty. The expectation of God then is the mere outworking of His requirements—put simply, as Jesus Himself said, "If you love Me, keep My commandments" (John 14:15), and "Why do you call Me Lord, Lord and do not do the things I say?" (Luke 6:46).

This latter point partially answers a question that we secretly ask when it comes to doing the things that we think are expected of us. Why? Or even, why bother? This questioning attitude itself comes from a position of security and comfort in our overall lives, and the sin of it is as old as faith itself, as Moses pointed out to the Israelites in Deut 8:11–17. The picture is familiar to us in the West after the initial euphoria of coming to faith in Christ; after a while we become "Christianized" and comfortable in our "church life," or we simply become "less enthused" and "less dynamic" in our relationship with Jesus. And so, we start to feel condemned for doing so and being this way. I would suggest, though, that the conviction we feel from the Holy Spirit is not one of condemnation (though we mistake it as such for that is how we generally are told we should feel) but one of hankering for us to start taking our own relationship with Jesus seriously. It is "the personal" and "the honest" that Jesus wants from us and has always wanted from us. Consider the words of King David: "Why are you cast down, oh my soul?" (Ps 42:5). We see from this statement two things: firstly, we see that David talks directly to his soul as if it is separate from him and that it needs a talking to and, secondly, that frequently this feeling of what we think is condemnation when we are distant from God is actually our souls hankering for Him. It is to David then, again, that we turn to for the solution to this, for he understands that to nurture the soul is the ultimate requirement and responsibility of the individual in our relationship with God. He takes a stand, and he declares his intentions in a manner that we would do well to imitate—these are the "I will" and "I shall" statements found across his psalms (see Ps 34). The Devotionist King David takes responsibility for his own faith and his own relationship with God because he knows that no one can do it for him. He has to do this on his own, to make it his responsibility. But note by saying, "I will do this and that," he means that he has not been doing so before and that he realizes that this is the only solution to his current state; so it is with ourselves. We must take a stand and draw close to God because that is what we want to do and will do—if not for our own sakes, then simply because we do love God. This is, of course, the heart attitude that God has always wanted. We do these things not for our own prestige or glory but because we love Him. We draw near to God knowing that He will draw near to us in return because we wish to be with Him. Dare I say, we should learn to become jealously protective of such times, for they are more than a privilege, they are connecting with the divine Creator of the universe who is beyond compare and yet wants, chooses, desires, and is so passionate Himself for you that He wants to be with you and to be trusted by you. This is the mystery of Christ. It is beyond comprehension and yet it is true.

And yet, and yet, we come back to the "Yes, I want to, I see that now, but how?" question that will always occur. The full answer to this question is broadly the subject of the remainder of this book, but for now the only biblical answer that could be given is again threefold.

Firstly, realize that if you are a Christian, then you are already indwelled by the Holy Spirit and that He is there to be your guide, to lead you to Jesus, and to conform you to His likeness. This is His function and utmost desire, for He knows that this is the will of God in your life.

Secondly, all you have to do is ask, as Jesus said, and you will receive. Ask the Holy Spirit to teach you His ways (as David would say in Ps 25:4–5, as an example) and to guide you. Ask Him to explain the ways of God. But more than that, ask Him for the transformed mind that will help you see the things of God as God sees them, in beauty and majesty. For Jesus came not to condemn but to give us life in all its fullness. To appreciate life in all its fullness, we must first see it as He does. And we are not to be apprehensive of the future or of events, for "God has not given us a spirit of fear, but of power and of love and of a sound mind" (2 Tim 1:7). Note when Jesus first starts His last discourse with His apostles, He starts with the most beautiful words, "Let not your heart be troubled" (John 14:1). And when Paul is discussing the second coming, he explains all these matters and then says that we are to comfort and edify each other because of these things, and we are to be encouraged by the second coming and all the glorious events surrounding His establishment of the millennial reign—but note, we are also not to be fearful either (John 14:1, 1 Thess 5:11). For the ultimate future is in God's hands; what He wants from us now as individual, ordinary Christians is simply to focus on Him, to love Him, and to honor Him in all that we do. To live, in other words, with Him and for Him but within our everyday lives, for our everyday lives to be lived in every way that reflects who we are and whom we represent in the world and to the world. He wants our inner light to so shine that it is noticeable externally to others who will see God within us (Matt 5:16), but to do that, the fires of our hearts need to be continually stoked through our own devotion personally to Him.

And finally, we must "let" the Holy Spirit do what He's there for. This is a small yet powerful word and probably one of the most reverent words there is for the Christian, for we are not to let our hearts be troubled and to

> let the peace of God rule in your hearts, to which also you were called in one body; and be thankful. Let the word of Christ dwell in you richly in all wisdom, teaching and admonishing one another in psalms and hymns and spiritual songs, singing with grace in your hearts to the Lord. (Col 3:15–16)

Only by letting the Holy Spirit rule within us and lead us and guide us do we truly get to the position where God wants us to be—sheltered and in His complete care—so we can look up and focus on what matters: Him alone.

An Abundant Life

As we consider during the course of our discussions the impact of the Positional Blessings on the believer in relation to our devotion, its perhaps instructive to consider one of the reasons Jesus gave for why He came and by extension why these blessings were bestowed upon us—a reason I would suggest is little considered and dwelled upon by many Christians, but one which in fact absorbs our whole daily relationship and devotion with Him.

In John 10:10, Jesus states that "the thief does not come except to steal, and to kill, and to destroy. I have come that they may have life, and that they may have it more abundantly." This word "abundantly" in New Testament Greek has the same connotations in meaning and description as it does for us today, such as "exceedingly" and "to a much greater degree,"[1] with the implication here that we are to expect, through Jesus, a

---

1. *Strong's* 4052 and 4053.

life that is not only more full but more complete and intense (one could even say vivid) than it otherwise would be. We might think that this element of Christ's teaching is somewhat lost on many Christians today, but to be clear, Jesus is speaking of our lives now on earth, not just that which is before us in heaven, where logically Satan can have no influence.

Unlike Satan, the Lord Jesus came to give not to get, and when He comes into our lives, He also comes to give not to get. He comes so that people may have life in Him that is meaningful, purposeful, joyful, and eternal. This abundance is given to the believer upon salvation, it is a gift from God. It is not to be earned, but it is to be appropriated. The application question, therefore, which must now be asked is, *How can I appropriate this abundance in my life?* Before we look at the answer to this question, we have to posit a former one—namely, *What is an abundant life?* The answer to this is, as is true with so many biblical questions, held within the correction: not what but who. For an abundant life is Jesus. It is caused by Him, sustained by Him, authored by Him, and is all to His glory. Eventually even this "who" will in fact become "us," as we become one with the Father and Jesus in a unification that is eternal and inseparable and all to the glory of God alone (John 17:20–26)!

Eternal Life

An abundant life is a life that begins the moment we come to Christ and receive Him as Savior and goes on throughout all eternity. The biblical definition of eternal life is provided by Jesus Himself: "And this is eternal life, that they may know You, the only true God, and Jesus Christ whom You have sent" (John 17:3).

This definition makes no mention of length of days, health, prosperity, family, or occupation. As a matter of fact, the only thing it does mention is knowledge of God. This is the key to a truly abundant life. So, while we as believers will share eternity with our Savior, in biblical terms eternity for the believer starts immediately upon salvation. For once we are with Jesus in heaven, we will certainly know Him, so John 17:3 must be talking about our life before then (for if it were otherwise, what he says is pretty self-evident). Indeed, the apostle Paul says that one day we will see God face-to-face and will know Him, but for now what we have and see is but a shadow:

> For now we see in a mirror, dimly, but then face to face. Now I know in part, but then I shall know just as I also am known. (1 Cor 13:12)

This Life

The truly abundant life belongs solely to those who are given it by Jesus, for truly from God's perspective, everyone else cannot have what He would regard as an abundant life. Just as nonbelievers are unable to discern the things of God, and therefore eternity, so abundance in God's eyes must be considered in relation to His own sovereignty. Abundance, therefore, can only be appropriated firstly by the true believer and secondly only in a manner which glorifies God. Just as God has always been interested in the heart of believers more than their works, so abundance too must reflect this divine principle. Abundance therefore is spiritual abundance, not physical—it can't be anything else, for everything material is fading away. And if abundance is spiritual, it must therefore be part of that which is imparted through Positional Blessings and therefore must also include the devotion of believers—hence why an abundant life can only come as we set our minds more and more upon what concerns God and less upon what concerns ourselves. Our interest should be in what is of eternal value, not the temporal:

> If then you were raised with Christ, seek those things which are above, where Christ is, sitting at the right hand of God. Set your mind on things above, not on things on the earth. For you died, and your life is hidden with Christ in God. (Col 3:1–3)

But again, I would say, how does this help us to appropriate this life more abundantly? To have an abundant life is to have a spiritual life—and this is only right. Our position in Christ means that we are now in God's household, and in God's household He comes first. In other words, we must learn the divine principle that He must increase in our lives while we must decrease (John 3:30). As we are indwelled by the Holy Spirit—and the role of the Holy Spirit is to convict us of sin in relation to the world (that is anything that puts God second place) and to point us to Jesus (John 16:7–14)—so this is what causes us to be dissatisfied with ourselves and our lives when we are not "abiding" in Jesus. And this too can only be achieved as we develop our understanding of what it means to abide or live in Christ; in order to do that and to develop our understanding and knowledge of Jesus, so we must nurture our souls and spirits through private devotion dedicated to the Lord.

To "abide" is to live, continue, or remain; so to abide in Christ is to live in Him or remain in Him. According to Rom 8:1 and 2 Cor 5:17, when a person is saved, he or she is described as being "in Christ." Therefore, abiding in Christ is not a special level of Christian experience, available only to a few; rather, it is the position of all believers. The difference between those abiding in Christ and those not abiding in Christ is the difference between the saved and the unsaved, at one level, but there also appears to be more than that both in the words of Jesus and also those of the apostle John (See John 14:21, 15:4–7, 9–11; 1 John 2:3–6, 3:6).

This is not to say that there are "super-Christians," for the emphasis should be upon the word "ought" in 1 John 2:6: "He who says he abides in Him ought himself also to walk just as He walked." What John is saying here is the same as saying that our only reasonable response (Rom 12:1)—to all the amazing things that Jesus has done, to the fact that He is God, to the fact that we were bought at so high a price (1 Cor 6:20), and to the fact that through mere faith in Him, He has blessed us with every spiritual blessing—should be to walk in a manner worthy of Him (Eph 4:1). However, this is, as always, with the caveat that we cannot possibly do this out of our own strength (for that would be works) but must rely on that of the Holy Spirit. Indeed, as the following passages show, we are only able to abide in Christ because of the Holy Spirit within us:

> Now he who keeps His commandments abides in Him, and He in him. And by this we know that He abides in us, by the Spirit whom He has given us. (1 John 3:24)

> No one has seen God at any time. If we love one another, God abides in us, and His love has been perfected in us. By this we know that we abide in Him, and He in us, because He has given us of His Spirit. (1 John 4:12–13)

The Standards of Jesus

Thus, it is becoming clearer that developing an understanding of what true abundance and abiding mean, is synonymous with developing understanding and knowledge of Jesus. And yet at the same time, the Bible states that believers already have the "mind of Christ" (which seems awesome and yet impossible at the same time): "For 'who has known the mind of the Lord that He may instruct Him?' But we have the mind of Christ" (1 Cor 2:16). Surely, then, a knowledge of Jesus must entail an understanding of His mind as well. But in all seriousness, how can we possibly possess, or even be expected to possess, the mind of Christ, which by definition is divine and perfect and must be the same as the mind of God the Father? I would say, you look at His characteristics or how He behaved in relation to those around Him and the world in general. And when you look at these traits, they are all totally those that one would want to have and to show to others. For He not only shows and demonstrates His authority and all the attributes of God but also those qualities that we as His bride would look for in our perfect groom, or of a people to their God and leader. For He is also protective of us (Matt 16:18), true (1 John 5:20), faithful (1 Thess 5:24), just (John 5:30), without deceit (1 Pet 2:22), innocent (Matt 27:4), blameless (Heb 7:26), obedient to the Father (John 4:34, 15:10), and zealous (Luke 2:49; John 2:17, 8:29).

This shows us just how completely and utterly impossible it would be to have the mind of Christ of our own accord—and yet the Bible says that we already do. This once again shows that we cannot do anything but for the Holy Spirit, for it is simply impossible to attain to such goals without God the Holy Spirit assisting us. And neither should we, for to try to do so under our own strength is insulting to the Holy Spirit within us. In similar manner, it is only through the work of the Holy Spirit within us that we are also given the ability to behave like Christ, especially when it comes to our fellow believers. This starts first and foremost with a recognition that there is no inequality in the household of God, for we are all equal with one another both in this life and in the life to come (Rom 12:4–5).

This wonderful truth about the divinely ordained structure of the body of believers implies a depth of relationship that goes way beyond the superficial. Indeed, when we examine the phrase "one another" in the Bible, we discover that it is one that appears multiple times in the context of the believer's relationship with each other (see Rom 12 and 15, Col 3, and elsewhere). It is the onus on how we are to treat each other within the body of Christ that again is extremely difficult to undertake with consistency of heart and love, given our fallen natures, and hence we must, as always, lean upon the Holy Spirit for strength and guidance. The connection between our Positional Identity and how we are to draw on the Holy Spirit to assist us in our relationship with one another is no more perfectly summarized than by the apostle Peter:

> Since you have purified your souls in obeying the truth through the Spirit in sincere love of the brethren, love one another fervently with a pure heart, having been born again, not of corruptible seed but incorruptible, through the word of God which lives and abides forever. (1 Pet 1:22–23)

It is only with the Holy Spirit within us that we could possibly even attempt "sincere love," let alone to love with a pure heart, for only God is good and pure. Hence, this is where Christianity is truly countercultural, for our motives for loving one another become sacrificial in that they come from hearts that are aligned with God and not from those of self-gain or aggrandizement. This of course, is only possible through the atoning work of Christ and the indwelling of the Holy Spirit, as the apostle Paul makes plain:

> Therefore if there is any consolation in Christ, if any comfort of love, if any fellowship of the Spirit, if any affection and mercy, fulfill my joy by being like-minded, having the same love, being of one accord, of one mind. Let nothing be done through selfish ambition or conceit, but in lowliness of mind let each esteem others better than himself. Let each of you look out not only for his own interests, but also for the interests of others. Let this mind be in you which was also in Christ Jesus, who, being in the form of God, did not consider it robbery to be equal with God, but made Himself of no reputation, taking the form of a bondservant, and coming in the likeness of men. (Phil 2:1–7)

The benchmark of how we are appropriating not just the mind of Christ but the whole concept of abundance is evidenced and manifested through our own demeanor—namely, the fruits of the Spirit. For the fruits of the Spirit are the manifestation of the mind of Christ within the believer—there is no difference whatsoever between the two, for the mind of Christ is also "love, joy, peace, longsuffering, kindness, goodness, faithfulness, gentleness, self-control" (Gal 5:22–23). But these fruits of the Spirit are just that, fruits of the Spirit—namely, they cannot be attained naturally but must be developed in the believer by the Holy Spirit Himself. We appropriate them by asking for them. For they are not to be self-made. We must humbly recognize this need, and by recognizing this need we submit to the Spirit and become "Spiritually minded"; and as we are now indwelled by the Holy Spirit, so our minds must become transformed in keeping with the God Himself living inside us:

> For those who live according to the flesh set their minds on the things of the flesh, but those who live according to the Spirit, the things of the Spirit. For to be carnally minded is death, but to be spiritually minded is life and peace. Because the carnal mind is enmity against God; for it is not subject to the law of God, nor indeed can be. (Rom 8:5–7)

> And do not be conformed to this world, but be transformed by the renewing of your mind, that you may prove what is that good and acceptable and perfect will of God. (Rom 12:2)

An abundant life, and therefore a devotionist life, can only come through a change in thinking, as our minds are transformed, and so our whole perspective changes. As we draw close to God, so He draws closer to us (Jas 4:8), and as that happens so the concerns of the world become less meaningful in our lives. And when we feel ourselves lapsing, then we should meditate on and draw near to Him in humility and thanksgiving:

> Only fear the Lord, and serve Him in truth with all your heart; for consider what great things He has done for you. (1 Sam 12:24)

> Listen to this, O Job; Stand still and consider the wondrous works of God. (Job 37:14)

Although we seem to be naturally desirous of earthly, temporal things, as Christians our perspective on life must be revolutionized as we are indwelled by the Holy Spirit and have our minds transformed by Him (Rom 12:2). By definition, this should and must change every perspective that we have. This, obviously, includes what constitutes abundance and, less obviously, how we perceive what devotion actually is, our part and participation in it, and what its function is for us as believers. While this is the subject matter for the remainder of our discussions in this book, it is worth just pausing and thinking through these beautiful words from Isaiah concerning the reciprocated relationship between believer and God:

> You will keep Him in perfect peace,
> Whose mind is stayed on You,
> Because He trusts in You.
> (Isa 26:3)

The Privacy of Devotion

W<small>E SPOKE PREVIOUSLY ABOUT</small> character formation, about how the Holy Spirit leads and guides us to conform ourselves to the image and mind of Christ. We discussed previously that this is only feasible with the help of the Holy Spirit and, by definition, is only available to those who are indwelled by Him. And as all Christians are indwelled by the Holy Spirit, so this is available to all who believe in Christ, with no caveats nor exceptions. It is available to all who believe and all we have to do is ask and we shall receive. We discussed how this is also conjoined with our own responsibility to ask and to be determined in our own will to dedicate ourselves to the Lord in this way—hence the determination we see in the "I will" statements found in the psalms. And, of course, we discussed how the heart is willing and the flesh is weak. We have discussed and elaborated upon the consideration that this is the ultimate goal of the relationship that God has always wanted.

We have discussed much so far about the external and the internal and about how the two are inseparable but must be internalized. What we need to talk through now, though, is the subject of the privacy of devotion. I dislike the term "subjectivity" in this context and think the words "individuality" and "liberalism" infer too much in the wrong direction (though they are not without merit in this context). What do I mean by this? I mean privacy is the deeply personal realm of an individual's inner relationship, individually with Jesus. How one dedicates one's devotion, how one engages with our Lord, and where (whether through personal conversations, through music, art, walks in the countryside, solitude, reflective times, or times of private contemplation), what transpires and is discussed (or not) or felt or shared with a person and Jesus is between them. It is privacy because it is possessional by the individual and deeply personal and internal. And, yes, it is individual and perhaps subjective in that what works for one person may not work for another; this is how it should be, and God wants it to be, because we are all different and were made to be so.

Part of the being a Devotionist is learning to enjoy life in all its beauty, not for its own sake but by doing so, we are to worship the Giver of life. Life was given not earned, and it therefore should be treated as a gift; for we did nothing ourselves to give ourselves life, and so this appreciation needs to be nurtured. It is the internalization of this nurturing process to do all in the name of the Lord, to decide where your treasure lies, to dwell upon all that is good and pure, to love and appreciate your brethren, that is the start of the internal development that manifests in and through your devotion. We do these because we love the Lord, not to gain His favor. We choose to nurture our souls, which we do not do if we do that which is against Him. We choose to honor God. We choose life in all its fullness. We choose to believe that eternal life starts in this life because that is what the Holy Spirit has told us through the Scriptures and what the Holy Spirit within us testifies to us as truth. We choose the fruit of the Spirit as the model for our behavior and choose to ask the Holy Spirit to help us. For without His help, all we do is as mere works to be blown away as dust in the wind.

This is the privacy of devotion for it is internal, individual, and personal to each of us. Each heart is different, and God wants a different relationship with each of us. No two relationships with God are the same—how can they be when we are all different and yet being conformed to His image. We should never compare one relationship with God with another, though of course, being sinful, this is the very first thing we do. We should first be so thankful that we have any relationship with Him at all, and then all will flow from there. Dwell upon His goodness and all that He has done for you—every one of us who are members of His household. This alone is enough for a thousand years of fellowship. Giving thanks—or should I say more personally, giving appreciation for who He is, how He is, and all He does and will do for us—is the foundation for any good relationship, and so it is with God. These are the means to "perfect that which concerns me" (Ps 138:8).

Nurturing the Soul: The Hidden Key to Our Personal Relationship with God

Our soul is what God is interested in, and nothing else should matter to us because nothing else matters to God. What the Bible says about our "heart" is actually the condition and consideration of the health and position of our soul. Our soul is what connects us to God. It is integral and yet distinct; it is personal to each one of us. And yet we see in the psalms that the soul can become distressed and downcast as we withdraw from God and become distant from Him. Psalm 23 has the plea of the writer to restore his soul (Ps 23:3a), expressed with the twofold appreciation that while restoration of the soul comes from God alone, we must take the initiative to ask. Note that David does not elaborate on how he expects God to restore his soul, it's just that he knows that if he asks, the Lord will—and so with us too. Note, too, that he does not elaborate on what he expects the Lord to do or what he has to do to assist. What we do know of David is that He was a great musician and poet who loved to meditate on God (by which He did not necessarily mean His word, but rather on all His attributes). What we see here is that the method of restoration is not prescriptive to all in some kind of "one size fits all" mentality that we are all expected to conform to when our souls need nurturing or indeed when it comes to devotion.

But the starting point has to be that it matters to you what happens to your soul, to even want to nurture it and to do so for the long haul. But as we have said before, the nurturing of the soul is actually the action and function of the Holy Spirit within us, and we know that the ultimate role of the Holy Spirit is to point us to Jesus and to assist in conforming us to His image alone. Unless our effort to nurture achieves this aim, then it is worthless and not of the Holy Spirit. This becomes a vital consideration when it comes to how we nurture and must be ever mindful of whether or not Jesus is actually being honored in what we do, listen to, the way we worship, what we are singing, reading, and most importantly what our own heart attitude is.

Many parts of God's created order around us give us clues and patterns that assist us in our deliberations of God and assist us when we seek to understand more of His ways. Hence, we see David look to the stars and ask, "What is man that You are mindful of him" (Ps 8:4), and we see Jesus constantly using horticultural imagery when describing our relationship with God and the coming kingdom. It is as such, then, that we can consider the nurturing of the soul—for the very word "nurture" implies cultivation and growth.

It might be helpful to see the nurturing of the soul in just such a horticultural way: all plants and seeds need taking care of, need nurturing, in order to establish, grow, and flourish. And is it thus with our devotion and the nurturing of our soul—we take care of it, we feed it, we water it, and we let it bask in sunlight. Just as photosynthesis is a closed system (you need all the components in place to function and without one it does not work), so nurturing our soul can be viewed in the same way. We need all of these to nurture, for without one, the nurturing does not happen.

Light: Jesus said "I *am* the light of the world" (John 8:12, emphasis mine). He is the light that destroys darkness. Just as the warmth of the sun is only really felt when the clouds are removed, so it is with us too; Jesus's light can burn away the clouds both within and outside us. But we need to let it. His is the glory and His light alone can provide the energy that we need to grow and to draw near to Him. Jesus is the glory of God, and as we draw to Him, His glory reflects onto us. This light is transferred from Jesus to us without our knowing (see Exod 33). How we let His light shine on us is actually how we perceive His glory. How do we do that? Well, we proclaim His glory (1 Chr 29:11, Isa 40–48), we proclaim His works (Ps 77), we meditate on His goodness and His majesty when we consider His ways and wonder at His creation and the wonder of Jesus, and we talk of His goodness to each other. This is how we bask in His light, and it is tonic for the soul.

Water: Water is an image of the Holy Spirit in the New Testament, but it is also the image of the life that Jesus gives the believer: living water. It is only this water that can quench our thirst for God. The Spirit teaches all things and leads to Jesus. But His role is sanctification to make us more like Jesus. Both the goal and path of sanctification now is the fruit of the Spirit, and this should be our focus when we draw close to God: our sanctification through the empowerment of the Holy Spirit. It is as we sit at the foot of the cross and wonder at all He achieved for us that then we can start to get up and walk in the Spirit. Jesus is the means by which we can walk in the Spirit—He is the One who is the object of our faith and the purpose of our walk.

Feeding: All Scripture speaks of Jesus, and so we feed ourselves not just through the word but through Jesus Himself. Jesus is the bread of life, not the word. Hence, we are not to make the mistake of worshiping the created rather than the Creator, or the word rather than He who inspired the word. Yes, we need to feed on the word of God, but more than that we need to be fed on Jesus, for Jesus is the word and He alone is the bread of life.

It goes without saying that the very word and concept of nurturing involves constant monitoring and "care and attention." Our devotional life is exactly the same as this. And if we are not careful, we become so easily distracted and lethargic that when (and if) we resume, we do so with a sense of obligation and guilt. This is because we too easily approach devotion as something that is legalistic and programmatic, and to be honest that is why it too becomes dull. This then is everything that devotion is not meant to be. So what's the answer? Again, it is held within the words of Jesus as He ushered in the new way of the bride of Christ; this new way is defined by Him as "abiding in Him and He in us." While it is easy to focus on what the word "abiding" means to us, in this context it is actually amplified by the simple word "in." To abide is full immersion in Christ: it is Living Devotion. The most holy and necessary practice in our spiritual life is the presence of God. That means finding constant pleasure in His divine company, speaking humbly and lovingly with Him in all seasons, at every moment, without limiting the conversation in any way.

"But how?" I hear you ask. And how can we, when we feel so wretched and inadequate before God, not spending time with Him when we feel that we ought to or even that we ought to *want* to, even when we don't? We will be addressing this during the course of this book in the light of our Positional Blessings, but in the meantime, I bow to the wisdom of Brother Lawrence:

> I consider myself the most wretched of men, full of sore and corruption, and who has committed all sorts of crimes against His King. Touched with a sensible regret, I confess to Him all my wickedness, I ask His forgiveness, I abandon myself in His hands that He may do what He pleases with me. The King, full of mercy and goodness, very far from chastising me, embraces me with love, makes me eat at His table, serves me with His own hands, gives me the key of His treasures; He converses and delights Himself with me incessantly, in a thousand and a thousand ways, and treats me in all respects as His favorite. It is thus I consider myself from time to time in His holy presence.[1]

1. Brother Lawrence, *Practice of the Presence*, 36–37.

As we reach the end of part 1 of this book, I guess we have finally come to the point where we have to be honest and say with Paul that it's not just that the heart is willing but the flesh is weak, but that even if I wanted to draw close to God, or to perhaps "practice devotion," I do not know how to. What I can say is that if that is the case, then you are halfway there already. I know that it's not particularly helpful of me to say that there is nothing proscriptive to what you must do and how you must do it, and that what works for some won't work for others because we are all different and God knows this. But what I can say is that it all starts with a heart attitude and an acknowledgement that you can do nothing except with the help of the Holy Spirit. This is what Jesus meant by basically saying all you have to do is ask. If there is one thing that Scripture is very clear on, it is that it is God's heart that you know Him more. It is God's heart that you fellowship with Him, that you learn of His ways, and that you love Him more and more.

What we are too little told and realize is that God actually wants us to ask and has always done so, as is evident from King David's plea to God, "Show me Your ways, O Lord; / Teach me Your paths" (Ps 25:4), through to Jesus's very direct and simple, "Ask, and it will be given to you; seek, and you will find; knock, and it will be opened to you" (Matt 7:7). Remember, we are indwelled by the Holy Spirit, and it is His function and delight to point us to Jesus. The Holy Spirit is God, and all we have to do is ask Him to point us to Jesus and the Father—in effect asking Him to do just what He said He would do. Remember, God will never give His glory to another (Isa 42:8), and hence the very desire of wanting to draw closer to God must come from the Spirit within us. The answering by God of these requests simply serves to give Him the glory, having been instigated by Himself in the first place in a divinely inspired closed loop system that is the entirety of Christian living and all doctrine.

All this is to say that it's actually very simple: we are to ask for help to be able to do these things. If you have difficulty in prayer, ask to be able to pray. If you feel that you feel closer to God through music, then listen more to true worship and draw close to Him through that. If your soul is nurtured through walks in the countryside, then undertake those with the purpose of giving God the glory for all that He has given us to enjoy in our lives. This is the abiding in Christ that we spoke of before. All He wants and all He has ever wanted is for the full immersion of our dedication to Him. He will guide us, individually, into what that looks like. As with all things, it will take commitment, but when we fail we know He will always be there for us; when we become distant, He will always call us back; when we condemn, He will remind us where we stand in His household and that there is no condemnation for us from Him. And He is patient and kind, long-suffering and compassionate. God is understanding of our ways and our weaknesses, which is why we trust in His loving-kindness. He wants us to bask in His beauty and His love for us. He has done everything for us, for He alone is complete. And yet while He alone is worthy, it is He who has set before us eternity, rewards for no reason, and treasures for us to behold that are beyond compare. And in the meantime, He wants our hearts not to be troubled, for He is in control of all things. "Comfort My people" He said to Isaiah (Isa 40:1), and so with us today. Let the peace of God rule in your hearts, bask in holiness, and in the beauty and in the privacy of your devotion.

PART 2

The Precious Gates of Devotion

The Heart Attitude of the Devotionist

KING DAVID HAS THE honor of being the only person in Scripture described by God Himself as being "a man after My own heart, who will do all My will" (Acts 13:22).[1] This makes David, of course, very much a type of Christ, who is the ultimate embodiment of the will and heart of God; hence we should give due consideration as to what it was about David that led to this honor. The first clue can be deduced from the fact that David was described as such in 1 Sam 13:14 before he became king, while he was still a lowly, unknown, insignificant shepherd, unknown to anyone outside of his family, and even considered by them as to be of so little worth that he was not even put forward by his own father.

There are so many elements to this that we could draw out in relation to devotion, but we should explore just three before we proceed. Firstly, the ways of God are not our ways. God looks upon the heart of the believer, never to that person's so-called status; it is the heart, as we have discussed already, that is of most interest to the Lord. The parallel to this is that a lack of worth in the eyes of the world rarely, if ever, correlates with the worth that the believer has in God's eyes and heart. David, as his psalms make clear, knew his identity and worth came from the Lord and knew that the opinions of others were of no import to God and should be

1. Cf. 1 Sam 13:14.

of no import to us either. Secondly, it is this very lowliness of this status that God Himself elevates. David would have known his seeming insignificance, and by knowing, he consequently exemplifies that humility before God is a prerequisite to a full understanding of Him and His ways. It has always been thus, and rightly so, for God is sovereign and He will never give His glory to another (Isa 42:8). As Jesus so beautifully explained, it is the poor in spirit, the meek, and the heavy-laden who will seek the Lord and find His kingdom. Thirdly, we can assume and infer from David that he had what we can describe as "devotional contentment," in that had his transition into being king never had happened, his heart would have remained content in his role as shepherd, devotionally devoted to God. This contentment comes from an understanding and appropriation of his position with God in His household and a complete appropriation of the purposes, ways, characteristics, and attributes of God and how they all combine to give those who love Him the full eternal security given to the individual believer whose heart is aligned with God's.

It is within the psalms that we can seek and discover the heart attitude of David as a Devotionist. What lies behind the emotion and conviction that David displays in the psalms is, of course, a heart that is not divided when it comes to his devotion. He is always abundantly clear who owns his heart and where his hope, because of that, comes from. These are the traits that we can posit were appropriated by him in his early years in the wilderness with his sheep. It is important for our purposes here as we explore these matters as ordinary Christians to remember that while a shepherd, David would have had no clue as to what lay ahead of him. For he was not being prepared, or groomed, for kingship—as far as he would have been concerned, this was his lot in life. And he loved the Lord anyway. Hence, we see the application to us as we seek to explore what it means to be a Devotionist and how we can learn from David's heart as the example given to us that best reflects God's. David's devotional traits, as we can describe them, start from a position of reflection and realization of just who God is and what He is like. From this comes the heart attitude of just longing to be in His presence. This goes beyond mere knowledge of the Scriptures, for we can assume that David, as a lowly shepherd spending months away in the wilderness on his own, would have limited access to the Torah (and indeed he barely mentions the law in the psalms, much like Jesus, in fact, in His ministry), taking nature and prolonged periods in the presence of God contemplating His ways and regarding His attributes, as displayed in nature and the stars, as his guide and tutor. This produces a deep, precious, and profound hunger for God that can only be satisfied by being in His presence. David realized above all, and shows us beautifully in the psalms, that our souls must be nurtured and cared for if we are to be satisfied as God's creatures and especially as members of His household. David shows us that as it is our souls that connect us to God, the responsibility is ours to cherish and nurture them above all else. This then leads to God's ultimate will in our lives that through Him and through Him alone we can have peace. This is His desire for us, and it is ours to receive, for it is already prepared for us, if we only seek it.

These are the not only the traits of the Devotionist but form, if we can adapt an analogy from David himself to metaphorically describe them, entry points or gates through which the Devotionist might enter into the presence of God. If nurturing the soul is the aim and focus of devotion, then by examining how David and the other psalmists reference the soul, we can draw various inferences from the way they describe their nurturing interactions with it. They identify the needs of their souls as an effective, and actual, longing to be in the presence of God—which is the ultimate aim of all devotion—and portray the soul's reactions to this anticipated and needed presence. We have imaginatively harmonized these themes and analogies and consolidated them into a typically Davidic image, metaphorically representing and visualizing them as a series of "gates" (inspired by Ps 118:19), through which the believer can enter as we endeavor to systematically approach our own devotion, or rather our own efforts to nurture our souls through devotion. Hence, we have coined the term the "Precious Gates of Devotion." They are "precious" not only for the believer as they represent the means of entry into the presence of God, but precious also because they are personal and intimate. By definition, something that is precious is subjectively valued by the beholder and, thus, God values us as we value our intimacy with Him:

> How precious also are Your thoughts to me, O God!
> How great is the sum of them!
> If I should count them, they would be more in number than the sand;
> When I awake, I am still with You.
> (Ps 139:17–18)

What is clear from the psalms is that the soul needs nourishing, as we have said. What is also abundantly clear is that David and the other psalmists recognize this fact and have identified its needs and what occurs prior to being nourished, during the nourishment, and after it has been nourished. This is extremely helpful for our own purposes as we seek to create a framework for our own devotion that is biblical, spiritual, and true to the heart of these Devotionists who have set before us exemplars in exploring the presence of God, many of which flow from, let us not forget, a man who is uniquely described as being a man after God's own heart.

Prior to Being Nourished

While we have to give the writers of the psalms their due creative license through their use of song and poetry, it is fascinating to see how they address the needs of the soul as if it were almost a separate entity for them, yet obviously intractably linked to our minds and bodies. It is spoken to, reasoned with, cajoled, and examined in manners which reveal much for us as we seek to nurture our own souls and seek deeper experiences and understanding of God through and within our devotion.

We see this developed in a way that possibly reflects our own experiences as we consider ourselves and how we are when it comes to devotion and periods of it. What is meant by this? It appears that the Devotionists are aware that there is connection to the behavior, mood even, of their soul and their own feelings toward God and their desire to spend time with Him. This starts and develops as follows.

Self-Examination

> Why are you cast down, O my soul?
> And why are you disquieted within me?
> (Ps 42:5)

The really interesting point to note first here is that in our general lives as Christians, there are frequently times when we feel down, despondent even, regarding our faith and are generally dissatisfied with our relationship with the Lord. Perhaps this manifests in our feeling disconnected from other Christians, in feeling guilty about not reading our Bibles enough, or in a multitude of other disengaged emotions. The answer to this that the psalmist gives is that this is a feeling that comes directly from our souls—it is our soul's demeanor that affects our own emotions when these emotions pertain to God and our connectivity with Him. Thus, to ask the question as David does here is to recognize this fact: our souls are the link between us and God and act as the bellwether, so to speak, of the health and strength of our connectivity between Him—note, not *whether* there is a connection, but the strength of the connectivity between us at any given time. The expectation of the psalmists is that it is God's desire that we should fellowship with Him, not whether they were entitled to do so. They knew they were entitled to this direct access, these expressions of honesty, frustration, and love, because they knew that the way God looked upon them was as the righteous ones, and this was only because they knew that He knew their hearts were aligned with Him. That's why the psalmist could honestly say such things as,

> Vindicate me, O Lord,
> For I have walked in my integrity.
> I have also trusted in the Lord;
> I shall not slip.
> Examine me, O Lord, and prove me;
> Try my mind and my heart.
> For Your lovingkindness is before my eyes,
> And I have walked in Your truth.
> (Ps 26:1–3)

This then is also the fundamental starting point for us as we ask the question, "Why are you cast down, O my soul?" (Ps 42:11). For we ask the question from the position of people who are in the household of God, who know that there is no condemnation because we have peace with God. Thus, we can ask the question out of concern rather than guilt or fear of the answer. But we must also be prepared to receive the answer to the question, and sometimes it's as simple as there being a lack of time spent with God or it's "You've let your anxieties and concerns for this world run away with you and run you away from the comfort of the presence of God." But other times, it is also because of other factors such as undealt-with sin. And in still others, we see the soul concerned with the bigger picture of wider issues pertaining to the state of the world in particular, as to how it affects what we can term "His household"—it is in these instances that we see the soul most likely preparing us for times of what we call intercession, whether corporately with other believers or in our own time. We see these scenarios played out in the psalms as the soul responds to the questions asked of it with the simple reply: there's a lack of time spent close to and in the presence of God.

It is part of our human nature that we find excuses and reasons for not looking to spend time with God, especially in our times of personal devotion. The only result, though, is a downward emotional spiral into despair as we use all sorts of excuses to excuse ourselves. And our souls become downcast.

Lest We Forget

> He has redeemed my soul in peace
> from the battle that was against me,
> For there were many against me.
> (Ps 55:18)

> For You have delivered my soul from death.
> Have You not kept my feet from falling,
> That I may walk before God
> In the light of the living?
> (Ps 56:13)

Unfortunately, we too easily forget and too easily adopt the comforts of the world and assume and appropriate its disinterest in the matters of God, and so our souls become downcast. Sometimes we need to take ourselves in hand and remind ourselves of just who it is who saved us and who it is who has bestowed upon us the privileges of salvation and righteousness that have been gifted to us, not through or because of anything we have done but simply because of the unmerited favor that God has chosen of His own accord for His own reasons to bestow upon us. We need to remember again and again, as we too easily forget, that we are nothing without God and that our salvation belongs to Him alone and is because of Him alone. We are only able to gain access to Him because of what He has done and because (let us never forget) He really wants us to have access to Him. As Jesus said to Adam and Eve as He walked in the garden of Eden, "Where are you?" (Gen 3:9), so He asks the same of our souls daily, hourly, "Where are you?" We forget that when it comes to devotion, this is God's heart for us. It is a mutual thing; it is not one-way with an impersonal, remote God, but it's direct, relational, and it matters to God. As such, it matters to our souls. This, then, is the feeling we have when we are separate through our own deliberate fault or through our own necessity of dealing with life as ordinary Christians (the purpose and spur of writing this book).

Separation Through Sin

> I said, "Lord, be merciful to me;
> Heal my soul, for I have sinned against You."
> (Ps 41:4)

The Bible is consistent in showing us that sin separates us from God. It is only logical then that the soul, as David says in Ps 41:4, needs healing because of sin. Now, obviously the soul cannot get sick to need healing, but this sin amounts to a physical feeling of sickness that can only be rectified through forgiveness by God. It is interesting that David attributes this feeling of sickness to the soul, as well as its impact on us physically too. Consider these words of his:

> O Lord, do not rebuke me in Your wrath,
> Nor chasten me in Your hot displeasure!
> For Your arrows pierce me deeply,
> And Your hand presses me down.
> There is no soundness in my flesh
> Because of Your anger,
> Nor any health in my bones
> Because of my sin.
> For my iniquities have gone over my head;
> Like a heavy burden they are too heavy for me.
> My wounds are foul and festering
> Because of my foolishness.
> I am troubled, I am bowed down greatly;
> I go mourning all the day long.
> For my loins are full of inflammation,
> And there is no soundness in my flesh.
> I am feeble and severely broken;
> I groan because of the turmoil of my heart.
> (Ps 38:1–8)

Here we see that the effect of sin is as a physical weight upon David, and this is true as our sins literally weigh heavily upon us. There is so much in this passage that we could delve into here to examine the heart of the Devotionist, but for now let's just look at two aspects. Firstly, it is important that we note that David describes his sin as "foolishness" (verse 5), and we know from elsewhere in the psalms that according to David, "The fool has said in his heart, 'There is no God'" (Ps 14:1). And so, by extension, if sin can be looked upon as foolishness, then sinning entails a denial of

God. Sin is a denial of God in that the act of sinning is actually a rebellion by the believer against the attributes of God—meaning that when we sin, we deliberately ignore His attributes of omniscience and omnipresence. God is all-knowing, so why do we think we can deceive Him, even in the secret places of our heart, when He knows all about us? He is omnipresent and hence He is there when we sin—"Where can I go?" (Ps 139:7) as David would say. And hence, the seriousness of sin is that we effectively deny these attributes, and this is what physically and spiritually pains our souls when we do so.

In addition, there is also an argument to say that there is the "sin of separation," as well as "separation through sin." As we have discussed previously, all God requires of us is our heart, and His whole desire is for us to be in constant connection and fellowship with Him. When we are not so, it pains us and our souls. When we deliberately hide ourselves, as it were, then we are replicating Adam and Eve, who tried to hide themselves from the presence of God; we see in this ridiculously futile action the immediacy of the effect of sin in promoting the denial of God's attributes, for this is again tantamount to denying the omnipresence and omniscience of God. This is why and when separation itself can become sin, which must be rectified because deliberate and prolonged periods of separation from God are not only unhealthy for our souls, our relationship with Him, but are in effect diminishing our respect for these attributes which do not change, though we behave as if they have. Prolonged periods of separation are tantamount to disinterest, at best, and profound disrespect for who He is and what He has done and will do, at worst. And that is sinful, to put it mildly. Thankfully, though, our God is not capricious; and this is not to condemn, for there is no condemnation for those in Christ Jesus. But whenever we have been distant or elusive in our relationship with God, when we seek to rectify that, God is always there, always loving, always forgiving, and always tender in His loving-kindness to those whom He loves.

Affliction and Anxieties

Naturally speaking, we are all too prone to withdraw from God at times when we need to do the exact opposite. Times of affliction and anxiety, whatever the cause (and they are many and frequently compound on each other), affect our complete selves—mind, body, and spirit. It is the soul's reaction to these that interest us here, for again we see that the only remedy is one of more, not less, of the presence of God. It is always God who is our shield and our defense. He is the only constant in whom we can always trust. But it is within, not apart from or outside of, these times of tribulation and anxiety that God comforts and delights the soul. He does this within the storm, so to speak. Even though it sometimes feels like we are going through the valley of death, emotionally or physically, God comforts us and restores us within ourselves. I cannot think of a better example than these times to prove that it is our hearts that God is concerned with most, and His comforts are for our souls, not necessarily for our physical or emotional state: "In the multitude of my anxieties within me, Your comforts delight my soul" (Ps 94:19). As always, God is interested in how we respond to these times of tribulation. Faith materializes here not just in wanting the problem solved or the anxiety for it to be removed, but in how we regard the issue or the perspective we have on the problem:

> In the day of my trouble I sought the Lord;
> My hand was stretched out in the night without ceasing;
> My soul refused to be comforted.
> (Ps 77:2)

Honesty in Affliction

The entirety of Ps 88 is a poem of angst from the godly in the face of affliction. It is a painful cry to understand pain and anguish in one's life when it comes from all around, even from loved ones and friends. It may seem odd to us that the psalmist lays the cause of this calamity at the feet of God Himself as He cries out to God and correctly identifies the impact of this calamity: "For my soul is full of troubles, And my life draws near to the grave" (verse 3). And yet this honesty of pleading with God when in the depths of travail comes from a heart that knows that there will be no recrimination for doing so. This heart also knows that while these afflictions are caused by external factors and come from other people, God in His Providence and in His attributes knows of them too—even to the extent of being accused of being the cause of them!

"Why would God do this to those whom He loves?" we too easily and perhaps lazily ask. The answer is that despite the hyperbole, there is nothing that is being complained of that is actually physically life threatening here. Emotions run high when one is downcast, and perhaps even paranoia can come in when we are being disciplined, for God does do that. He will discipline those whom He loves (Prov 3:11–12) if we are deliberately, consistently wayward from Him for long periods of time. The word of God does, after all, convict and is able to separate bone from marrow for it is living and powerful to do so (2 Tim 3:16–17, Heb 4:12). Psalm 88 then can be read as the desperation of one who recognizes that this disciplining is coming from God and identifies all His spiritual and emotional maladies as having a root cause. Thankfully, though, we also know that the Devotionist will be able to recognize these symptoms for what they are—namely, deviation from the fellowship of God. The solution is always clear from the psalmists themselves:

> Keep my soul, and deliver me;
> Let me not be ashamed, for I put my trust in You.
> (Ps 25:20)

> I have hated those who regard useless idols;
> But I trust in the Lord.
> I will be glad and rejoice in Your mercy,
> For You have considered my trouble;
> You have known my soul in adversities,
> And have not shut me up into the hand of the enemy;
> You have set my feet in a wide place.
> (Ps 31:6–8)

The hunger for justice and deliverance from oppression is a powerful motif not only throughout the psalms, but generally in the life of any believer. But it is precisely because God is the God of justice that our souls and the Spirit within us cries out for justice—and yet this cry in itself will always point us to Jesus. Just as the Hebrews knew that ultimately justice belongs to God alone, so it came to be synonymous with the time of the Messiah when justice would rain down from above and all afflictions would be wiped away (Amos 5:24). And so our afflictions not only point to our own position of salvation (and hence the grace and mercy of God to us now as we contemplate the realities of eternal life) but also point us to the times of hope before us: the time when we will be forever with the Lord, whether on earth or in heaven, whether in our glorified bodies or in our spiritual state.

Longing for the Presence of God

David's question as to why His soul is downcast is answered not in a recriminatory way, as we would expect, but through the generation of the feeling of longing to be in His presence. This feeling is of course reflected in our own lives. When we have been away from loved ones, we miss them and we long to be back with them. This is the same response our soul has then when we spend time—especially too much time—away from engagement and connectivity with God. Poetically, the image given is more than just longing, it is "panting," hankering, thirsting, yearning to be with God:

> As the deer pants for the water brooks,
> So pants my soul for You, O God.
> My soul thirsts for God, for the living God.
> When shall I come and appear before God?
> (Ps 42:1–2)
>
> O God, You are my God;
> Early will I seek You;
> My soul thirsts for You;
> My flesh longs for You In a dry and thirsty land
> Where there is no water.
> (Ps 63:1)
>
> My soul longs, yes, even faints
> For the courts of the Lord;
> My heart and my flesh cry out for the living God.
> (Ps 84:2)

This is the heart and soul then of the Devotionist. Our times with God are precious to us, hence when we are away then our soul's light becomes as if put "under a basket" (Matt 5:15) and we become dimmed and our shine begins to lack luster (to mix metaphors). The answer the psalmist gives is simple: refocus back onto God, consider His ways and the hope we have in him.

> Why are you cast down, O my soul?
> And why are you disquieted within me?
> Hope in God, for I shall yet praise Him
> For the help of His countenance.
> (Ps 42:5)[2]

---

2. Notably repeated in verse 11.

Expectation

Longing produces expectation and expectation compounds longing—the two are inseparable both in our personal lives with loved ones, and the same is true between ourselves, our souls, and our God. But where does this expectation that produces longing come from, if not from the Lord himself? As the psalmist says,

> My soul, wait silently for God alone,
> For my expectation is from Him.
> (Ps 62:5)

But what is this expectation, and expectation of what? Quite simply the expectation of the Devotionist is the presence of God. That said, it is also an expectation built on the solidity of the one of whom we are expectant. It is based on the trust, confidence, reliability, and loving-kindness of this person. When we are expectant of the presence of God, our expectation is that of engagement with His divinity. The implications of this need to be digested and absorbed by all who wish for the presence of God, and this is what our expectation really needs to encompass—our direct engagement with the Creator, the One who is all-knowing, all-powerful, and who is love, grace, truth and mercy. This is our God, and so of course we are to be expectant of Him to be divine. But this expectation comes not from a position of fear or remoteness but, as we said earlier, from the position of familial intimacy. Our expectation is only of goodness, for that is what God is.

> For He satisfies the longing soul,
> And fills the hungry soul with goodness.
> (Ps 107:9)

Our expectation is that of loving-kindness, for God is love and is kindness. Our expectation is that of the miraculous, for He is divine and nothing is impossible for God. Our expectation is life in all its abundance, for that is what He has promised, even among the trials and tribulations of everyday life. Our expectation is that He will honor His word, for the entirety of the word is truth (Ps 119:160). Our expectation is that He will cure our anxieties and satisfy our souls:

> In the multitude of my anxieties within me,
> Your comforts delight my soul.
> (Ps 94:19)

> My soul shall be satisfied as with marrow and fatness,
> And my mouth shall praise You with joyful lips.
> (Ps 63:5)

Our expectation is that He will be as God in our lives and that He is more than able. And so, as we contemplate entering into His presence, our hearts and souls rejoice together, as so eloquently stated by the apostle Paul:

> Now to Him who is able to do exceedingly abundantly above all that we ask or think, according to the power that works in us, to Him be glory in the church by Christ Jesus to all generations, forever and ever. Amen. (Eph 3:20–21)

Psalms 42 and 145 are excellent to read in their entirety, meditate upon, or pray though as we prepare to enter into God's presence. Psalm 42 asks the soul questions, the answers to which are basically to look to the Lord for our consolation, and as we consider His works and hope in him, we soon realize that there is no reason to be downcast.

The Cross and the Empty Tomb

All this is to say that as we prepare to enter into the presence of God through the Precious Gates of Living Devotion, so we pause to consider first and foremost both the cross and the empty tomb. When we look upon the cross, of course, we see our sin nailed to it; but our Savior is not there. We recall the scourging and the insults and the manifestation of the sheer magnitude of grace personified before our eyes as the Creator of all things suffered for us; but our Savior is not there. When we look into the tomb and see the cloths that wrapped Him, still stained with our sin, His sweat and blood still clearly visible, the air still thick with the aromas of oil and perfume, yet our Savior is not there. For when we look upon the cross and the empty tomb, we crouch and prostrate in awe at the mind of Christ, the will of the Father, and are in awe of this perfect sacrifice. And we marvel at the power and authority demonstrated through the death and resurrection of the Lamb of God who would do this for us and for His glory, to make a mockery of all principalities and powers, putting to death sin and death. But when we gaze upon the cross and search the tomb, our Savior is not there—for He is at the right hand of God, with the earth as His footstool, where He wonderfully, remarkably, impossibly is still making intercession to the Father for us. This is our Savior who said that even though He was going, He would send the Comforter and Helper to be with us, to guide us, and to dwell in us so we can live for and love Him as He deserves. And our souls remind us continually, "For you were bought at a price; therefore glorify God in your body and in your spirit, which are God's" (1 Cor 6:20). And rightly so, for this is our God, and this is how abundantly He loves us and is now imploring us to look to Him in His splendor and magnificence to join the host of heaven in declaring, day and night,

> Worthy is the Lamb who was slain
> To receive power and riches and wisdom,
> And strength and honor and glory and blessing!
> (Rev 5:12)

. . . and all of our devotion.

The Precious Gates of Devotion

Open to me the gates of righteousness;
I will go through them,
And I will praise the Lord.

Psalm 118:19

It would not be incorrect to state that the division into three of factors that pertain to God occurs throughout the Bible, and hence to do so would be neither biblically nor spiritually unorthodox—think Father, Son, and Holy Spirit; the way, the truth, and the life; faith, hope, and love. In keeping with this, I have drawn out from the psalms and elsewhere three "Precious Gates of Devotion" as "entry gates," a means of consolidating our thinking around how we can enter into the presence of God. These are obviously metaphorical in nature and yet at the same time biblically spiritual. The purpose of portraying these in such a way is the attempt to establish a means through which we can begin to prepare our hearts and souls to enter into the presence and, as we shall discuss later on, remain in the presence of God.

These gates we have not only termed collectively as "precious" (for that is what they are) but have taken inspiration from Scripture to name them individually. We are told, for instance, in Acts 3:2 that one of the entry gates into the temple was called "Beautiful"; hence, we have adopted this practice to describe not only their individual function but also their individual qualities. By naming them in this way, we can start to explore the entrance into God's presence through how the psalmists themselves address their own souls when preparing to be in His presence. I am also of a mind to consider the vast gates and gatehouses that are detailed as the entry points into the millennial temple of the Messiah in Ezek 40–41 and ultimately into the very presence of God as a further development of this metaphor for how gates can have rooms and interconnecting passageways that can in themselves be explored. This then becomes symbolic and helps us to visualize the passage from one to another that I think we can adopt and adapt for our purposes of creating a visual concept of gates as metaphors for entering into the presence of God.

While they can be considered in some ways sequentially—as in passing through from one to the other until we finally enter into the light of God's presence—they are three-in-one. For the gates themselves, while plural (like the Godhead), are in fact one (like the Godhead). We have set out below what can be seen as the three "entry gates" that lead into the presence of God, and there is one "continued presence gate," or exit gate, which we will explore through which the believer takes the blessings of the presence of God into everyday life. In this section, we shall explore the entry gates first and have termed these as follows:

- The Gate of the Consideration of the Divine
- The Gate of Transcendental Trust
- The Gate of Familial Confidence

Gate 1: The Gate of the Consideration of the Divine

> Bless the Lord, O my soul!
> O Lord my God, You are very great:
> You are clothed with honor and majesty,
> Who cover Yourself with light as with a garment,
> Who stretch out the heavens like a curtain.
> (Ps 104:1–2)

> When I consider Your heavens, the work of Your fingers,
> The moon and the stars, which You have ordained,
> What is man that You are mindful of him,
> And the son of man that You visit him?
> (Ps 8:3–4)

As we consider the divine, so we see our own futility and humility in the presence of God. As we contemplate and perhaps even ponder the ways of God, so we are drawn toward Him, and when we do this, so we become absorbed in the light of His countenance. His ways are not our ways (thank goodness), and the more we contemplate the divine, the more we become appreciative of the privilege that we have as Christians. But sadly, too few of us do "consider" the ways and works of God for just what they are and whom they signify and glorify. How often do we contemplate God? Not what He does for us, not what He can do for us, and certainly not what we purport to do for Him, but God Himself, His ways, His works (the fact that He does them, how He does them, and why), and His attributes for what they are? For most of us, I would say, the answer is, sadly, not very often if at all. And we are the poorer for it.

This is why the first "gate" is that of "Divine Consideration." It opens into all devotion and is displayed in both elaborate and simple ways, with words such as "blessed are You" (1 Chr 29:10) or "hallowed be Your name" (Matt 6:9). It starts from a position of acceptance and recognition of the fact that seems, strangely, to be missed by many Christians today: God is divine and He is holy, and while we who are redeemed are very much part of His family and have incredible familial privileges, He still deserves and requires to be honored and revered. In Malachi, God asks a very simple yet hugely profound question:

> A son honors His father,
> And a servant His master.
> If then I am the Father,
> Where is My honor?
> And if I am a Master,
> Where is My reverence?
> (Mal 1:6)

The comprehension and appropriation of belief in God's divinity is foundational to our faith. Without due thought to it, we cannot pray in honesty, we are unable to grasp His blessings, even our Positional Identity becomes meaningless until we comprehend in whose hands we rest. Indeed, without an understanding of His divinity, we have no appreciation of the Godhead, let alone who it is who dwells within us, as we discussed previously. The more we think about this, the more we should be in awe and wonder:

> By the word of the Lord the heavens were made,
> And all the host of them by the breath of His mouth.
> He gathers the waters of the sea together as a heap;
> He lays up the deep in storehouses.
> Let all the earth fear the Lord;
> Let all the inhabitants of the world stand in awe of Him.
> For He spoke, and it was done;
> He commanded, and it stood fast.
> The Lord brings the counsel of the nations to nothing;
> He makes the plans of the peoples of no effect.
> (Ps 33:6–10)[1]

Consideration of His Works

We must grasp and absorb the concept and depth of the divinity of God. We should meditate upon it and let the thoughts about it sooth us as well as compel us into endless awe and wonder. And this not just at His power and magnificence but at His ways, His characteristics, and above all at how He chooses to demonstrate Himself to us through His work (past, present, and future) both corporately and individually, in history, and in our everyday lives. For our purposes regarding devotion, as we remember His works, so we actually honor Him, and as we honor Him, He draws closer to us. We are, as in so many other ways, too quick not to recall His many wonders, both big and small, and always forget to give Him the glory even for the smallest things in our lives. This Gate then becomes about putting matters in their right perspective first; and as all is enveloped in God's glory and His attributes, so is our continued passage through the most Precious Gates.

> Nebuchadnezzar the king,
> To all peoples, nations, and languages that dwell in all the earth:
> Peace be multiplied to you.
> I thought it good to declare the signs and wonders that the Most High God has worked for me.

---

1. See also 1 Chr 29:10–13, Rev 19:4–7.

> How great are His signs,
> And how mighty His wonders!
> His kingdom is an everlasting kingdom,
> And His dominion is from generation to generation.
> (Dan 4:1–3)

Consider the passages below concerning the imperative to recall and remember His works, for to do so brings solace to our souls and warmth to our hearts. Blessing upon blessing is heaped upon His people, not least through the most wonderful position in His household where He has placed those who believe. This privilege belongs to all who believe, but oh, how we should dwell upon that which we might not consider to be His works, but which are His works and wonders, nonetheless. Consider, we should, the cross, the resurrection, the ascension of Christ, and His soon return in these ways. We should consider how He orchestrates the past, the present, and future to fit His eternal plans and fulfillment of His prophetic words. As we see all that goes on around us, so we see His works and word synonymously being outworked, literally, in tandem and in unison. When we see His Providence in our lives, in our salvation, and in the joy of being blessed so abundantly through the indwelling of His Holy Spirit, so we should declare endless gratitude for His infinite grace and loving-kindness to us:

> I remember the days of old; I meditate on all Your works;
> I muse on the work of Your hands.
> I spread out my hands to You;
> My soul longs for You like a thirsty land. Selah.
> (Ps 143:5–6)

> The works of the LORD are great,
> Studied by all who have pleasure in them.
> His work is honorable and glorious,
> And His righteousness endures forever.
> He has made His wonderful works to be remembered;
> The LORD is gracious and full of compassion.
> (Ps 111:2–4)

Genuine Humility

> O my soul, you have said to the Lord,
> "You are my Lord,
> My goodness is nothing apart from You."
> (Ps 16:2)

Honesty with God to the extent shown in the Ps 16:2 quoted above can only emanate from a strength of self-awareness that itself can only come from a profound internal recognition of humility in front of the Lord that is not only required but acquired through deep contemplation of the position of the believer in the presence of God. It is also representative of an understanding that every believer should have regarding themselves in the relation to God's providential plans. This realization is perhaps the first and most important step in all devotion.

This is why the first Gate is that of "Consideration," for reverence can be the only true product of contemplation and consideration. And from it comes forth awe and wonder, spontaneous praise and worship, and sheer marveling at His ways. What's more, it has ever been thus from His devoted ones, as we see from the outpourings that seem almost irrepressible expressions of wonder from King David and from Paul and down through the ages. Consider this for example from nine hundred years ago from Bernard de Clairvaux, the Cistercian monk:

> You may know this from personal experience. If not, believe one who does—not me, but the holy man who said: "you are good, O Lord, to those who hope in you, to the soul that seeks you" [Lam 3:25]. So, what is God? With respect to creation, its end; to election, salvation; to himself, He alone knows. What is God? All-powerful will, all-benign power, eternal light, immutable reason, blessedness supreme. Creator of beings to partake of him, He quickens men to perceive him, disposes them to desire him, enlarges them to receive Him, justifies them that they may deserve him, fires them with zeal, fertilizes them that they may bear fruit, directs them in the way of justice, moulds them to kindness, contempers them to wisdom, strengthens them to virtue, visits them with consolation, enlightens them with understanding, preserves them unto immortality, fills them with felicity and keeps them safe in His encircling arms.[2]

---

2. Bernard de Clairvaux, as quoted in Matarasso, *Cistercian World*, 90.

Reflective Moments Between Gates

To move and journey from one Gate to another is seamless, for though they are separate, they are yet one. And yet, as we pass through each Gate and enter the next, we should pause to reflect upon what the Spirit has been teaching us and then prepare our hearts and souls to pass through the next Gate. With this first Precious Gate, there is just so much about the magnificence of God that we could dwell upon that perhaps sometimes it is as well to simply state with the psalmist,

> Great is the Lord, and greatly to be praised;
> And His greatness is unsearchable.
> (Ps 145:3)

Gate 2: The Gate of Transcendent Trust

> Cause me to hear Your lovingkindness in the morning,
> For in You do I trust;
> Cause me to know the way in which I should walk,
> For I lift up my soul to You.
> (Ps 143:8)

For the righteous, trust is the natural response to the attributes of God. Because of who God is, our understanding of His ways produces greater trust in Him—we can trust Him and have confidence in who He is and why. We can trust in His word, His loving-kindness toward those whom He loves, and that when He does discipline us, He does so out of love, never out of malice. But more than this, as we prepare to go through this Gate, we need to understand that because of who He is, God expects us to trust Him. It is a requisite of our entrance, and it is proof of our understanding of His fidelity and power, when our own is so feeble.

The Gate of Transcendent Trust, then, is one that leads onwards towards His presence, and we pass through it with faith in God for who He is. To truly trust God means that we can continue to enter into His presence with the full assurance that He will be to us all that His word says He will be, that His attributes are reflective of His very nature, and that He is utterly constant in this—and hence trustworthy. The trust that God delivers transcends faith and material analysis. It transcends the boundaries of doubt, the limitations of apprehension and the depths of anxiety, and enables the believer to soar into new heights of love and ecstasies of hope.

As we pass through this Gate, we do so on the basis that we trust Him to be for us and not against us, that He will never leave us nor forsake us, and that we can rest in the sure and certain knowledge that He is not only worthy of our trust but trustworthy to the utmost—no one else, nothing under heaven and on earth, can match this for the believer. It is because of all these things that we can trust Him to the utmost. Transcendent trust then becomes a Positional Blessing for the believer, for it is because of what God has done through Jesus for us that we can always and without hesitation know that we can always trust Him:

- Trust in His loving-kindness

    How precious is Your lovingkindness, O God!
    Therefore the children of men put
    their trust under the shadow of Your wings.
    (Ps 36:7)[3]

- Trust in His ability to see us through in times of trouble

    Be merciful to me, O God, be merciful to me!
    For my soul trusts in You;
    And in the shadow of Your wings I will make my refuge,
    Until these calamities have passed by.
    (Ps 57:1)

- Trust Him in times of affliction

    In the day of my trouble I sought the Lord;
    My hand was stretched out in the night without ceasing;
    My soul refused to be comforted.
    (Ps 77:2)

- Trust Him to comfort us in all our anxieties

    Unless the Lord had been my help,
    My soul would soon have settled in silence.
    If I say, "My foot slips,"
    Your mercy, O Lord, will hold me up.
    In the multitude of my anxieties within me,
    Your comforts delight my soul.
    (Ps 94:17–19)

---

3. See also Pss 25:6, 20; 26:3; 40:11.

Trust and Faith—Hand in Hand

While it is true that faith is defined in Scripture as "the substance of things hoped for, the evidence of things not seen" (Heb 11:1), trust can be seen as being based on experience. Faith and trust, though, clearly go hand-in-hand; for one without the other makes the one false and the other inept. And thus, the Gate of Transcendent Trust is mirrored with fortified faith, for the more we genuinely trust the Lord in every way, in all that He has said and has revealed both through His word, through creation, through history, and through our lives, so our faith is enriched and enveloped in His loving-kindness toward His people.

How God Views the Faithful

It shows God's heart and nature that He has revealed His heart for His people and preference toward them. Our courage in devotion is just as King David says in Ps 31 quoted below, that the Lord Himself will strengthen our hearts because of our hope in Him. Hope then becomes synonymous with faith for, as we know, without faith it is both impossible to please God and to have hope. Our hope is in God alone for He alone is the only one who is in control of all things, and He alone holds the entirety of creation in His hands; He alone is trustworthy and true, and He alone is constant and full of grace and mercy. Which is why when we contemplate these things our hearts and souls exclaim alongside the psalmist,

> Oh, love the LORD, all you His saints!
> For the LORD preserves the faithful,
> And fully repays the proud person.
> Be of good courage,
> And He shall strengthen your heart,
> All you who hope in the LORD.
> (Ps 31:23–24)

As we have seen before, the reaction to such truths from too many Christians will be that of self-recrimination for their own perceived inadequacies of faith. But this, as we have said, is not how God sees it. The only requirement of faith that God has is faith in His Son, Jesus Christ. This is the faith that saves, and it is the only faith that is required of us—to ask for any more is to edge toward our own merit and our own glory and hence must be rejected out of hand for God will never give His glory to another (Isa 42:8), which is why salvation is by faith, not works. Why? Lest we should boast—meaning that by earning something which is not ours to earn, we claim the glory for something that is not ours to claim. (Eph 2:8–9).

> For I say, through the grace given to me, to everyone who is among you, not to think of himself more highly than He ought to think, but to think soberly, as God has dealt to each one a measure of faith. (Rom 12:3)

To some, it would appear, the clear statements of Scripture are never enough. When it comes to faith, we are all too ready to compare ourselves to our peers, to others in the past whom God has used mightily, and to the great men and women of God as detailed in Heb 11. But we forget that these are the exceptions that prove the rule that we all have been given faith (Rom 12:3) but that God at His sovereign discretion distributes faith as a gift from the Holy Spirit to those who are in need at a particular instance, or as He sees fit in His own sovereign wisdom for His own sovereign reasons (1 Cor 12:7–9).

> But the Scripture has confined all under sin, that the promise by faith in Jesus Christ might be given to those who believe. (Gal 3:22)

We must remember that we all have faith and that faith in Christ is imparted to us as a part of our Positional Identity: those who are in Christ have faith. That is the equation, and it is that simple. The faith of one believer therefore is no greater than that of another believer, for there is only one faith and there is certainly, in God's eyes, only one faith that counts:

> There is one body and one Spirit, just as you were called in one hope of your calling; one Lord, one faith, one baptism; one God and Father of all, who is above all, and through all, and in you all. (Eph 4:5–6)

It is of vital importance, as we consider faith in relation to the Gate of Transcendent Trust, to comprehend that as faith and therefore trust become positional for those in the household of God, there is never any condemnation directed at the believer by God when our faith and trust seem diminished and unworthy in our eyes. For there is no condemnation for those in Christ Jesus, as we have said before (Rom 8:1). Certainly, faith can be given as a gift in exceptional circumstances, but it is also part of the fabric of our Positional Identity, to the extent that those in the household of God are also defined as being one and the same with the "household of faith" (Gal 6:10).

A further aspect that we need always to remind ourselves of as we prepare to enter into His presence and as we reflect upon and consider our own faith and trust in God is that faithfulness is as much part of the nature and character of God as are His other immutable characteristics and attributes. Put simply, God is faith and He is unconditionally faithful toward those who believe. Scripture is absolutely emphatic about this, and when we consider entering into His presence, we do well to understand this aspect of His nature, for His fidelity to His people is attached, in His eyes, to His own sovereignty (Jer 31:35–37, Matt 16:18):

> Therefore know that the LORD your God, He is God, the faithful God who keeps covenant and mercy for a thousand generations with those who love Him and keep His commandments. (Deut 7:9)

> Ephraim has encircled Me with lies,
> And the house of Israel with deceit;
> But Judah still walks with God,
> Even with the Holy One who is faithful.
> (Hos 11:12)

> Let us hold fast the confession of our hope without wavering, for He who promised is faithful. (Heb 10:23)

> But the Lord is faithful, who will establish you and guard you from the evil one. (2 Thess 3:3)

Put quite simply, the only reasonable response to this faithfulness is as declared by the Devotionist King David. Our own devotion, we dare to say, should emulate such openness and reverence, such love and understanding:

> I have not hidden Your righteousness within my heart;
> I have declared Your faithfulness and Your salvation;
> I have not concealed Your lovingkindness and Your truth
> From the great assembly.
> (Ps 40:10)

> I will sing of the mercies of the LORD forever;
> With my mouth will I make known
> Your faithfulness to all generations.
> (Ps 89:1)

Faith and Trust Produce Hope

> Our soul waits for the LORD;
> He is our help and our shield.
> For our heart shall rejoice in Him,
> Because we have trusted in His holy name.
> Let Your mercy, O LORD, be upon us,
> Just as we hope in You.
> (Ps 33:20–22)

Hope is a word that has become virtually meaningless in common parlance—people speak of hope being associated with the most menial of events (such as catching a train on time) or banal desires (such as finding something fashionable to wear). But for the Devotionist, our hope is not based on material objects, subjective theories, or even in other people, but in the only person who is worthy of our hope, for "by Him all things were created that are in heaven and that are on earth, visible and invisible, whether thrones or dominions or principalities or powers. All things were created through Him and for Him. And He is before all things, and in Him all things consist" (Col 1:16–17). It is wise, therefore, to hope in Christ, and because Christ lives, so our hope is living and able and powerful and true. So when the Devotionist enters into the Transcendent Gate of Trust, our hope is based on the Reality of God in our lives as discussed previously. It is tangible, real hope based on sustained veracity of promises and proven fidelity encompassed with unrelenting love and power. This is devotionist hope—the living and true hope in the power of the resurrection, hope in eternal life, hope in the once again fulfillment of Scripture. This living hope that is not ill-defined but actually based on lived and experienced understanding so that hope for the Devotionist is not nebulous but in actuality is expectation, hope in itself for the believer becomes "certainty." For when God says something, it is as good as done and nothing will alter the fact. What is to come in the future according to His word and precepts is as certain as if it has already happened. And thus, we are to take comfort in this, for the future is in the palm of God's hand and thankfully He has declared that the believer's future is secured within His eternal plan and purposes. This promise and this position have already started, in this life, if we only apprehend their truth and availability.

Our hope is not just in this world but in the world to come, and in this we trust in God's word to be true that what He has said will happen, will. We trust Him with our salvation and for our futures in this world and the next. Biblical hope, because it comes from the Holy Spirit within us, always points to Jesus who is the culmination and completion of our hope. And hence hope becomes longing and expectation of the coming of Christ and the establishment of the kingdom of God:

> We give thanks to You, O God, we give thanks!
> For Your wondrous works declare that Your name is near.
> "When I choose the proper time,
> I will judge uprightly.
> The earth and all its inhabitants are dissolved;
> I set up its pillars firmly." Selah.
> (Ps 75:1–3)

> Let the heavens rejoice, and let the earth be glad;
> Let the sea roar, and all its fullness;
> Let the field be joyful, and all that is in it.
> Then all the trees of the woods will rejoice before the Lord.
> For He is coming, for He is coming to judge the earth.
> He shall judge the world with righteousness,
> And the peoples with His truth.
> (Ps 96:11–13)

> Let the sea roar, and all its fullness,
> The world and those who dwell in it;
> Let the rivers clap their hands;
> Let the hills be joyful together before the Lord,
> For He is coming to judge the earth.
> With righteousness He shall judge the world,
> And the peoples with equity.
> (Ps 98:7–8)

Reflective Moments Between Gates

When we dwell on these things and pass on toward the next gate, so too our souls have moved from the states of reverence that we held as we passed within the Gate of Contemplation through to complete and utter revival, resuscitation via the Gate of Transcendent Trust. As we prepare again to move forward, our souls are warmed and become comforted, for they know what lies ahead as they take the final step through the next glorious Gate: the Gate of Familial Confidence. And as we step forward, we also glance back and exclaim to God in unison with our souls,

> Oh, how great is Your goodness,
> Which You have laid up for those who fear You,
> Which You have prepared for those who trust in You
> In the presence of the sons of men!
> (Ps 31:19)

Gate 3: The Gate of Familial Confidence

> To You, O Lord, I lift up my soul.
> (Ps 25:1)

> Rejoice the soul of Your servant,
> For to You, O Lord, I lift up my soul.
> (Ps 86:4)

> Cause me to hear Your lovingkindness in the morning,
> For in You do I trust;
> Cause me to know the way in which I should walk,
> For I lift up my soul to You.
> (Ps 143:8)

Where does such confidence come from that David knows that he does not need to fear God with any harm or any retribution against him? Despite his many failings, the Devotionist King David knew that his own righteousness came not from himself but from the Lord. He knew, without doubt or wavering, that God was true and just and would always honor His word. He knew that his relationship with God was not based on his own abilities but upon the faithfulness of God toward those whom He loves. Importantly, David knew that he was nothing special and had not earned these blessings or position but that they came through to him by the grace and unmerited favor of God that God bestows on all whose hearts are aligned with Him, who hear His voice and value His ways as treasures above all things and beyond compare. And before we all think that this is impossible to attain, we realize that this is just the point, for the attaining was never meant to be by our own works or merits, but by the pure blessings of God.

The righteous are able to enter the presence of God boldly because of their understanding of their position as His children. As a child runs toward a parent in love, confidence, and happiness, so the child of God is entitled to do so with God. This is not overfamiliarity toward a superior, but the appropriated rights of those who are deemed to be adopted, are described as being heirs and coheirs with Christ Himself, and are beloved of the Father and the Son and the Holy Spirit. This is the confidence and the belief that is required from the believer by God in order to pass through this Gate and into His presence.

This sense of familial confidence can only come from deep within our consciousness. It is more than just knowing the ways of God, and it is more than just acknowledging the facets of His majesty and greatness. It is subliminal and sublime absorption of His many, profound, complex and yet so simple ways embodied within His complete, unmitigated, and unconditional love for those who are in Christ Jesus. This is, as we have said, perfectly captured in the beauty of the picture of a child running toward a parent or grandparent, where all the complexities of relationships that we find so inhibitive and difficult to analyze as adults are of no relevance. This behavior, though, in itself bears witness to both experienced and expected love and joy at being in the presence of the one who is loved. This then is the familial confidence that the believer enjoys with God. It is the privilege that we behold, and it is only the believer who is entitled to this. It was ever the case with the righteous of the Old Testament and the believers in the New Testament; while it is a familial confidence that is built upon the foundations of understanding, trust, faith, and hope, it is perhaps more important to see that it is more than that, it is deeper and more subliminal, as we said. This familial confidence within the individual and the people of God is in fact the divine plan of God that will culminate in our ultimate unification with the Godhead (John 17:21–23) while enjoying the blessings of unity with God in this life. This Gate is the one that leads to this unity in the here and now; it is enjoying the blessing of fellowship with God from our undeserved position of being considered members of His household, citizens of heaven, and children of God who have been redeemed, renewed, recreated, and sealed by the Holy Spirit, destined to be with the Lord for all eternity, considered holy, highly esteemed, cherished, valued, and loved unconditionally as the bride of Christ.

What is devotion if not enhanced and experienced love and the desire to learn to love the Lord all the more? As we bask in His light, our souls are nurtured through the Spirit. The Spirit is our Comforter and Guide, and so He comforts us and our souls and envelops us in God's love. His presence is love divine; it has an intensity which defies description and analysis and yet is there. It is both a consuming fire and an everlasting ocean whose depths are unmeasurable and whose extent is beyond infinite. It cannot be contained and has no boundaries; its power is unassailable and its beauty unimaginable. This is why, with the psalmist, we say that "such knowledge is too wonderful for me" (Ps 138:6) and why we are left with the Spirit within us calling out with unmitigated familial confidence and joy as we enter into His presence (Rom 8:15, Gal 4:6).

What then is this love so perfect? It is perfect love; it is love so pure and holy that it is what sustains the very universe itself. It defies all, encompasses all this, and emanates from the very Author of life itself. The very act of creation and creating came from love of God for Himself alone; it came because of the love of God the Father for His Son—for all was created by Him and, most crucially to comprehend, for Him (Col 1:16). God did not have to create but chose to do so, not out of vanity but out of love for the One for whom it was created. And because it was created out of divine love, so salvation and redemption is shown to come because of this love as well: "For God so loved the world that He gave His only begotten Son, that whoever believes in Him should not perish but have everlasting life" (John 3:16).

Hence, it is because of this love, knowing that we are loved by God, knowing that we have the personal peace that belongs to every single believer, and knowing that we are sustained through the Spirit of love, that we have comfort, and because of comfort we have confidence. You cannot have confidence unless you already have comfort first within yourself. You have to have the rock of comfort to be confident. Confidence must be based on that which is solid, otherwise it is a house built on sand. Our comfort is God Himself. The Spirit is the Comforter, so this is our comfort: God Himself is our rock and our shield.

The Gate of Familial Confidence is the final entrance into the divine presence. It is the passageway through with we are to pass and is necessary to enter as His children. This is the Gate that opens into the love supreme, the oceans of life and love, where there is no darkness and only warmth, welcoming, safety, security, and sanctuary. This is the true domain of the bride of Christ. This is where we belong and feel most at home. This is what and where our souls long for: being with Christ and ever in His presence—forever, for all eternity—basking in His divine light. This is what we were created and recreated for, and this is our destiny, our identity, and our belonging. For Jesus Christ loves His bride as unconditionally as the Father loves the Son. And as the Spirit leads, so we follow. And as we enter, so our souls rejoice, and our spirit is united with the Holy Spirt in crying, "Abba, Father!" (Rom 8:15, Gal 4:6).

As we look to leave these Precious Gates, we do so with joy and wonder, for we know that His word is true, and we have full confidence in our Positional Identity and His mighty blessings that He has bestowed upon us so that we are certain that

> the Lord is near to all who call upon Him,
> To all who call upon Him in truth.
> (Ps 145:18)

Patience in the Outer Courts of His Presence

We are told in Gal 5:22 that patience is one of the fruits of the Holy Spirit. To wait on the Lord and to be still enough to hear His voice is truly not only a fruit but a gift from God. Patience implies peace as it does also perseverance and calmness. These are all qualities in our lives which are difficult to attain, especially now within our instant satisfaction culture. Waiting and patience do not come easily to us now. But perhaps there is also, in the delay and in the waiting, a lesson to us: perhaps we need the calm and to pause for a while in quiet and solitude (whether mentally or physically) in order to be able to contemplate the Lord, His ways, and His countenances. It is difficult enough to discern His voice at any time, let alone amidst the rush of life. So, to teach ourselves to wait rather than rushing head on into the next thing is, in itself, a valuable spiritual lesson. And as we wait, we have the chance to reflect on what and whom it is we wait on. And as we wait, so we learn that eagerness and yearning can also be a by-product of patience; for nowhere does it say that patience is passive.

> Wait on the Lord;
> Be of good courage,
> And He shall strengthen your heart;
> Wait, I say, on the Lord!
> (Ps 27:14)

> Truly my soul silently waits for God;
> From Him comes my salvation.
> My soul, wait silently for God alone,
> For my expectation is from Him.
> (Ps 62:1–2)

Waiting in the Outer Courts of His Presence

As we wait, our souls are calmed and excited at the same time. Just as a child is quieted yet never fully satiated, so only the actual presence of God will ultimately do that for our souls. Our souls know this, and yet we can be assured as we wait that we have nurtured, fed, and are now ready:

> Surely I have calmed and quieted my soul,
> Like a weaned child with his mother;
> Like a weaned child is my soul within me.
> (Ps 131:2)

As we prepare to enter into His Presence, there is time that needs to be taken as we absorb within ourselves all that we have considered, been shown, and dwelled upon as we go through the Precious Gates. As we wait upon the Lord, this then gives us a further opportunity to quietly consider and reflect upon how the blessings that have been bestowed upon us are truly transformative, not only during our times of devotion but in how they become absorbed into our very way of thinking and believing. Once again, we see this in the psalms and how this is reflected in the heart attitude of these Devotionists as their appropriation of their knowledge and understanding of God and His perception of them as His people permeates their own devotional outpourings and how they engage with and encounter God through their devotion. It is instructive that God uses poetry and song as the means to articulate this, for these genres themselves are more representational of the complexities and beauty of what is being portrayed, as dialogue and prose become clumsy and lack the imaginative fluidity necessary when contemplating the response of our souls to the wonders of God, as well as the struggles and glories of being His people within the context of the outworkings of His divine plans.

To categorize some of these "absorptions" in the manner in which they are manifested through the psalms becomes instructive to us not only when using them for our own devotions, but by extension, we can use them as "soul-nurturing subject titles or themes" to guide us in our contemplations and considerations during and after times of personal devotion—whether reading Scripture, in private prayer, or simply while meditating on the ways of God. Therefore, as we wait on the Lord in our consideration of them, we can ask of the Lord to further reveal to us His heart as we align our souls through various expressions:

- Awe and Wonder at God

> When I consider Your heavens, the work of Your fingers,
> The moon and the stars, which You have ordained,
> What is man that You are mindful of him,
> And the son of man that You visit him?
> (Ps 8:3–4)

The Devotionist knows that all glory and honor, praise and majesty belong to God. He is above all and yet He actually desires to be with us, His family. This is the mystery that all who know the Lord contend with, and yet they come to fully accept that this is so because He wants it to be that way.

- Praise, Thanksgiving, and Gratitude

> Let us come before His presence with thanksgiving;
> Let us shout joyfully to Him with psalms.
> (Ps 95:2)

Once we accept this position and appropriate all the spiritual blessings that are freely available to us and when we combine this understanding with that of our familiarity with the uniqueness of this state as being validated by God, then not only is our only reasonable response one of gratitude but also one of joy at the peace we have with God.

- Received Peace

> The Lord is my shepherd;
> I shall not want.
> He makes me to lie down in green pastures;
> He leads me beside the still waters.
> He restores my soul;
> He leads me in the paths of righteousness
> For His name's sake.
> (Ps 23:1–3)

The recognition that peace is available to those who trust and have aligned themselves with God is a theme that underscores the heart of

David, for he knows that while this peace is only his at the discretion of God, it is peace that is received and stored as a precious gift. Such peace as shown in Ps 23 can only come from a heart that truly accepts that God is by nature compassionate, loving, and caring and has appropriated that this relationship is not one-sided or adversarial in any way but is convivial and familial in the way that one can be utterly at ease with the other. Psalm 23 is the expression of one who is at perfect ease with the subject about whom it is being written, is thoroughly immersed in this ease, but knows from whom that ease comes and why.

- Loving-Kindness

> Cause me to hear Your lovingkindness in the morning,
> For in You do I trust;
> Cause me to know the way in which I should walk,
> For I lift up my soul to You.
> (Ps 143:8)

That the kindness of God is defined and enveloped in His love is a revelation that comes directly from the Lord Himself. This is no mere indifferent generosity as that between a superior and a subordinate, but sincere, heartfelt, passionate compassion like that shown between a loved one and the object of that love. The loving-kindness of God embodies all His blessings and gifts. For these are made available not through vanity or the hypocritical need for self-glorification but from the purity of intensions that only God can have. This is why they are so special and why His loving-kindness is both received and sought. Once tasted, it is addictive in its purity and beauty. To those who believe and have tasted of the goodness of God, His loving-kindness is all-sustaining and all-encompassing in how He treats those whom He loves. As we seek Him through our devotion, then, this is the characteristic of God for which we most yearn—for while we have received so copiously from Him, so His loving-kindness is that which we can never be satiated of. It is the framework of His grace and our faith. It is that which encapsulates His ways with us: His constant patience with us and His utter loyalty on our behalf, even when we are so fickle in return. It is His loving-kindness toward us that we should most dwell upon, for it is this that best describes and encapsulates all His intensions for us.

- Longing for His Presence

    > As the deer pants for the water brooks,
    > So pants my soul for You, O God.
    > My soul thirsts for God, for the living God.
    > When shall I come and appear before God?
    > (Ps 42:1–2)

A period of waiting enhances the anticipation, and longing ensues. This is the enduring state that is required from us to truly experience devotion with God. This is not the ecstatic experiences of the cults and even of the mystics, but it is a need. It is a need that our soul clearly hankers for—a thirst, as the psalmist says. A thirst, as Jesus said to the Samaritan woman at the well, that only His presence in our lives can quench. To be in fellowship and in His presence should be the pinnacle object and sole interest of every believer. For when we are absent from the Lord, then we dry up, wither, our spiritual strength is sapped, and we become lethargic, disinterested, unmotivated, and apathetic. The soul, though, during these times, as we have discussed, becomes downcast, distressed, even parched. Hence when we recognize this, we see the need for nurturing and for watering with the ways of God. Our souls long to be in His presence, for only He will satisfy them. Our earnest desire then is to be with Him, basking in His light, comforted, fortified, edified, equipped, never condemned, only loving and being loved. Such is the presence of God and it is worth waiting for.

To wait for and upon something has become almost countercultural in the West. Periods of delay before we receive something or are satisfied are virtual misnomers to us now. Whether we look at this historically, biblically, or both, the expectation of all who have sought to encounter God personally have always anticipated periods of waiting, periods that might require considerable effort and discipline to be expended by the "seeker." We see this throughout the Scriptures and even from Jesus Himself. This is why patience, forbearance, and long-suffering are synonymous with the Holy Spirit, and through Him we can endure this waiting for from Him, and through it, we also learn. God is interested in our aligned hearts and transformed minds, and it is during these periods that His Spirit works within our souls to shape our characters—which is why, in themselves, these periods should be considered blessed times of connection, correction, and cultivation of the character of God within us.

PART 3

The Participation of Devotion

The Precious Gift of Positional Devotion

Preamble

The basic premise for "Positional Devotion" is that as far as God is concerned, the believer is now in a state or position in the household of God that is permanent and eternal—this has always been part of the sovereign plan of God. It was unilaterally instigated by God and is unchallengeable, though many seem reluctant to see it in all its beauty and magnificence. But beautiful it certainly is, as well as liberating. The only reverential response to this for the believer is to accept this humbly and with awe and wonder at the magnitude of God's love, grace, and mercy toward us, and to thereafter acknowledge this in our faith, walk, and life in Christ. We have argued previously that it has always been the case that the whole desire of God has only ever been for a people dedicated to Him in their heart. We have also argued that the vast majority of believers across the expanse of both Testaments have been "mere" ordinary believers and have only ever both been able and required to be devoted to God within an environment of the "real world," and argued how this has been outworked throughout time. Thus, we consider the heart attitude of the righteous in the Old Testament to be transferred to believers in the new covenant, wherein those that believe are able to enjoy even greater spiritual riches through the appropriation of what we defined as their Positional Identity as being part of the household of God.

We will argue that the appropriation by the believer of the beauty and veracity of the Positional Blessings through Positional Devotion is the key to having an abundant life and enjoying peace with God. It is available to all who believe on account of their position in the household of God, for it is a divinely given gift and is there to be received with joy and appropriated with thanksgiving. It is the key to peace with God, peace with one another, and abiding with Christ. But it is through the consideration of what we have termed the Precious Gates of Devotion that we put forward below as hopefully helping believers to enter into the presence of God not just through times of personal reading of Scripture and of prayer, but through absorption and abiding that goes beyond these temporary experiences into a more permanent condition.

Abiding Through Positional Devotion

> Therefore I also, after I heard of your faith in the Lord Jesus and your love for all the saints, do not cease to give thanks for you, making mention of you in my prayers: that the God of our Lord Jesus Christ, the Father of glory, may give to you the spirit of wisdom and revelation in the knowledge of Him, the eyes of your understanding being enlightened; that you may know what is the hope of His calling, what are the riches of the glory of His inheritance in the saints, and what is the exceeding greatness of His power toward us who believe, according to the working of His mighty power which He worked in Christ when He raised Him from the dead and seated Him at His right hand in the heavenly places, far above all principality and power and might and dominion, and every name that is named, not only in this age but also in that which is to come. (Eph 1:15–19)

Such is the heart of God for the believer, not just for the religious elites, spiritually superior, those in ministry, or those who teach in Bible colleges—no, it is the heart of God that every believer should know Him in this way. That it is achievable by all is also implicit in its unconditional and ubiquitous proposition. As we have said right at the start of this book, it is to the detriment of modern Christianity that most believers are never actually instructed on this availability for all. The reader will note that Paul here is calling on God's sovereignty in asking Him to reveal these truths to the believer. Such is the pattern throughout Scripture: it is God's own desire to reveal more of Himself to us, and it is the very purpose of the Holy Spirit within us to point us to Jesus and to conform us to His image, but we have to take the responsibility and ask.

The nurturing of our souls is the most fundamental activity of the believer; it is, in effect, our sanctification and is therefore to be considered the "will of God" (1 Thess 4:3). As discussed, the premise we have put forward is firstly that the requirements of God apply to all believers and that the most fundamental requirement of God is our devotion to Him. All else is detail—I hesitate to say unnecessary detail for it is outlined in the Bible and therefore must be seen to be "profitable," but profitable in a biblical sense can only mean that which enhances our understanding of the character and nature of God and also draws us closer to Him. Indeed, we can even go one step further in our clarification of this matter, for the trap for the believer can be to study and learn of the intricacies of the Bible while forgetting that it is divinely inspired, hence missing the spiritual interpretation and application of it, for we are to worship in spirit and in truth. But as we have said previously, paradoxically we are told within the Scriptures that Scripture itself is not the only place where we can learn of God, and hence Positional Devotion must also include the internalization of the external through the absorption of the divine as manifested in beauty and goodness, both of which emanate and reflect God's glory.

The parallel truth that we must accept and absorb is our Positional Identity within the household of God. As our sanctification is the will of God and as we will be transformed into His likeness, so we participate with the fellowship between the members of the Trinity. As we conform to and absorb this unity, we abide with Christ. To abide therefore is both positional in the household of God and participatory in the work of the both the Holy Spirit and the Son. As we accept that once we believe and are indwelled by the Holy Spirit, so our position in Christ becomes irrevocable and unconditional, this then frees us to participate in the privileges of relationship and access to God.

There is then a freedom in limitation. If we accept what the actual requirements of God are for us, this leads to a freedom of expression and exploration of our devotion that is devoid of unnecessary and "unrequired" detail and effort. For the limitation is freedom in that God clearly defines what is expected and therefore what is required—thus limitation is a positive, while freedom is given through participation with the role and function of the Holy Spirit dwelling within the believer. The Holy Spirit's role and function within the believer is sanctification, the process of pointing the believer to Jesus and conforming us to His Image. Thus, devotion is our participation with this process, and hence devotion is participating with the Holy Spirit as we become one with the Father and the Son through Him (John 17:2–23). This is abiding or being or becoming holy as He is holy. It is the participation in the work and function of Holy Spirit that is only available to believers by merit of being indwelled by Him. Hence, when we then combine this "freedom-giving-limitation" with the "life-giving-access" of our position, then we are able to appropriate this into our "freedom-given-participation" called Positional Devotion.

Positional Devotion and the Precious Gates of Devotion

We examined before the attributes and approaches of the Devotionist King David as revealed in the psalms. These point us to a heart attitude that emanates from the devotional and manifests in the manner of engagement with God. These then are the gates of the righteous in the Old Testament, as they open and reveal for the believer the courtyards of heaven and the presence of God.

Previously we outlined these Precious Gates—individually as the Gate of the Consideration of the Divine, the Gate of Transcendental Trust, and the Gate of Familial Confidence. It is our contention, as argued in part 1 of this series, that these Precious Gates are the spiritual manifestations of those who already appreciate their status and standing with God through belief fundamentally in His attributes and characteristics; these spiritual manifestations produce the devotional desire of those whose hearts are aligned with God and by God. Already in the Old Testament we see that those who fully grasped the true nature of God and His whole desire for each individual believer were able to lay hold of the magnificence of God's ways in a manner that was deeply, personally spiritual and permeated through their entire being, as we shall briefly discuss below in relation to King David and Mary, mother of Jesus. These words, poetry, comments, and speech, though incorporated within divinely inspired Scripture, emanate first and foremost from those whose hearts are aligned with God. When first written or spoken, those who did so, of course, did not know that they would be incorporated into Scripture. As such, they reveal the quality of the hearts of those who, before they were chosen by God, were ordinary people with ordinary lives, distinguished by what was clearly a devotionist mindset already aligned with God. King David was a shepherd first and his precious psalms reveal his depth of knowledge and experience of God that he developed while still a shepherd. One only needs to think about the heart behind the words of Ps 8:1, for instance, to recognize in him perhaps a hankering for a time when he would have spent so much time on his own in the wilderness with his sheep, marveling at the wonder and greatness of his creator God, the Lord. The same is true of Mary, mother of Jesus: her venerated and so beautiful Magnificat reveals a, probably very young, maiden's heart that is already aligned with God, who truly understands Him, His nature, and purposes and is already wonderfully and magnificently expectant of Him. Her response to Gabriel does not just come out of nowhere, so to speak, but from a well of nurtured devotion that she draws on deeply as she accepts the most magnificent of duties and responsibilities from a position of deeply ingrained and appropriated understanding of the promises and nature of God. The almost unimaginable dignity and immediacy of her response is all the more inspiring when considered as the spiritual fruit of a committed Devotionist, dedicated in her profound love of God and understanding of His ways.

Both David and Mary show that as ordinary people first and foremost, they knew the "Reality of God" in their lives and lived with hearts aligned to Him; the fact that they were then chosen by God in the ways they were does not obviate this. But it is important to remember that they were not chosen by God because they were like this, though no doubt God loved them for it. The point is that prior to being chosen, they obviously had no idea that this was going to happen to them—it just came out of nowhere—and the point being that even if it hadn't, both would have just carried on loving the Lord with all their heart and mind and lived their lives in this devotionist mindset, content just to be part of God's household, no matter what.

It is important, as we shall discuss in the concluding section of this book, to realize that devotion in and of itself should never be the end for the believer. Devotion for devotion's sake is unbiblical in that it is unprofitable for God's purposes and intentions for how we conduct ourselves in the world around us within the confines of the Realities of God. There is always in Scripture a "so that" clause after any call for sanctification or description of the required characteristics of the believer. This "so that" is that we become the people of God that He wants us to be. That we become "doers as well as hearers," as the apostle James says (Jas 1:22). Thus, devotion becomes the preparation ground where we engage with God directly, spiritually; it is where we nurture our souls so that we love God more and love one another with a heart that is aligned with God's. Hence, we see with the everyday believer, from the foundation and perspective of our irreversible position, that we can learn to walk worthily as well as to stand for God and withstand all that the "world" and "life" throws against us. Secure in the knowledge of our position and the indwelling of the Holy Spirit, we do not need to be confused, concerned, or apprehensive as we read of the behavioral expectations of believers as outlined in passages such as Rom 12. For the Lord knows that without the Holy Spirit within us, we do not have any chance of ever being able to fulfill these. Imagine, for a moment, what it means to truly "love without hypocrisy" (Rom 12:9). How can we possibly do this on our own, for our natural and fallen instinct is always "self-first," and so normal love is always predicated by this instinct and is never actually the genuine, unconditional love that can only ever be exhibited by God Himself and is so beautifully described by the apostle Paul in 1 Cor 13:1–8. And so, the Holy Spirit within us is the One we have to turn to, to help us and to conform us, to give us this required transformation of our minds. Consider, too, the fruit of the Spirit, for they are called the fruit of "the Spirit" for a reason—they are His fruit in us, not our own fruit in us.

It is only with the Holy Spirit that we are able to assimilate these attributes, and it is only with His help that we are able to nurture and absorb them in our lives; through His help alone they become our very character and personality. Such is all the more apparent when we consider what it means when we are, seemingly so implausibly, told that we already possess some of the very attributes of God, such as the mind of Christ (1 Cor 2:16). To have Jesus Christ's mind is surely so utterly unattainable for any mere mortal that it must only be a considered a perfect condition embedded within our imperfection, a situation that, though we are being perfected through the ongoing work of the Holy Spirit, will only be rectified as we are made perfect by God himself (1 John 3:2). And yet 1 Cor 2:16 clearly says that we have this mind now, so it can only mean that with the Holy Spirit within us, we are able to represent to others and attest to, even as a shadow or as a part of its own glory, what this marvelous condition might even vaguely produce from such inherently flawed vessels as ourselves. Thus, it is the Holy Spirit who works the work of renewing and transforming our minds so that we "may prove what is that good and acceptable and perfect will of God" (Rom 12:2) within ourselves (and hence our devotion) and, as always, externally so that our light will "so shine before men, that they may see [our] good works and glorify [our] Father in heaven" (Matt 5:16).

This is the point that is made abundantly clear throughout Scripture, in both Testaments: without the Holy Spirit we are left bereft of any chance of ever living up to the standards of God. But, for the believer, we can go even further, for without an understanding of our Positional Identity, we consider such instructions with potential trepidation, anxiety, and inadequacy. This can lead to times of self-doubt in our faith and even in our own salvation as, when we measure our own lives against these requirements, we feel shame and condemnation. But our transfigurative and transformative Positional Blessings say the exact opposite of this. These Positional Blessings say that we have peace with God and that there is no condemnation for those in Christ Jesus because we are already beloved members of His household. There is nothing more that we need to do to improve our standing in God's eyes, for we have done what He wants—believe in His Son—and what He wants now is our love and devotion. That's all.

Just as Jesus said that the Sabbath was made for man not man for it, the same is true when we consider these imperatives and instructions for believers. These only become acceptable to God when they are undertaken from a position of love and trust in Him—otherwise, they become works and are fruitless. They are there for our benefit—for us to lead lives that are pleasing to God, yes—but also are there for us to learn more of Him in that what we struggle with now will one day be perfected by Him and by Him alone. We are called to be holy as He is holy and at the same time are already holy in His eyes, but one day what we see in part now will be completed in Jesus and by Jesus as we are made like Him and are joined in unity with Him. All and everything we struggle with now in this life will be perfected in Jesus. This is what Jesus meant when He said that He alone is "the way, the truth, and the life" (John 14:6) and that He alone is "the resurrection and the life" (John 11:25), for to Jesus—and therefore now to us—"the life" is not just our transitory time here but eternal life with Him, forever and outside of time. That is *the* life. And for the believer, this eternal life starts the moment of salvation with all of its heavenly blessings freely available now (Eph 1:3). Albeit—marvel upon marvel at the greatness of God—this too is only in part or as a shadow of that which will be fully consummated once we are with the

Lord and are translated into His image. Truly, as the apostle Paul says, "to live is Christ, but to die is gain" (Phil 1:21), which for us is so beautifully complemented by 1 John 3:2–3: "Beloved, now we are children of God; and it has not yet been revealed what we shall be, but we know that when He is revealed, we shall be like Him, for we shall see Him as He is. And everyone who has this hope in Him purifies himself, just as He is pure."

The Precious Gift of Positional Devotion

Positional Devotion starts with the conviction of the believer that these Positional Blessings are true and are truly gifts from God. And if what they amount to is true for the believer, then they must be applied not just theoretically but in a living way. Once they are fully grasped and appropriated, then they become living and powerful and able to radically impact the believer's life with Jesus in a transformational way that is at the very heart of the purposes of God for each and every believer. Moreover, the very nature of what the truth of these blessings imply is that this transformation is in fact a "right," and it is available to, and can be appropriated by, all who believe. Positional Devotion can be likened to a gift from God that He has preprepared for every single believer to receive and own upon their salvation. It is up to the believer to accept this gift and to enjoy to the full its contents, for they bring life, peace, comfort, and confidence in our status in God. This is the status that affects our entire relationship with God and is no more evidenced than in our approach and entrance into our acts of devotion through what we described as the Precious Gates of Devotion. Positional Devotion emanates from all these things, undergirded by our agreement and adoption of the Positional Blessings that have been unilaterally bestowed upon us by God: it is a heart recreated and realigned with God; it is a mind transformed and being transformed by the beauty of the precious gifts that God Himself ordained and bestowed upon us. And it is acceptance of these gifts as being living and letting them dwell richly within us that produces the aligned heart that God requires from us—fully aligned, fully transformed, fully accepting, fully grateful, and fully at peace with the Author and Finisher of our faith, the Prince of Peace Himself.

Positional Devotion then is devotion that is built upon and sustained by these truths. These truths become the bedrock, the foundation for the believer's life, for they are hewn from our acceptance of, and belief in, the perfect sacrifice of God to Himself, the death of Jesus the Messiah on the cursed tree of the cross. The impact of these truths can be summarized when we look at the emotional impact of them as they reach the crescendo devotionally in the words of Jesus: "I will never leave you nor forsake you" (Heb 13:5). And if He will never leave us, then He is always with us. And if He is always with us, then this must include every aspect of our lives, including our devotion. And if Jesus is with us in our devotion, then we miss the totality of that if we are ignorant of, or (worse) fail to appropriate, the completeness of all that He has achieved and given us. For there can be nothing lacking from God that is not promised either for this life or the life to come—to doubt this is to misunderstand, misrepresent even, the very nature of God as shown us both in Scripture and in creation. God is never, and never can be, lacking in anything for He alone is perfect, and hence His gifts and promises must be perfect too—by definition. If we only focus on all He has achieved, then we miss out on the other half of what He has given us. It is when we appreciate both that we become complete in Him, and not until that point. The impact of these on our devotion means that we know that we are one with the Lord and that when we let Him down, He will forgive us; and when we come before Him, we need not be fearful or have trepidation. The heart of the Devotionist here becomes full of wonder and joy at our God's grace and His mercy toward us. Our gift of Positional Devotion becomes precious in that it was bought at so high a price—the death on the cross of our Lord and Savior. But Positional Devotion is not retrospective but driven by the power of the resurrection to translate us into the kingdom of God, to transform our lives, to draw us close to God, to sanctify us, and to ultimately conform us to the image of God. Nothing else can compare, this side of heaven, and indeed that is the point—for the participation in eternity for the believer started the very moment of salvation.

Positional Devotion is awe and wonder at the heart of the One who ever thought of these awesome and awe-inspiring Positional Blessings. For before the foundation of the world, God's plan of redemption included these mighty measures of divine grace and generosity. God's love for His Son knows no limits, and hence who are we to limit what He chooses to bestow on those who believe in His Son? This is the exchange that we are dealing with when it comes to our position in Christ; it has nothing to do with our own merit and everything to do with the immeasurable and incomparable love that God the Father has for His Son. It has nothing whatsoever to do with anything we may think we are or even what we think we may achieve for God, and it has everything to do what Jesus achieved through His death and resurrection. Our position in Christ is to God's glory alone—for He will never give His glory to another—and because of that, to not accept this position or to deny it or to limit it, or to diminish it any way whatsoever, is tantamount to denying the attributes of God in terms of His limitless power and infinite love. When we grasp this, then our devotion becomes "Positional Devotion" and is transformed as we are transformed.

Positional Devotion and the Reading of Scripture

Let the word of Christ dwell in you richly in all wisdom, teaching and admonishing one another in psalms and hymns and spiritual songs, singing with grace in your hearts to the Lord.

COLOSSIANS 3:16

Scripture Immersion

MY FOCUS THROUGHOUT THIS book is on the everyday believer, what God requires from us as ordinary Christians, and how we enhance our relationship with Him within this context. As ordinary Christians, we know that we are never going to be academic theologians or even necessarily expert biblical exegetes. We are told endlessly from the pulpit and elsewhere of the absolute need to spend as much time as possible, every day, "in the word," and other such commonplace Christian phraseology. This has become almost orthodoxy in some Christian circles so that to challenge it and confront it feels almost heretical. But, if we are to be honest, realistically we are not able to do this given the pressures of everyday life, and as such either end up feeling condemned or unmotivated, apathetic, and resentful. The reality really is that we think and feel that we know we ought to be doing this (for we have been told endlessly that we should) and so cover it up with ourselves and our Christian friends, and even with God—which only then serves to further the sense of guilt and resentment.

Accordingly, while this section will look at how we engage with Scripture, there are three things then that I want to address, first of all, head on:

1. What God requires from us is a relationship based on love, not obligation.
2. He wants us to know Him, but He is to be found not just in words.
3. He wants us to know Him, but He is to be found not just in Scripture.

Love, Not Obligation

Why do we bother reading the Bible at all? As I said, most of us will never be, nor would ever want to be, theologians or Bible experts; most of us are extremely busy and yet conversely also have significant amounts of leisure time. As Christians, we are told to make time for God, to get up early to read "the word," and to use our leisure time for God, whether that be for church activities or evangelism or whatever works are deemed necessary. Now, there is nothing inherently wrong with this. Of course, reading the Bible is an important part of getting to know God. But it is the reason why we do so that matters: it is the same as in the Old Testament, as we discussed before, as all things must be undertaken from the position of being heart-aligned first with God so that no matter what is undertaken, it is done to His glory. How is God's glory reflected in the act of our Bible reading? It is done so by the fact that we approach it as if it is the very word of the Creator of the universe, God Almighty and God All-Powerful, written by Him. We are therefore to read it expectantly and in awe but also in love for Him and who He is. Ephesians 1 says that it is Paul's heart that we grow in our knowledge and appreciation of Jesus. We do this through Scripture, yes, but not only this, as we shall expound upon in subsequent sections.

Many ordinary Christians struggle not only with finding the time and motivation to read the Bible on a regular basis (and end up feeling guilty and condemned for not doing so), but even when they do so, they encounter a book which is hard to comprehend and seemingly largely irrelevant in their contemporary, personal context. Too often, reading the Bible then comes from a spirit of obligation, which inevitably leads the believer to feel even further removed from God, and hence the purpose of reading becomes null and void. But part of not wanting to do so is perhaps because we are not shown what to do. We read the Bible almost in a vacuum of "expected understanding," and when that "understanding" is not there in the first place, the only natural response is frustration, disappointment, dissatisfaction, and ultimately disinterest. To be honest, there are no easy ways around this. Reading the Bible takes time, effort, and patience—with the key word being patience, which is where we start to see the glimmer of something different. We live in a microwave mentality world where we expect instant knowledge and gratification. And yet our understanding does not increase. If the goal, as we said before, is that our "understanding" increases, then we need to perhaps think again about how the ordinary Christian approaches the reading of Scripture. And therein lies the difference: patience and Scripture, when combined, means we have one of the fruits of spirit with the words that are inspired by the Spirit. Hence, positionally speaking we know that we already have both patience and understanding from the Holy Spirit, for it is He who dwells within us. It not only His responsibility to reveal His word to us, but in fact revelation can come from Him alone as He will not give His glory to another. Hence, the double-sided coin of God's sovereignty and man's responsibility comes forth again: He teaches and reveals, but we have to ask Him to do so. Of course, this request comes from the heart that is aligned with God (whether we feel aligned is irrelevant, for as far as God is concerned, if you are a believer, then you are aligned with Him), and the very fact that you ask, or even want to ask, means that the Holy Spirit within you is prompting you. And if the Holy Spirit is within you, then by definition you are saved and your position in Christ is secure for eternity—all the blessings and privileges are open and available to you. All you have to do is ask. From this rock of assurance, all else is feasible and possible for every believer concerning their relationship with and devotion to the Lord.

Acceptance and Access

Perhaps this could be expounded upon more clearly by examining a key passage pertaining to how our Positional Blessings combine with the word of God into Positional Devotion:

> Let the word of Christ dwell in you richly in all wisdom, teaching and admonishing one another in psalms and hymns and spiritual songs, singing with grace in your hearts to the Lord. (Col 3:16)

Within this passage we see the apostle Paul draw together four key devotionist concepts that enhance our understanding of how we engage with and experience Scripture: allowance ("let"); abide ("dwell in"); abundance ("richly"); adoptive ("you").

Allowance ("Let")

The word "let" is a tiny but incredibly powerful word for the Christian Devotionist. The manner in which the apostle uses the word "let" in this instance implies a gentle command, or rather a concerned suggestion, with hints that to do so would definitely be to our benefit. It implies that we are to "allow" and "stop resisting" or "stop putting up barriers." Importantly for our understanding and purposes here, it also has connotations of humility in the form of compliance with a greater force. With the Holy Spirit within us, it means that we can rest assured in His goodness and trust totally in His intensions for us as believers—we can trust in Him to do what He says He does and draw us ever closer to Jesus. We are told elsewhere not to resist the Holy Spirit (Acts 7:51), and here the clear implication that to stop resisting and just to relax and allow Him to lead and guide and teach us is not only to our benefit but is actually honoring what He wants to do. It is, in other words, a reverent response to His divinity and our privilege of having Him within us. And, again importantly, we should consider it as such, for to do so is the starting point of Positional Devotion.

Abide ("Dwell")

The word "dwell" in Scripture immediately brings connotations and images of the tabernacle in the Old Testament, or the holy of holies where God lived and literally dwelled or tabernacled among His people. We are also told of Jesus that He, too, tabernacled or dwelled among His people (John 1:14), and Jesus Himself, in His unbelievable revelation of the future unified relationship between God and His people, outlines a time when we will be one with the Godhead. Hence to allow the word of God to "dwell" within us means that it is to reside, to inhabit, and to literally tabernacle within us. Thus, we are to let the word of God do this, to literally tabernacle within us so that it permeates everything—all that we think, do, and say, even down to our very being, so that our characters and ultimately our very personalities are shaped by it and we physically embody the fruit of the Holy Spirit.

Additionally, the word "dwell" implies a living, continuous activity. When the word of God dwells within a believer, it is not only a living relationship but a participatory one whereby the believer and the Holy Spirit work symbiotically, as it were, as one to absorb God's word into our very beings. This is not absorption for absorption's sake but as always has the purpose of conforming us to the image of Christ in that the will of God is our sanctification, and hence this absorption is necessary as we seek its manifestation through the essence of the Spirit in our lives. We are told that the word of God is living and powerful, but this is true in positive ways as it lives within us to empower us to live and walk in God's precepts, Jesus's standards, and the Holy Spirit's fruit.

Abundance ("Richly")

Lavish nourishment perhaps sounds suspiciously self-indulgent for most Christians; it seems a little excessive or even hedonistic—the very concepts that we are told are un-Christian, unholy even. And yet, here we are; when it comes to the word of God, we are to allow it to dwell richly, lavishly, deeply, indulgently within us. This what our souls are really longing for all the time: deeply satisfying nourishment, satiation to the utmost, as our spirit meets with the Holy Spirit within us through the word of God. If this sounds mystical, then so be it, for it what we are discussing is a mystery as it pertains to the divine interaction where absolute divinity meets absolute abundance. This is why only those who are indwelled are able and allowed to see and understand the things of God, for it is only through this mystical union that the miraculous and Spiritual is understood (see 1 Cor 2).

Adoptive ("You")

Such as we have said is open and available to all who believe—not just those in ministry, or the priestly class, but everyone. Every ordinary, everyday Christian is exhorted in this passage to just "let." We should take huge comfort from this, that such as we have described is available to all. Just as there is no distinction between those who are in the household of God and as there is no partiality with God, so this richness is not exclusive to those who believe themselves to be more spiritual or more holy. In fact, the exact opposite scripturally is true, for the wise are to be dumbfounded while those who are meek, humble, and poor in spirit will be enriched and blessed beyond measure. This is the nature of God; and hence this must be the way that He set forth for His children to engage with Him through Scripture and through devotion to Him as a whole.

There is, in addition to this, an implied position for the believer that the believer must approach this from the standpoint of an acceptance of their own imperfections, when confronted with God and His word. There is also an acceptance that Scripture is the very word of God and that it therefore has the right to be respected, and we are to expect it to conform us to His expectations of us. And there is the implied beautiful concept of access—there is no indication here that our access to God will be in any way conditional or restricted.

He Wants Us to Know Him, but He Is to Be Found Not Just in Words

> LORD POLONIUS. What do you read, my lord?
> HAMLET. Words, words, words.
> LORD POLONIUS. What is the matter, my lord?
> HAMLET. Between who?
> LORD POLONIUS. I mean, the matter that you read, my lord.[1]

This very famous exchange from Hamlet encapsulates how when reading anything, one can be reading but not absorbing or even comprehending what is written—our eyes are running over the words, but there's little or no connection between what is being read and the brain, in terms of engaging with the text. The sentences are mere words strung together, and when the reader is asked about them, the reader has no recollection what's being discussed or the subject matter and is even sometimes

---

1. Shakespeare, *Hamlet*, act 2, scene 2, lines 190–94.

so distracted that they are not aware that they are even reading. This is, unfortunately, so very true for many of us when we read the Bible—and to be clear, it happens to all of us (and it is not just the Bible, clearly; the same is true for any type of reading, including when singing). We all get distracted, and our minds stray elsewhere, and we find that we can "read" entire passages and look back and not realize we have done so, having little or no recollection of what we have just "read."

The Bible is no ordinary book if we are to believe what it says it about itself (2 Tim 3:16). Perhaps in terms of devotion, we need to start our thinking about it differently by changing not only the way we read it but also even how we refer to it when reading for devotion. For devotional reading is not the same as studying the Bible and is not even the same as what can be termed "daily reading." Here changing the word "Bible" or even "Holy Bible" to the word "Scripture" perhaps begins to alter the mindset of reader, as it has greater connotations of reverence for what it is, as well as being a distinct differentiator, for nothing else can be called "Scripture." What, then, is devotional reading of "Scripture"? Devotional reading is contemplative, reflective, and participatory, rather than cursory at one level or studious at another. It is, though, purposeful in terms of being undertaken for personal benefit and edification, using Scripture as the mirror to our souls that it is and thereby edifying and nurturing our souls through it: nurture is the purpose and "Godliness" is the goal, with devotion as the means. The purpose of devotional reading is to become more Christlike—any other reason is superfluous and is mere vanity. To become like Christ is motivation, means, and destination all in one, for nothing else matters and all else is mere "works" in God's eyes.

He Wants Us to Know Him, but He Is to Be Found Not Just in Scripture

As we said before, it is perhaps paradoxical that it is from Holy Spirit–inspired Scripture that we are told that God is not just revealed in Scripture, for we are told in Col 1:16 that all things were created by and for Jesus Christ. Hence, it is only right that our devotionist heart looks outside of Scripture, too, for inspiration and nourishment of the soul; indeed, not to do so yields a danger of restricting God into set confines of revelation. Such, unfortunately, can be the case for Christians who become too confined and restricted in their relationship with God and miss out on the expansiveness of what a truly devotional relationship is, or can be, with Him.

While it is true that we get to know God through His word, this is only true to an extent, or in part. What we see dimly in Scripture is also revealed through beauty, goodness, and wonder at and within the world and universe that we occupy. These are qualities that our souls grasp for and that we see glimpses of in others, through creation and the creative arts. The word itself is created, and we must remember that it is the Creator not the created whom we worship. Our God is living and is ever present, so when it comes to devotion, we must search for His presence not just in His book but in how else and where else He has chosen to reveal Himself. If we seek we will find, and He is to be found everywhere, including within ourselves, for that is where God dwells as His Holy Spirit; and, of course, by extension He is to be found in other believers too—if only we could see it and recognize it. We see this in the letters of Paul as he identifies first the things within the various believers that are deemed laudable because, and only because, he sees them coming from God. Seeing the positives in others regarding their behavior in a Christian context is an excellent way of seeing the work of God in others. To identify this and to give God the glory for it draws oneself closer to God in the process as we see His activity in His works and Providence.

While it is good and proper to look for God in the wonders of the world and in beauty, our heart here is for the ordinary Christian, and as we are all different, one has to be conscious that not everyone is conditioned to be appreciative of, or is as sensitive to, beauty as others may be. So where then is God to be sought and found? We have discussed that the Holy Spirit dwells within all believers, and yet perhaps too little do we consider that God is to be found within ourselves—"Where can I go from Your Spirit? Or where can I flee from Your presence?" (Ps 139:7) as the Devotionist King David said. How lightly do we all carry such wonder within us and how we should all gape in wonder along with Paul as he entreats us, "Or do you not know that your body is the temple of the Holy Spirit who is in you, whom you have from God, and you are not your own? For you were bought at a price; therefore glorify God in your body and in your spirit, which are God's" (1 Cor 6:19–20).

We who believe can all seek and find God within us. This is the beauty that we carry wherever we are and whatever we are doing for His presence is always there, and all we need to do is look for it and keep looking for it until it is found in all its beauty. Thus, we can take such assurance of the work of Holy Spirit from the wisdom passed down through the ages via those whom He has indwelled before us:

And even though you feel His nearness through the gift of devotion or knowledge or in any other way, do not rest content with this feeling as though you had fully found Jesus. Forget what you have found, and always desire Jesus more and more, so that you may find Him more fully, as though you had so far found nothing. For consider this, that however great your experience of Him may be—even though you were carried up in spirit to the third heaven like Saint Paul—you have not yet known Jesus as He is in His glory. However deep your knowledge and experience of Him, He utterly transcends it. Therefore, if you wish to find Him as He is the realms of love and joy, let your soul never cease to long for Him in this present life.[2]

---

2. Hilton, *Ladder of Perfection*, 57–58.

Devotional Reading

To LEARN OF GOD is the goal of all personal reading of Scripture. It is different from study and theological analysis (though both, of course, should be approached as sacrificial offerings to God and undertaken with the purpose of learning of Him and His ways); it is where the living word meets our living hope. But where do we start?

Reverent Expectation and the Mirror of Scripture

I would say that we start with the expectation that Scripture will do what it says it will do. We can describe 2 Tim 3:16 and Heb 4:12 as being the "mirror of Scripture" for they set out how Scripture itself reveals our true hearts and intentions as we examine ourselves properly through them:

> All Scripture is given by inspiration of God, and is profitable for doctrine, for reproof, for correction, for instruction in righteousness that the man of God may be complete, thoroughly equipped for every good work. (1 Tim 3:16–17)

> For the word of God is living and powerful, and sharper than any two-edged sword, piercing even to the division of soul and spirit, and of joints and marrow, and is a discerner of the thoughts and intents of the heart. (Heb 4:12)

Thus, when reading the Bible with a devotionist heart with devotional intent, we must anticipate that we will be taught, inspired, edified, convicted, and comforted because this is what the Holy Spirit does and who He is. As it is inspired by the Holy Spirit, it is the only book that has the right, as it were, to do this to us—to expose our hearts, to make us uncomfortable as our sins are exposed, but also to give us huge comfort as we contemplate our awesome God and the position He alone has given us in His household. We are to expect the divine and the miraculous, and we are to expect to see God, to envisage His glory, to love His attributes, and to marvel at His ways; while His ways are not our ways, they are all the more magnificent for it.

But if the purpose of devotional reading is to enhance our knowledge of God, how do we go about it? The most logical place to start is right at this point then. We start, in humility and awe, to enquire of each and every passage or book or letter, "What does this reveal about the nature of God and His purposes for us in conforming us to the likeness of His Son?"

Take for example the whole history of Israel. The passage in 1 Cor 10:6 explains that its history was to be an example to us. We are to learn from them, not to directly apply them to ourselves or even to our own situation. They point to God's patience, justice, His hatred of hypocrisy and heresy, His unconditional and enduring love for His people, and His utmost sovereignty in the lives of His people and the nations as a whole. This is our God. He is the God of wonders and there is none like Him. We should read of the miracles of God and Jesus with awe and wonder. We are to see the history Israel as the outworking of God's promises and prophecy as to what would happen to them if they obeyed, or otherwise, His voice and His instructions, to see it as the effectual fulfillment of what He said would happen to them in Deut 28–30. The entire history of Israel from the days of Moses to the present day is in effect an outworking of what God said would occur if they obey His voice and when they disobey His voice. And we are to take comfort in that He stands by His prophecies, for they will truly come to pass as they are undertaken with His very reputation and sovereignty at stake (Jer 31:35). Our very reaction should be amazement and never complacency or indifference, no matter how many times we read it. Think for example of what power it takes to create, to part the Red Sea, to direct entire nations to suit His purpose, and to know all things in the minutest detail. Think of the mind that can speak the universe into being, that defines and establishes the concept and existence of beauty across multiple senses and dimensions, that is and creates love, and that is, by definition, all-powerful. This is our God, and it is our privilege to be considered members of His household. This wonder and awe should then be at the core of our reverence as we explore how to develop this relationship and how we learn to love Him all the more for it. As we truly perceive that it is this power that keeps us, so we can absorb and know for certain—deeply, permanently within us—that there is nothing that can separate us from the love of God in Christ Jesus.

Inspired by the Holy Spirit

One of the most important ways to approach Scripture from a Positional perspective is to remember that the Bible is not just literature but a divine message. This is not to say (in fact very far from it) that the traditional basic rules of literary understanding should not also apply; but it is to say that it should also be approached with respect and reverence, and in a manner that reflects the fact God is not confined and is Spirit. For instance, when we remember that it was God who chose to inspire the writers of the Bible and to reveal Himself through it, we can start to ask questions of it within such a frame of reference. Therefore, from this we can start to search for answers as to why the Holy Spirit chose to reveal certain things to certain people and at those particular junctures in place and time.

A classic example of the above can be found in the book of James, the first book written/inspired after the long gap between the Testaments.[1] One can argue, therefore, that this is in itself of particular interest for what is said and how the Holy Spirit then serves to guide the new believers in the faith. We can ask questions about what is different in what is being mentioned, what is new, what is not being said, and why. This then opens in our personal reading various channels to explore that help us to connect closer with the passages and thereby closer with God.

Positional Devotion and Unnecessary Pitfalls

While the goal of devotional reading is spiritual growth, we should be wary of inconsistencies of interpretation that can actually end up causing more harm than good—and can unfortunately remain embedded in our understanding of certain passages and doctrine as a whole. Such instances

---

1. Fruchtenbaum, *Messianic Jewish Epistles*, 212.

fundamentally occur around misappropriating promises or instructions and generically applying them to people or situations to which they have no actual relevance or connection. We too easily miss standard literary interpretation techniques and seemingly throw them to one side when it comes to the Bible. Classic examples of this are when taking something that is said to one particular group or set of people at a certain time and in certain instances, and applying them in a broad, sweeping manner to all people thereafter without any regard to context or historical setting. While it is true that we are to seek God's heart throughout Scripture, this in no way justifies misinterpretation dressed up as spiritual insight. This fact is vital when devotionally reading or studying Scripture. For example, so much erroneous teaching has come from simply misapplying what Jesus says to one set of people at any given time and sweepingly applying it to all believers thereafter. The life of Jesus was a life lived pre-resurrection, by definition, and within the context and confines of the Law of Moses—hence, His teachings and life must be seen in that context. And this makes His actions and teachings all the more remarkable because of their context and all the more wonderful as He defines the new covenant and new way of the bride of Christ in John 14–17.

Examination, Not Exegesis

God understands that we are all different and as such knows that when it comes to reading the Bible, we will all approach it in differing ways. As we said before, we are not all called to be theologians or biblical exegetes—though this is in no way meant to discourage anyone from delving into such matters. However, the Bible is full of passages that are seemingly obscure, and so rather than being deflated by them, we should perhaps instead develop from them methodologies that assist not only in the interpretation of these passages but can be developed to provide devotional interpretative techniques and exercises. Through this we can seek methodologies that approach such passages that will draw out the personal lessons that God may want is to learn about Him and about ourselves and our devotion to Him. Ultimately this is how we can edify each other through such passages.

Reading Scripture and Positional Devotion

Participation with the Holy Spirit in our devotional reading of Scripture is essential if that reading is to nourish our souls. God is Spirit, and we miss the meaning and desire of God if we do not read and contemplate Scripture both in the light of its Author but also in participation alongside the Holy Spirit. This is the missing ingredient for most everyday Christians' "relationships" with the Bible. It should become a spiritual exercise to encounter and learn more about God—it should become soul nourishment and spiritual edification. It is this participation with the Holy Spirit through the Scriptures that differentiates devotional reading from studying or nonparticipatory reading (discussed further below). It is this participation that makes these forms of reading personal and even intimate as the individual engages with Scripture privately and expects private instruction, comfort, and even correction at times as the mirror of Scripture exposes our inward parts; and it also elevates our souls as we, individually and personally, are drawn into the presence of God.

Personal devotion should become a form of worship for the believer. As it takes time and commitment, so it is a sacrifice to the Lord and should be regarded as such. Devotion is no ordinary exercise, for it is entering into the divine presence of our Lord. And as with the sacrificial system, we should undergo an element of preparation before entering into His presence.

Reverence in Contemplation

The best way to commence any time of devotion is to start with contemplating who it is we are about to engage with, whether through reading or prayer. He is our God and He is worthy, holy, and, by definition, pure. And so to think on Him is to start to dispel all consideration of anything that is unworthy and impure. Perhaps then, it makes sense to let Scripture speak back to Him by reading such passages as 1 Chr 29:10–13 and to emphasize and take note of the number of times David uses "You" and "Yours"—the emphasis, and only acceptable form, of all true worship is back on God and not on ourselves. In other words, we start by focusing on Him rather than ourselves. This is the best way to dispel impurities—namely, by speaking out that which is pure.

Purification

Since we are already forgiven and have been cleansed by the Holy Spirit, such is our state that while we do get sullied by the world around us and our hearts within us, this in no way affects our Positional Identity. We do, however, need the ongoing process of transforming our minds to that of Christ; in order to do so, we need to leave behind our worldly thoughts and clear our minds of sin and concerns of the world. While we are already accepted by God and have peace with Him, we do continually need to so become acceptable receptacles of God's revelation.

Heart Alignment and Expectation Through the Reality of God

We too often forget that it is God's greatest desire for us to know Him better and to draw close to Him. As part of our mental preparation, then, for entering into a time of devotional reading, we should remind ourselves of the privilege that we have to have fellowship with the divine in these times. This always involves a heart alignment that refocuses us on the Reality of God in our lives and the expectation that He will lead, guide, and hopefully speak with us during these times of devotion. In other words, we must learn to open our minds and hearts up to His instruction and the appreciation of His beauty through Scripture. How do we do this? As discussed before, the easiest, most reverent, and biblical way is simply to ask, "Lord teach me Your ways," for by doing so we show humility, acknowledgement, and expectation all in one go.

The Immersive Reading of Scripture and the Precious Gates of Devotion

As we seek to engage with God through our reading, the contention here is that the believer can use the Precious Gates of Devotion as a means to explore more deeply our own reflection in the mirror of Scripture and to seek unity with God through them. Using each one, we seek to dig deeper, spiritually, into the text and our reactions to it. In other words, we can use these as entry points into greater understanding of God and His ways. These are the metaphorical gates then that open into the inner courts of worship and devotion.

Gate 1: The Gate of the Consideration of the Divine

All of Scripture is inspired by God, and we are to learn of His ways through it. Therefore, we should seek Him through each passage, to see how His attributes are reflected in it and to be enriched as we consider just how beautiful He is in His majesty and grace. How intricate, intense, and utterly consistent He is as shown through the word. And as we consider these in relation to each passage, therefore we gain greater and greater understanding of Him as we stand in awe of Him and yet marvel at our privilege of knowing Him and being considered part of His household.

The only reasonable response to the majesty of God as revealed in Scripture and in creation is awe, wonder, praise, and gratitude. Our reaction to each passage and each time of immersive reading must be to praise God for who He is, His word, what He has revealed of Himself through it, and importantly, what He has revealed about ourselves. Thanksgiving for this is expected from God. He expects gratitude from us for who He is and what He does. This again needs to be our reasonable response to the revelation given in His mercy and needs to be framed in the light of the fact that this has only been feasible because of the Holy Spirit within you, leading and guiding and ever moving us closer to Christ and Christlikeness—which in itself should only ever produce awe, wonder, and eternal gratitude!

It is perhaps here that we need to look again at what Jesus Himself says about the word of God and His own relation to it, for within these statements we see that in His own words, He is interwoven into Scripture itself:

> You search the Scriptures, for in them you think you have eternal life; and these are they which testify of Me. (John 5:39)

> Jesus answered and said to them, "You are mistaken, not knowing the Scriptures nor the power of God." (Matt 22:29)

For the purposes of our discussion on immersive reading, these two passages taken together are immensely revealing in a number of ways. Firstly, before we delve into what is said, let's consider to whom Jesus was speaking when He made these statements: namely, the religious elite of the time who had been trained since childhood in the Torah and who would have literally been able to recite vast passages of it from memory. To say therefore that they do not know the Scriptures is to point to a much deeper issue in Jesus's mindset. This deeper issue is exposed by Jesus in His typically penetrating manner, for they certainly would have known the Scriptures in the technical sense, but they utterly miss the point of them, and by doing so they expose themselves to a lack of understanding of them and the true heart of God that is revealed through them. Perhaps the best way to explain this is to paraphrase Jesus from elsewhere regarding the Sabbath, and state that "Scripture and the law of God was written for man, not man for the law and Scripture"—meaning that Scripture is a path, a way that always points to God, and is not meant to be a formulaic set of rules that actually keep people from God (see also

Jesus's exposure of the end results of this in Matt 23). This then leads to the second point that the purpose of Scripture is to reveal Jesus—to see Him in it as He is revealed in both Testaments—and through this to not just to learn more of Him but to "see" Him as the literal embodiment of the Godhead in all glory, power, dominion, and sovereignty over time, history, prophecy, and creation.

> For if you believed Moses, you would believe Me; for He wrote about Me. (John 5:46)

> "Ought not the Christ to have suffered these things and to enter into His glory?" And beginning at Moses and all the Prophets, He expounded to them in all the Scriptures the things concerning Himself. (Luke 24:26–27)

> Then He said to them, "These are the words which I spoke to you while I was still with you, that all things must be fulfilled which were written in the Law of Moses and the Prophets concerning Me." (Luke 24:44)

It was not just the not knowing of the Scriptures that Jesus reprimands the religious elite of in Matt 22:29 but also the ignorance of the "power of God." This is phrased by Jesus as if this was a deliberate form of ignorance, even a dismissal of the evidence so clearly held within Scripture. In context, Jesus is exposing their disbelief in the concept of the resurrection, as if they thought that such a thing would be too hard for God. To say anything like this is in fact gross blasphemy. For to limit God's power in any way is to state that God's power is finite, and if finite then that necessarily and logically opens up the possibility of there being a greater "god" who has infinite power—which of course, all of Scripture is adamant against for we are told repeatedly that "there is no other" God (Deut 4:35, 39). By accusing them of blasphemy in this way, the irony here is that Jesus is accusing them of exactly the same thing that they try to stone Him for repeatedly and ultimately bring Him before the high priests for in Jerusalem.

However, for our purposes here in relation to immersive reading, we see that an understanding of Scripture cannot be separated from an appreciation of the wider aspects of the nature and attributes of God. We cannot read Scripture and doubt what it says about God, about what it says about Him, His ways, or His divinity as revealed in creation and miracles. God is not to be confined or boxed or limited in anyway—for all power belongs to Him and He alone is wise—and so our immersive reading must reflect this; we must not only see God through the Scriptures, but more than that we must wallow and take huge comfort in the attributes of God, for this is "our Father" and "our God" of whom we are reading. He is "ours" and no one else's. And as we read of Him in Scripture this way, so our hearts swell for the love that is revealed to His people who love Him, for the care and the jealousy He shows for us, and, as we said right at the beginning, for the extreme measures He has undertaken to draw to Himself a people "unto Himself"—that is, a people aligned and devoted to being dedicated to Him. This is what we learn to read and see, and when we do so, we then start to understand and dwell richly in His word.

There is one characteristic of God's that must be embedded within our souls when it comes to any consideration of His attributes and all His works, within which I would include Scripture itself (where this is most greatly revealed), and that is His glory, and exactly what it means to God that He possesses it and how it is to be treated. For Isa 42:8 says,

> I am the Lord, that is My name;
> And My glory I will not give to another,
> Nor My praise to carved images.

The starting point of all logical analysis is the setting of a single premise, and if any subsequent argument or point distracts from or contradicts that single premise, then it must be ignored for it is antithetical to the argument being made. This then is how we should view this single statement from God as to how He views Himself and His name. That God will not give His glory to another may seem technical, but I would argue it is in fact integral to how we must view all that is discussed and revealed in Scripture. This is especially important for immersive reading, as it can easily be used as a quick sense check against problematic verses and more importantly as a sense check for and against how we read certain doctrines and interpretations of Scripture. To illustrate what I mean here, take the doctrine of salvation by grace. Ephesians 2:8–9 states clearly that salvation is by grace through faith—meaning that it is both sovereignly instigated by God (grace) but yet is instigated through our responsibility (faith). And to further clarify the issue, Paul then continues to say that salvation is "not of works, lest anyone should boast" (Eph 2:9). This cannot be clearer: salvation is from God, not earned by man. Why? Lest man appropriates any of the glory that is due to God alone for salvation by claiming that he earned it or did something to earn approval from God. To be clear, what I am saying in no way negates man's responsibility here, hence "through faith"—it is just that salvation itself is to the glory of God, as it is Him who set its parameters in the first place and solely, uniquely, and unilaterally instigated it through Christ. It is our responsibility to respond. We see here, then, that salvation very clearly accords with Isa 42:8. And the same can be applied to virtually every other doctrine too (such as gifts of the Spirit; premillennialism versus postmillennialism; who gets the glory, man or God?)—even the very sacrifice of Jesus proving His divinity, for only the sacrifice of God to Himself fulfills the righteous requirement of God by not giving His glory to another. Thus Isa 42:8 becomes an incredibly useful benchmark for us to use quickly when assessing doctrine, prophecy, and even general interpretation. It also assists within our times of immersive reading as it clearly always points everything back to God's heart, which therefore always assists in aligning our own with His—that is, at the end of the day, why we engage in immersive reading and all devotion in the first place.

Consideration of His Works

> To you it was shown, that you might know that the Lord Himself is God; there is none other besides Him.... Therefore know this day, and consider it in your heart, that the Lord Himself is God in heaven above and on the earth beneath; there is no other. (Deut 4:35, 39)

The consideration of the works of God as within Scripture serves the greatest purpose known to us: the revelation of who He is, what He has done, what He will do, and why. This revelation is the peculiar prerogative of those who are believers, indwelled by the Holy Spirit, as 1 Cor 2–3 shows us. This then leads on to the further point of consideration: what we actually regard as the works of God. For our immersive reading and consideration purposes, I would posit that these "works" fall broadly into three main categories.

Metanarrative Works: The Way

Metanarrative works are those that fall into the overall sovereign, providential plan and purposes of God as shown in creation, history, prophetic fulfillment, and eschatology (end times). We should, as members of the household of God who are indwelled with the Spirit, begin to recognize as God's works aspects that others would miss. We should see the world through this lens and marvel at His creative works and see them as such. For example, while creation can be recognized by all as a work of God, so too are His acts through fulfillment of His plans through history and prophecy which demonstrate His divinity and sovereignty over all things. Thus, we are to see both the fulfillment of the prophecies concerning the first advent of Christ as part of this metanarrative; and of course, we should see the prophecies and the prophetic portents of the second advent in the same way (see Matt 24). As we see potential fulfillments of the prophecies of Jesus pertaining to His second coming in Matt 24 happening in our own time today, for example, we should recognize these are the works of God fulfilling what He said would happen; and thus we should give God the glory and praise His holy name, even when such events seem very unpalatable to experience ourselves. The same is obviously true when we consider the words of Paul in 1 Tim 4:1–3 and 2 Tim 3:1–5 regarding the end times, and that of Peter in 2 Pet 2 as he describes God's perspectives on false teachers (in parallel with God's perspectives on heresy and false prophets as detailed throughout the Old Testament but especially in Jeremiah). The ultimate metanarrative throughout all this, though, is that everyone should choose life over death and that it is God's heart that none should perish, that all should have eternal life (2 Pet 3:9). These are the works of God and the fact that they are happening, as they must happen, should give the believer hope and comfort for they show that the Scriptures are true and reliable and that God is sovereignly in control, for as He said to the prophet Isaiah, "Indeed I have spoken it; I will also bring it to pass. I have purposed it; I will also do it" (Isa 46:11)—the proof of prophecy is such that devotionally it is immensely spiritually edifying as it strengthens our transcendent trust in God. This is the comfort available for those who trust in the love and nature of God—available and applied in our times of personal, private devotion.

Positional Works: The Truth

The works of Christ through His death, resurrection, ascension, and return are the central themes of the whole of Scripture for all point to and speak of Him. These works of Christ are to bring great comfort to us as we see them and read of them, search for them and seek to comprehend them. But it is the heart enrichment and soul consolation that can be sought through the consideration of the Positional Blessings, which have been bestowed upon each and every believer, that are of note to us as we engage in immersive reading and private devotion. These Positional Blessings are, in and of themselves, the works of God in us and are as miraculous as the parting of the Red Sea. The transitioning of one from darkness into light, from an unbeliever to a believer, from an enemy of God to a member of His household, from one who is dead in trespasses and sins to a new creation with a heart of flesh that is aligned with God, these are true miracles that only God can perform. And when we see them as such, so our hearts rejoice, for it is because of Jesus that we are redeemed, forgiven, indwelled by the Holy Spirit, recreated, sealed with the Holy Spirit, and now have peace with God. These Positional Blessings are just that—they are gifted to us not through any merit of our own but through the unfathomable magnanimity of our triune and wonderful God.

Transforming Works: The Life

Transforming works are the ongoing, sanctifying activity that the Holy Spirit undertakes within us as He executes His commission to conform us to the image of Christ, which in this life we participate in through our devotion (as we have been saying throughout this book). In some ways, these can be seen as the transitioning works between our old lives and our eternal ones. These are as much the works of God as anything else and should be considered and glorified as such.

Understanding Scripture

First Corinthians 2:13–16 answers one of the very fundamental questions that any believer has regarding themselves, the word of God, and unbelievers: "Why is that believers can understand the word of God and others can't?" The answer, of course, is that revelation has to come from God Himself so that He gets the glory for our revelation—hence the role of the Holy Spirit. The real point, though, is not that it is only those who are indwelled who are able to understand the word of God, but that it is only they who are entitled to understand it. To think otherwise is actually somewhat insulting or grieving to the Holy Spirit—for to be indwelled by Him must, of course, make a difference. When we are recreated, reborn, and indwelled, this must, to be at all reverent about it, make for a fundamental difference between those who are and those who are not. Hence, it is only those who are indwelled by the Holy Spirit who are able to understand the word of God, which being inspired by the Holy Spirit can only be comprehended fully by those who have the Holy Spirit within them revealing to them the meaning of the Scriptures that He inspired. In other words, this is another divinely instigated closed loop, so to speak. Such, therefore, is to the glory of God alone (recall Isa 42:8). Hence this is a transforming work of God that we are to give Him the glory of. It becomes, therefore, part of our positional rights, as it were.

Teaching Us His Ways

The role of the Holy Spirit within us is, as we have said, always to point to and glorify Christ. It is His responsibility to do so, but it is our responsibility to ask. That this has always been the case is shown clearly in Neh 9:20 and also in the psalms, of course, where David and the other psalmists call upon the Lord to do just that—to teach us His ways, His law, His precepts. He has to be the one who shows us. He has to be the one who teaches us. He alone is our teacher, and according to 1 John 2:27 we need no other. Thus, to be indwelled by the Holy Spirit enables us to call upon the actual Author of Scripture to teach it to us, and all we have to do is ask.

Transforming Mind

As we learn more of Christ through the teachings of the Holy Spirt, not only do our hearts become further aligned and our souls become nurtured, but also our minds become transformed. The more we truly understand the ways of God, so the ways of the sinful and corrupt around us become more exposed and less and less palatable. As we draw closer to God through our devotion, so the Holy Spirit within us works to transform our minds as well as our hearts. This literal "change of mind" is, of course, pointing us to Jesus and is part of the overall sanctification process in giving us the desire for the mind of Christ. This work of the Holy Spirit is about character formation—meaning the molding of the believer not just into a superficial image of Christ (with connotations of false identity and false imitation of that which is Christian) but into the spiritual image as well. Mind, body, and soul must be transformed in the sanctification process. And this, therefore, is also part of the miraculous work of God within the believer. That it is gradual is true and that it is sustaining is also true—that it is to be desired, and that desire to be nurtured, is entirely and unequivocally biblical.

Sanctification, Conformity, and Unification

The post-salvation or post-justification process of sanctification encompasses much of what is discussed as the works of the Spirit within the believer in this life. That it is a certainty for all believers is factual for all who are indwelled by the Holy Spirit, whose role and function in the life of the believer can be summarized by the word sanctification. The process is an ongoing one requiring much patience and long-suffering from both parties (the believers with themselves and the Holy Spirit with the believers). In terms of devotional reading, the relevance is obvious as Jesus Himself asked the Father to "sanctify them by Your truth. Your word is truth" (John 17:17). Note who it is who undertakes the sanctification, and hence its achievement is not based on our merits or to our glory or satisfaction, or even upon our own processes, inclinations, or doctrine. And because our sanctification comes from God, it is as certain as it is ordained—we are already sanctified even though it is an ongoing process (Heb 10:10) in much the same way that we are already perfect while continuing to be perfected (Heb 10:14).

All things, everything in the Bible, draws together into the person of Christ. The span and plan of the Bible is that eventually all that is now will ultimately be consummated into God. This process occurs in stages both in the metanarrative of the sweep of history, the future reign of Christ, and God's ultimate plans for the entire universe. Always at the center of this is Christ. The same is true for the individual believer, for ultimately, we will be with Jesus and where He is we will always be. Our conforming to His image will be complete as we are made to be like Him. And thus, we will be unified with the Godhead—forever. This is our destiny and destination. That this is more than incredible is the actual point—for if it were not, then it would not reflect the nature of God. And this is the mindset that must be reflected in each and every believer as we approach God, for as each time we draw closer to God, then we enter into this divine picture and participate within it. We enter into His sphere which is separate and divine, Holy, mysterious, and majestic.

Too frequently, though, as we enter through this Gate, we forget to think on the reasons for God's works and for such magnanimity toward us who deserve absolutely nothing from Him. But this again is the point: it is not us that deserve anything, but Jesus does. That we believe and love His son is sufficient for God—for He alone has done everything else. Nothing else matters to God from us; all we have to do is love Him. This is our "required work," as we discussed previously. In missing this, we miss the very purpose of the works of God: love. But the love of God and from God is often seen to be too weak a reason for us to accept, for the concept of love has in itself become so corrupted to the modern mind. Hence, we look not to God but to ourselves, and this is where all error starts. Too many believers actually resist the love of God because of this old mindset within us. Under the pretext of thinking themselves unloving or indifferent to others, they virtually reject the love of God, which is in itself an unnecessary act of rebellion and error. After all, God's love to us is based on His nature, not our own inadequacies. The Devotionist, though, adores this love from God, embraces it, and allows it to envelop all that the Devotionist is and becomes. For the love of God to dwell richly within the believer is actually the ultimate goal of devotion; this is the love that transforms and love that edifies as we pass through these Precious Gates of Devotion, and it is the love that regards these gates as being precious.

Fruit of the Spirit and Abiding

Nothing that God does is without purpose, and all that He purposes is to His own glory. Sanctification is not only the will of God but also part of His purpose for us as believers. It is also His purpose that we grow in our knowledge and understanding of Him, that we nurture our souls, and that we live our lives with and through Him. Even more importantly it is clear that the purposes of God are also to become reflected in our own behavior and characters to the extent that, while they may be (should be) invisible to us, they are transparent to others—believers and nonbelievers alike. How is this manifested and attained? They are manifested to God's glory through the fruit of the Spirit and attained through meekness by asking for more of this fruit in our lives. Within our private devotional times of immersive reading, this involves asking God to perform His works of transformation so that not only can the fruit of the Spirit permeate our very being, but that these manifest so visibly from us that to others they reflect not us but God within us. This then entails abiding in Christ, as all that we are becomes a mirror of His divine reflection. Abiding is devotional participation, and in terms of devotional reading, participation in Scripture is learning to be conformed by it, challenged by it, and changed by it until such time as we are ultimately consummated through our unification with Him. Learning to abide through participation then becomes the purpose of the work of the Spirit within us through our times of personal devotion in the form of immersive reading—and it is to be seen as a beautiful and life-enhancing work of God.

Absorption of His Works

It is crucial again, and as always, to remember that while these works are post-redemptive, they are also not perfected in us yet and as such must be seen in the framework of our Positional Blessings—for while we are still imperfect, our God does not condemn those in His household. Where we fail to live up to His and our own expectations, He is gracious and loving to forgive us all and to help us and guide us with the Holy Spirit as we seek to "press toward the goal for the prize of the upward call of God in Christ Jesus" (Phil 3:14). This "pressing" mentioned by Paul as applied within our context of immersive reading and devotion requires us not to just read and move on, but to reflect upon our readings and bring them to remembrance, to celebrate them within ourselves and when we are with others:

> I remember the days of old;
> I meditate on all Your works;
> I muse on the work of Your hands.
> I spread out my hands to You;
> My soul longs for You like a thirsty land. Selah.
> (Ps 143:5–6)

> The works of the LORD are great,
> Studied by all who have pleasure in them.
> His work is honorable and glorious,
> And His righteousness endures forever.
> He has made His wonderful works to be remembered;
> The LORD is gracious and full of compassion.
> (Ps 111:2–4)

Genuine Humility

All of Scripture is replete with examples of how humility is a precondition to the miraculous works of God and His demonstration of His power. This is perhaps no more so than in the Gospels themselves, where those in need not only showed gratitude and awe post-miracle, but humility before the event in front of Jesus. This humility stems from not only a recognition of the distinction in status confronting the person but also from an expectation of an encounter with the extraordinary. It is a shame that the word supernatural has been corrupted in modern parlance and meaning, but in its true sense of being beyond the bounds of the physical world as we in our limitations see it, then this is precisely what encountering God should be like. As we engage in immersive reading then, this expectation should emerge from a preconditioned sense of humility regarding about whom we are learning and, more importantly, whom we are encountering through this exercise.

Reflective Moments Between Gates

As we pass through this first Precious Gate, we pause to reflect on the revelation of the attributes and magnificence of God that Scripture has revealed, and prepare our hearts and souls to pass through the next Gate. And such a revelation should never be kept within, but always produce the required reaction of declaring the greatness of God to all, simply stating with the psalmist,

> My mouth shall speak the praise of the Lord,
> And all flesh shall bless His holy name
> Forever and ever.
> (Ps 145:21)

Gate 2: The Gate of Transcendent Trust

> Blessed are all those who put their trust in Him.
> (Ps 2:12b)

To learn to completely trust God is in one sense the goal of all devotion, whether through immersive reading or private prayer; it is the end product that takes us into the wider world and our daily lives. It is so crucial to our normal lives that it overshadows almost everything else regarding how we live as believers. For trust is more foundational and structural than either faith or belief. If trust fails then all else fails—as is so true with everything in life, especially relationships. But our God, as is His way in so many matters, is totally transparent about this. He knows that He is the only One who can be trusted completely by His children and states as such emphatically in His word, and proves and validates Himself and His words through His actions in creation, history, and prophecy. Only the true God can state the following:

> "To whom then will you liken Me,
> Or to whom shall I be equal?" says the Holy One.
> Lift up your eyes on high,
> And see who has created these things,
> Who brings out their host by number;
> He calls them all by name,
> By the greatness of His might
> And the strength of His power;
> Not one is missing.
> (Isa 40:25–26)

The Bible is very clear as to what it says about its own divine inspiration—and abundantly so. The real question is whether we, as believers, truly believe this. For if we do, then this changes everything. For when we do so, we can learn to trust what it says about all things, and for our purposes of devotion, we can trust what it says about our Positional Blessings and take great comfort in our souls when it says such beautiful things about our relationship with God as,

> For I am persuaded that neither death nor life, nor angels nor principalities nor powers, nor things present nor things to come, nor height nor depth, nor any other created thing, shall be able to separate us from the love of God which is in Christ Jesus our Lord. (Rom 8:38–39)

The Gate of Transcendent Trust then is that which we pass through with the sure and certain knowledge that we can not only trust the Scriptures, for that is not even the half of it, but that we also trust God Himself as the divine mind behind the Scriptures. For while Scripture is that which is in one sense the created work of God, our calling is to worship and to trust in the Creator, not the created (Rom 1:25).

We are told in Ps 2:12 quoted above that those who put their trust in God are "blessed." Now why would this be? The answer is here within our devotion: we are blessed because we can trust in God and because we have allowed ourselves in some sense to release ourselves from our own inadequacies and to place ourselves in the care of the One who is almighty. We are blessed because we are able and entitled to trust Him; it is not misguided or impoverished or inadequate—no, our trust is based on the One who is not only utterly trustworthy but has included us among those upon whom He bestows His favor, whom in a sense He lets trust Him. This privilege of being able and allowed to trust God is because He alone has gifted the Positional Blessings that are the prerogative for those who believe, through the precious blood of Jesus.

Thus, our immersive reading is blessed because through it our existing trust that we have in the Lord is bolstered, as we see through the Scriptures how those within them hold onto the fact that we can trust Him, implore others to do so, and pity those who should be doing so but aren't for whatever reason. As discussed previously, we enter through these gates in the spirit of trust so we can

- trust in His loving-kindness (Pss 25:6, 20; 26:3; 36:7; 40:11),
- trust in His ability to see us through in times of trouble (Pss 57:1, 77:2),
- trust Him in times of affliction (Pss 77:2, 116:4),
- trust Him to comfort us in all our anxieties (Pss 17:19, 94:19).

Transcendent Trust and Fervent Faith—Hand in Hand

Trust, for the Christian, strengthens the heart aligned with the purposes and plans of God, and this strength then solidifies further into fervent faith. Fervent faith is the product of transcendent trust, and as the believer enters through the gates into the presence of God, through and during times of immersive reading and private devotion, so this faith becomes knowledge and knowledge becomes understanding, trust yields to hope and hope becomes certainty.

Certainty then becomes comfort for the believer during times of immersive reading and private devotion, so we are comforted by the fact that we need not be concerned about the future for our position in the household of God is certain and irrevocable. This means that we can progress with the requirements of God to love Him with all our heart, to be His people, and to strive for sanctification in the sure and certain knowledge that being indwelled by the Holy Spirit means that we have the Spirit within us to honor God and strive toward this upward calling. Thus, when we read the prophecies pertaining to the future events surrounding the end times and the second coming of Christ, we read them in the light of wonder at the future works of God but also with the aligned heart of those who are the bride of Christ, and therefore we are to take comfort in that what is destined for some is not destined for us. I appreciate that this is edging into what some might think to be contentious theology, but my point here is in relation to how we approach Scripture during our times of devotion. Namely, our comfort in our Positional Identity in Christ is not limited to just certain passages or books of the Bible but is to be found throughout once we see who we are in God's eyes, for it penetrates throughout the Bible, and always has. My point being that while others approach some passages with trepidation and concern, believers may approach the passages with certainty and comfort. Since all of Scripture speaks of Jesus and all points to Him, then as His bride, we read Scripture because it is about Him, to learn more of Him, and to learn His ways. He is the purpose of Scripture, we are not. And what He says of His bride, how He loves Her, how He regards her, and how He has foreordained Her perfect future as being perfected with Him, we who are His bride must reverently and respectfully take comfort in and not be distressed; as the bridegroom says, "If it were not so, I would have told you" (John 14:2).

Reflective Moments Between Gates

When we reflect on how the truth of God's word both nurtures and satisfies the soul, we do so not because of the words themselves or even because of the wonder of such constructs as "truth," but upon the Author of the word and the Giver and personification of "truth": Jesus Christ. Our reflections and considerations always draw us closer to Him in awe and wonder, and this, in itself, yields greater trust in Him:

> As for God, His way is perfect;
> The word of the Lord is proven;
> He is a shield to all who trust in Him.
> (Ps 18:30)

Gate 3: The Gate of Familial Confidence

Confidence for believers comes not from ourselves but from the Holy Spirit within us. Our confidence is in Christ, not in our own abilities or of our own merit. Such has always been the case, of course, for God chose the people of Israel not because there was anything of merit about them per se but because of His own unilateral promise to Abraham. And hence, as we know, the same is true for every single believer and, therefore, corporately as the collective body known as the church too. Our relationship with God through Jesus affects everything, as we have discussed, not least of which is the confidence we have in this relationship. This confidence then is the attitude we have as we approach our times of devotional reading, for we are able to immerse ourselves into them, and from this position, so we draw strength, comfort, solace, sanctity, and security. Such are the privileges available to all who believe in Jesus. For He is the foundation and rock upon which we can build our lives and upon which we can stand when we need to withstand the wiles of the enemy (Eph 6:9–11).

Consequently, as we enter in through this Gate, know that we do so with the heart of those that yearn to learn and see more of Him whom we love. For to love God with all of our heart and to learn of His ways is the core purpose of all devotion—that we can come boldly into His presence is purely owing to our acceptance of the pure and perfect sacrifice of Jesus. God's love for us because we believe should never be questioned, and as such it is with awe, wonder, and almost incomprehension at the generosity of God that we see Him wishing for us to refer to ourselves as beloved children, blessed in the Lord, and kept by the power of God. Hence, we see and find in Scripture through our immersive readings our identity, our belonging, our destination, and our utter privileges. Our purpose, through the Holy Spirit, is to appropriate these, to absorb them, and to apply them to our lives. They should shape our character, define how we treat each other, and should be so apparent to others that all recognize their transformative power: edifying and strengthening the faith and resolve of those that believe while intriguing, even drawing in, those that don't. All is to the glory of God alone for we are merely His workmanship, and our times of all forms of devotion are our times of being molded and yielding to the Master's craft of nurturing our souls and aligning our hearts with His.

Leaving the Entry Gates

As we look to leave these Precious Gates, we do so in full knowledge that to read and to immerse ourselves in Scripture not only serves to nurture our souls, and is not even just *part* of our full devotion, but produces life in all its fullness as we embrace the beauty of our faith:

> You will show me the path of life;
> In Your presence is fullness of joy;
> At Your right hand are pleasures forevermore.
> (Ps 16:11)

Practicing Patience in the Outer Courts of His Presence

> But you, O man of God, flee these things and pursue righteousness, godliness, faith, love, patience, gentleness. (1 Tim 6:11)

There is no point to having patience unless you can be assured of eventual satisfaction of what you are waiting for. Biblical, spiritual patience is never shrouded with the expectation of disappointment, but rather eventual blessing by God. But neither is it nullified with instant gratification—though, of course, that sometimes does occur at God's sovereign discretion. Hence, patience might be considered an unusual fruit of the Spirit but is clearly designated as such; we must by nature, therefore, be impatient. The Holy Spirit's role, as we have discussed, is to conform the believer to the image and character of Christ—namely, through what we term the fruit of the Spirit (Gal 5:22–23)—and thus the Holy Spirit's nurturing of this particular characteristic of patience within the believer becomes part of this process. But even further than this, according to both apostolic blessings given in Rom 15:5 and 2 Thess 3:5, patience is in fact an attribute of both God and Christ. Quite rightly, therefore, we see that patience comes to be considered a highly commended virtue by the apostles throughout the New Testament, to the extent that it in itself becomes synonymous with the believer's desired behavior, akin to a distinctive, Christian characteristic (Col 1:11, 1 Thess 1:3, 2 Thess 1:4, Heb 6:12, Jas 5:10). Indeed, as with both the peace of God and the richness of His word (Col 3:15), we are to "let patience have its perfect work, that you may be perfect and complete, lacking nothing" (Jas 1:4).

Godly patience, when it comes to devotion, materializes because there are times when God has ordained that there are circumstances and instances where we need time to understand and reflect and also time to savor what we are being taught and shown, whether that is through our times of study, reading, or prayer—and indeed through our overall nurturing. There are, perhaps even more frequently, periods where we need patience both within His presence and also as we enter. Impatience, being a tendency of us all, is not therefore an attitude with which to enter the presence of God. That we must learn "patience" and the need for it would appear as reflective of a human-centric rather than God-centric mindset that needs to be adjusted before we can enter into His presence. This is not to say that we are not able to enter into His presence boldly (in fact just the opposite), or indeed that we cannot petition urgently in times of urgency; it is to say that patience is a mindset that says, "Let Your will be done," and "Not my will but Your will." And this includes God's timings and His decisions.

Good Fruit with Patience

Waiting on the Lord takes many forms within the Gates of Devotion as we enter into His presence and are within it. We wait to understand passages in the Bible, even after we've asked for revelation. We wait to "see" Him through the text, and we even wait to appreciate its relevance at times—frequently, if we are to be honest with ourselves and with Him. Most importantly and distressingly, we are told in Scripture that we are to obey and hear His voice if we are to follow him, but what if we can't because we don't? The answer to this mystery and quandary is not simple, and to make it so would make the reader more prone to reject what is said as not only being disingenuous but even insulting in its feebleness. The truth is there is no answer that another person can put forward to this sensitive and deeply personal matter. There is no "box-ticking exercise" that everyone can undertake and then we will all hear from God. Neither is every individual like that, and nor is God. There is the mystery, though, that God clearly wants to communicate and have heard, but so few of us seem to genuinely do so.

I can only be honest here, as this entire book has come about through a search for honesty in our relationship with God and His relationship with us, His requirements and desires for us. Maybe patience in hearing Him is the key; I do not know and dare not say, in all honesty. If we do take the whole plan of God, though—how He has revealed Himself through creation, through history, and through prophecy; through individuals; and through the revelation of His attributes, plans, and nature—then they surely tell us that we should not just to seek Him in one place or through one means, and hence we are not to expect to hear from Him through just one medium, even if that medium is Scripture. God is integral and integrated into everything, and personal and personalized to every believer. To hear His voice, then, may start with learning to listen for it and perhaps even considering where and by what means we may consider hearing it and, most fundamentally, commencing by asking the Holy Spirit to help us to listen. That is all I can say.

The Comforter and the Comfort of Scripture

> For whatever things were written before were written for our learning, that we through the patience and comfort of the Scriptures might have hope. (Rom 15:4)

Finally, the reading of Scripture can bring great comfort, solace, and inspiration for the believer. That it has ever been the case for us who believe and therefore are indwelled by the Spirit is one of the wonders of the history of our faith. For just as "Jesus Christ is the same yesterday, today, and forever" (Heb 13:8), so must the Holy Spirit and His work be. Hence, we see the same Spirit at work in the lives of believers throughout history, and this is no more apparent in the attitude of those toward Scripture itself. I do not mean just in its veracity or its authority (as crucial to the believer as these are) but more in how it is regarded in its purity and capacity to transform, change, and comfort for it comes from the Comforter (John 14:26). Those who not only love the word of God but see it as a means to love God more know this and always have done. Consider these nine-hundred-year-old sentiments toward it, as a simple and beautiful example of this:

> Brothers, however cast down we may be by harassment or heartache, the consolations of Scripture will lift us up again, for all things that were written in former days were written for our instruction so that we, through steadfastness and the encouragement of Scriptures give us, might have hope. I tell you, brothers, no misfortune can touch us, no situation so galling or

distressing can arise that does not, as soon as Holy Writ seizes us, either fade into nothingness or become bearable. This is the field where Isaac walked in the evening meditating, and where Rebecca came hurrying towards Him and smoothed with her gentle charm the grief that had befallen him. How often, good Jesus, does day incline to evening, how often does the daylight of some slight consolation fade before the black night of an intolerable grief? Everything turns to ashes in my mouth, wherever I look, I see a load of cares. If someone speaks to me, I barely hear: if someone knocks I scarcely notice, my heart is turned to stone, my tongue sticks fast, my tear-ducts are dry. What then? Into the field I go to meditate, I reread the holy book; I set down my thoughts; and suddenly Rebecca comes running towards me and with her light, which is your grace, good Jesus, dispels the gloom, puts melancholy to flight, disintegrates my hardness. Soon sighs give way to tears, accompanied in their turn by heavenly joy. Unhappy are those who, when oppressed in spirit, do not walk into this field and find that joy.[1]

---

1. Aelred of Rievaulx, as quote in Matarasso, *Cistercian World*, 193.

Devotional Reading Methods

Methods of Personal Reading and Scripture Immersion

THE BIBLE STATES VERY clearly that all revelation comes from God first and it is God who teaches us His ways, but it is our responsibility to ask Him to do so. Hence, in the first instance we should take this at face value and always ask Him to reveal Himself to us through His word and to teach us and guide us and to ultimately point us to Jesus. This should always be the starting point of all devotional reading; if it is not, then we run the risk that all becomes as dust in God's eyes—worthless—for He sees our motives and desires dedication. He requires that we worship in spirit and in truth, and hence our personal, devotional reading must become a form of worship that is undertaken in truth and honesty both to God and to ourselves—meaning from a pure heart with the only motivation being the desire to nurture our souls through becoming closer to God and learning more of His ways.

To be clear, devotionist reading from the perspective of the Positional Blessings is different from both studying the Bible at one end and just reading the Bible for pleasure or as part of a daily routine. Devotionist reading is "immersive" and "participatory," for it involves the believer and draws us into the text for the only reason of enhancing our personal relationship with God in a private and subjective way that is personal to each believer who engages with God in this way. I have described pointers and methodologies, but these are in no way meant to be prescriptive and are simply there to guide and make suggestions.

The reader will probably also note that I have not sought to engage in various other forms of devotional activity that have been developed through the centuries, from Christian meditation to engaging devotionally through biblical art, music, and other forms of worship. I feel in some ways that these are peripheral to the context of the purpose of this book, and to be honest there are literally thousands of books on these subjects for the reader to find and to research in their own time. While I mention the concept of meditation in the section titled "Waiting in the Outer Courts of His Presence," I am of the opinion that the meditating that is mentioned in the Bible is based on a form of continual contemplation of God's ways and works that should not be specific to certain times or forms of devotion (Pss 77:6, 12; 119:15, 27; 143:5). David, for instance, mentions meditating on God in his bed, at night, and continually (Pss 1:2, 4:4, 63:6, 119:148), so technically meditation in the sense that is obviously described in the psalms is not how we imagine it today—it is more like continuous contemplation whereby the subject matter is pondered upon deliberately and deeply. While for our context here it is true that the psalmist speaks of times of meditating on the word of God (Ps 119:148), this is by no means the only subject matter that is meditated upon. The others can be summarized as being effectively the "whole council of God"—namely, His wonderful works (Pss 77:12, 119:27, 143:5), precepts (Ps 119:15, 78), statutes (Ps 119:23, 48), and the whole law (Ps 1:2). It is interesting that the psalmist mentions that his times of meditation in this fashion occur as he also brings to remembrance the ways and works of God, which then lead to these periods of intense reflection (Pss 63:6, 77:6, 143:5)—it is also intriguing that this occurs at night, when all is quiet and when on their own. This then applies directly to us as Devotionists, for it is when we are alone in the quiet places that we can reflect on God and recall His full council and think, pontificate, cogitate, and deeply reflect upon Him and the Reality of God in our lives. As such, it is a subject to which I will return in the section below on "The Exit Gate," but for now certainly the heart of David shown in Ps 143:5 applies to us as we consider Positional Devotion and the word of God through the lens of the Precious Gates:

> I will meditate on the glorious splendor of Your majesty,
> And on Your wondrous works.
> (Ps 145:5)

Devotional Reading Methods

I have put forth below methods of devotional reading that hopefully will assist in spiritual growth and soul nurturing. They are developed around the practical implementation of the injunction as discussed above to "let the word of God dwell in you richly" (Col 3:16), and within two of them I have also sought to utilize an interpretation of the Precious Gates in order to augment the methodology used from a devotionist perspective.

I explore within these methods how, when approached through the lens of our Positional Identity and the Positional Blessings, Scripture reading can become involved and personalized with the purpose of nurturing our souls and enhancing our devotion to God. To assist in this, I have also sought to explore how this can be enhanced by examining these methods in the light of what we described before as the Precious Gates of Devotion—my hope is that these can used to guide the believer through to a more spiritual understanding and experience with the word.

The three methods that are expounded upon are as follows:

1. Nurturing our souls through devotional "Lectio Divina"
2. Nurturing our souls through speaking Scripture and reflective reading
3. The personal examination method of devotional reading and contemplation

Following the discussions on these methods, there is section called "Post-Reading: Waiting in the Outer Courts of His Presence." This is a general section that can be applied to each of the methods after the time spent in engaging in these forms of reading Scripture. While we included this "waiting" discussion within the overall context of the Precious Gates of Devotion chapter previously, I have chosen to discuss it in a generalist way across all three methods, as I believe that by doing so, this will prove to be of most assistance to the practice of patience after each method is engaged upon.

Finally, I have also included a brief section entitled "Personal Study for Greater Gain." In the same manner as I mentioned about meditation above, the engagement of personal study of the Bible or of books about theology or of other matters concerning our faith is not to be considered "devotion" and hence falls outside of the scope of the focus of this series. However, it is a matter of sufficient relevance to be discussed, albeit briefly, if only for the sake of clarity.

Method 1

Nurturing Our Souls Through Devotional "Lectio Divina"

THE FIRST METHOD INVOLVES the combination of devotional reading with prayer and contemplation. This, for centuries, has been called "Lectio Divina" and was first developed by St. Benedict in the sixth century and further developed by the Cistercian monks in the twelfth century under Bernard de Clairvaux. It is essentially the means whereby the individual can engage with Scripture in a deeply profound and personal way through contemplation and prayer. While what is outlined below does not necessarily match the strict format of formal Lectio Divina, I have tried to adjust it into a method that hopefully will be of benefit by adapting it to the precepts of Positional Devotion.

This method has been used for centuries as a means of enhancing spiritual growth through concentration and consideration of small passages of Scripture or individual texts. This differs from general Scripture reading and is a deliberate selection of texts that serve to enrich and edify the believer. We now have peace with God, and so there is nothing wrong, and everything absolutely right, in focusing on passages that enhance our understanding of God and all that He has undertaken for us and given us. For the Holy Spirit's desire, as shown through the apostle Paul, is that we "may be able to comprehend with all the saints what is the width and length and depth and height—to know the love of Christ which passes knowledge; that you may be filled with all the fullness of God" (Eph 3:18–19).

The purpose of this method is to draw us closer to God and help us to enter into and sustain His presence as we focus on particular passages that reveal His nature and attributes and confirm our identity in Christ. This method has the dual function of deeply nourishing our souls while providing the greatest of comfort. It is for the solidification and augmenting of our faith to the deepest degree. Quite simply, this method is to focus us more earnestly on Jesus so that "the peace of God, which surpasses all understanding, will guard your hearts and minds through Christ Jesus" (Phil 4:7).

The steps are broadly as follows (and they assume that the previous steps of preparation outlined above have been undertaken already).

Step 1: Selecting a Text

Positional Devotion, we have said before, focuses on our privilege of being members of the household of God and all that Jesus has done for us through His death, resurrection, and ascension. I maintain that if the Christian were to do no more than contemplate on these texts, then we would be immensely blessed, for these alone are sufficient to nurture our souls and shine God's light into our hearts. Each text that reveals each of the Positional Blessings could be used to form a devotional pattern of reading and contemplation, and hence I have set out in the appendix a list of the passages pertaining to the blessings that we discussed before so that this can be used as a devotional tool to assist the reader.

A useful recommendation at this stage might be that having selected the text, one might want to either read it out loud at least a couple of times or possibly write it out slowly and carefully to give it due consideration and to "let" it absorb into your consciousness through such deliberate actions that involve different parts of the brain, through speech or hand and eye coordination.

Step 2: "Dwelling"

Contemplation of these Positional Blessings involves not mindless meditation but pausing, thinking, dwelling upon, and "letting" the implications of what has been given to us simply sink deep into our hearts, minds, and souls. This is concentration of and on Scripture as it is compressed within us.

Step 3: "Richly"

To focus the mind and heart in this adaptation of Lectio Divina, we seek to enrich our appreciation of Christ and nurture our souls through exploration of the text through the prism of the Precious Gates of Devotion. Taking each one gives our contemplation a means to focus and method of meditation.

Gate 1: The Gate of the Consideration of the Divine

As we commence the contemplation on each passage, our first point of entry is that of considering the divine nature of God as revealed through each of them. Each passage should be approached in awe at the heart of God for those whom He loves. It is impossible to fully comprehend what manner of love God has for those whom He loves, but when we consider these passages and let them literally become absorbed into our very being, so our hearts swell and we drift toward perhaps a deeper appreciation of all He has done for us. These Positional Blessings are so beautiful in that they reflect the very depth of the love that God has for His people—not just in the future but in this life, in the here and now. This is our God, and this is what He is like, our souls cry out.

Consideration of His Works

That each text represents a preordained work of God for His people in response to the complete and magnificent work of Christ is deeply humbling as we consider how such a mind conceives of such goodness for those of so little merit. Truly when we consider each text, we should cry aloud in unison with the psalmist:

> Oh, taste and see that the Lord is good;
> Blessed is the man who trusts in Him!
> (Ps 34:8)

Metanarrative Works: The Way

The contemplation of each text not only produces awe, as each can be set within the overall metanarrative of God's ultimate plan of redemption and restoration of all things to Himself. It is only humbling to contemplate that these blessings were considered from the foundation of the world, and activated as part and parcel of the overall redemptive plan. To place each one within this context is to elevate it to its rightful status within this eternal plan. This then serves to place the believer's positional privileges among this plan, for they mean that each believer is a both simultaneously a participant in and recipient of divine favor without merit or warrant, except through the will of God. Hence, when we consider these texts, we see God in creation (for we are recreated) and through Providence (for He has placed these blessings as available at any time to those who believe) and through the future (for these blessings are our proofs and seals of what our future holds, as revealed by God through His word).

Positional Works: The Truth

To accept each of these blessings as being true is truly liberating. That they are revealed to us at all reflects pure and utter love unmerited and grace unconditional. But we must accept them as blessings, and when we do so we must accept them for what they are—divine gifts that are bestowed upon all who believe. To understand them as such is truly to grasp their significance and the price with which they were bought by our Lord and Savior. They liberate for they mean that our future is secure and not determined by our own failings or successes, but by the almighty workings and power of God. Each text furthers this; each text cements this; each text adds layer and layer to complete this most magnificent of tapestries displaying to all of heaven and earth the ways of our God. To not see this, to ignore or to diminish this, is to greatly offend and affront our God. They truly are Positional Blessings and truly are true.

Transforming Works: The Life

Each text reveals the life available to every believer. As we build on the foundation of our belief and faith in Jesus, these texts then become stepping stones as we traverse the course of everyday life as Christians. They serve in our character development based upon our perceived and appropriated identity as the people of God, beloved members of His household, and cherished citizens of heaven. When we see ourselves as such, this life is the prelude to eternity. This is why Jesus said that He is "the life" and why He is "the resurrection and the life" (John 11:25), for with Jesus and because of the resurrection, we have eternal life—starting now and lasting forever (John 11:25, 14:6) This is as transformational as it should be given its divine authorship. But we must believe it, accept it, and apply it, and when we do so, our hearts align with God and our souls rejoice.

Genuine Humility

Jesus said that the "meek shall inherit the earth," and it is with this heart that we inherit what has been bestowed and made available to us (Matt 5:5). When due consideration is given to what Jesus achieved on the cross and through His resurrection, and when we add to this the unparalleled and unimaginably generous gifts given to us, the only genuine reaction to all this can be awe, wonder, and absolute gratitude.

Reflective Moments Between Gates

To contemplate the divine is one of the worthiest of exercises any Christian could undertake and spend a lifetime doing. The choice of texts would be endless, but maybe a few could include 1 Chr 29:10–14, Job 38–40, Isa 40–48, Ps 145, among many others.

Gate 2: The Gate of Transcendent Trust

As we have discussed before, trust in the word of God comes from an understanding of the value He Himself gives to His attributes and characteristics. As we contemplate these Positional Blessings, so the Gate of Transcendent Trust opens as we literally confirm openly in our hearts and audibly to our souls that "the entirety of Your word is truth" (Ps 119:160). And because it is inspired by God and God is truth personified, so we can trust these passages and texts to be true. We can enter into this divine exchange that God requires of us in the form of belief and trust—for we cannot have one without the other if each are to be true. Accordingly, it is because of this divine exchange that when we contemplate these passages, we know that we can, as we have said previously,

- trust in His loving-kindness (Pss 25:6, 20; 26:3; 36:7; 40:11),
- trust in His ability to see us through in times of trouble (Pss 57:1, 77:2),
- trust Him in times of affliction (Pss 77:2, 116:4),
- trust Him to comfort us in all our anxieties (Pss 17:19, 94:19).

Alongside and in parallel with this divine exchange is the further progression between trust and faith—for transcendent trust begets fervent faith. As we know that these blessings are true, so we appropriate them into our faith and our walk with God. But trust also transforms faith into something altogether more powerful: certainty. When we are certain of our position in Christ, our Positional Identity, then everything changes. Everything in life becomes clearer and more meaningful as we accept the certainty of what Jesus did and achieved on the cross and what the Father has bestowed upon those who believe; when we truly believe that nothing under heaven and earth can separate us from the love of Jesus, then the hope of eternal life and earthly blessings in this life itself is no longer nebulous, but certain. And with certainty comes comfort and with comfort, peace. Hence, trust is a prelude to ultimate peace. Oh, the wonder and joy that we have with our Lord!

Reflective Moments Between Gates

Once again, Lectio Divina is perfect for the Christian to focus the heart and soul on what sometimes just individual words or phrases can produce, in terms of the value they can create when time is given to them. Focus can be given by simply allowing the text to penetrate our souls.

> But as for me, I trust in You, O Lord;
> I say, "You are my God."
> (Ps 31:14)

Gate 3: The Gate of Familial Confidence

It may seem to be a circular argument that the consideration of the passages and text that speak of the familial blessings enhance our understanding of those blessings, but the full beauty of what they are both individually and collectively is only truly understood by those who are believers. Hence, the Gate of Familial Confidence is the Gate through which each believer is able to consider these blessings as truth, and the approaching of them as truth strengthens each one, links them, and integrates them to form an entry point into the presence of God that is beyond compare. It is with confidence that they are to be considered, and it is confidence that they inspire: confidence in who God is, what He does and has done for us; confidence in His ways and that He is truth; confidence in how He regards us now as His children; and confidence that He will include us with all of what He has planned as His precious bride of Christ.

That such passages strengthen our characters and our walk with God should in some ways be considered their divine purpose in their revelation. Thus, the purpose of such contemplation is not only to enrich our souls but also through that to equip us with the means to walk worthy of our calling (Eph 4:1), meaning that as these passages permeate into us, so we become wiser in our understanding of God and His ways. Consequently, as they shape and conform us, as they embed within us the beauty and majesty of God in His infinite love and generosity toward us, so we are also able to live in a manner that is pleasing to God, with characters bearing the fruit of the Spirit. May His light within us shine forth from us to others so that they, too, learn the of the peace and comfort available to all who believe, as we appropriate the Positional Blessings into our devotion and lives.

Entering into His Presence

Of course, Lectio Divina is defined by periods of consideration and contemplation on the word of God, and so to do so on those passages that speak of entering into this presence is both edifying and instructive to all:

> Let us come before His presence with thanksgiving;
> Let us shout joyfully to Him with psalms.
> (Ps 95:2)

Method 2

Nurturing Our Souls Through Speaking Scripture and Reflective Reading

THE WORD OF GOD, Heb 4:12 tells us, is living and powerful. It therefore has the ability to literally interact with our souls in ways that we do not necessarily see or immediately appreciate. For the ordinary believer, we can take what the Bible says of itself as being the "mirror of Scripture" and simply let it work within us through speaking Scripture and reflective reading.

Speaking Scripture

This entails the believer literally reading out loud passages or texts of Scripture, whether privately or among other believers. Scripture passages are read out loud at least once and can be reread quietly should the believer wish. The reason for this is threefold: Firstly, most Scripture was originally written to be read out loud, whether in public or in groups. Secondly, the speaking out loud of what is written can not only be an act of affirmation but can also assist in "lodging" the text further into the memory, thereby assisting in subsequent recollection. And thirdly, there is something undeniably mystical about letting Scripture speak for itself. Explanatory teaching or personal investigation is not always necessary, as we "let it dwell richly within us." It can be absorbed, and we can let it nurture itself within our souls and very psyche.

One can choose to do this with entire books of the Bible, preferably the shorter ones, or with the Epistles and preferably all in one go, or choose individual set texts or passages that are meant to be read as one, such as the psalms, of course, or the Sermon on the Mount (Matt 5–7), the Olivet discourse (Matt 24–25), John 14–17, other individual events in the Gospels, or of course passages that speak of the majesty and glory of God (Isa 6, Ezek 1, Isa 40–48) or are just pure, unmitigated worship (1 Chr 29:10–16). These can be just read and appreciated—not necessarily overly thought through as they are read, but just letting the words and images literally wash over you. In a group setting, the reading out loud of Scripture could also be accompanied by a period of "recitation" or "recollection" of the text, as members of the group retell what the passage said (without looking at their own versions)—this is a particularly good exercise to do to encourage greater recall and even understanding of the text or passage as retelling it in paraphrase serves to embed it deeper into our memories.

Reflective Reading

Often undertaken in conjunction with speaking Scripture, this can involve the reader then taking time to reflect upon what has been read, but not necessarily in an analytical or investigative way as discussed below, rather more emotionally spiritual. This can entail again asking questions of ourselves about the text and the issues it draws from us. One can immediately see then the benefit to the Positional Devotionist as one need not get concerned or distracted either by technical detail or theological nuances but can focus immediately on what matters to God—our love for Him and the nurturing of our souls.

Through this method, we can start to ask questions of the text to help us with our reflections, to make them purposeful in God's eyes and therefore fruitful in our desire for spiritual growth. This can be to take again what Scripture says of itself and ask questions of the passage accordingly, such as these:

- What do we learn of God through this passage? What attributes of His do we see and what do they point to?

- Are there elements in the passage that are particularly convicting of how you react to them in the light of knowing what displeases God and what pleases Him?
- As all Scripture points to Jesus, and as it is the Lord's will that we will be conformed to Christ's image, how can this passage help us learn to have more of the mind of Christ, as well as learn to love God more through it?

Using John 14:6 as a model, we can frame our questions around the fact that all Scripture is inspired by God and that it is the role of the Holy Spirit to point us to the truth, hence we can use Scripture itself to ask the following questions:

- The Way: How does this passage point me to Jesus?
- The Truth: How does this passage reveal God's true nature and my own heart?
- The Life: Certain of eternal life with Christ, how does this passage shape my character in this life?

These are then just a sample of the types of questions we can start to ask ourselves—how we then assemble them is a question of time and preference. One could use these as pointers for "journaling" or note-taking after having read a passage; or they could be points simply to ponder over in the instant and let the thoughts filter through us as we perhaps think on them again during the day or evening. Either way, it is perhaps good to spend a little time both meditating on these thoughts afterwards and consolidating them within us. Finally, though, we should also always give thanks to God for the passage and for what it has shown us—whether we believe it to be profound revelation or not is completely irrelevant. What we are thanking Him for is the privilege of being in His household and for being able to ask of Him in the first place.

Method 3

The Personal Examination Method of Devotional Reading and Contemplation

THIS METHOD STARTS WITH an honest appreciation that we should expect and encourage Scripture to read us as well as us read it. It is living and powerful and it pertains to and is from a supernatural being, and hence we should not be surprised when the reading of it produces the results that it says of itself that it will produce as the mirror of Scripture is held up before us (2 Tim 3:16, Heb 4:12).

It also starts with accepting and acknowledging that, as we have said multiple times already but needs to be repeatedly reenforced, the Holy Spirit will only ever point us to Jesus. If our studies and our deliberations do not end up doing that, then they are at best fruitless, at worst erroneous and potentially deceptive.

The stages that comprise this method can be summarized as follows.

Inquisitive Textual Examination

We start first by asking questions of the text or passage and framing it in reference to other biblical truths in both Testaments. While we set the passage within its historical and cultural position first, we must be mindful that in terms of our devotional reading, textual examination should be undertaken with reference also to the divine imperative that all is written by the Holy Spirit and all Scripture speaks of Jesus.

Characterization Examination

We next consider the motives and consequences of behavior. All actions are governed by motives and within the Bible can be framed not only within a historical and cultural setting but also within theological, providential, and prophetic context. This is especially important when reading the Gospels but the Epistles too—not to mention, of course, the Old Testament. For the Bible frames all within a theological and theocentric framework; and hence all character examination must be considered with this in mind.

The Consequences of Conduct

This is what God is interested in, for in God's eyes, conduct is judged in accordance with the outworking of the two great commandments around which the Law and the Prophets hang, as Jesus said. Everything is held within this frame of reference, and so every consequence of conduct is measured against these. This then starts to serve as a model as to how we can interpret and interact with the text, which is the next stage.

Inquisitive Personal Examination and Reflective Self-Characterization

This involves asking honest and searching questions of our own response to the text and the characters/events within the text. We then measure ourselves and these up against the requirements of God, particularly regarding the mirror of Scripture and the teachings of Jesus. Honesty and contemplative searching of oneself is imperative here as we search ourselves to assess our true reactions to the events and the individuals involved by asking questions: How would I have reacted? Am I like that as well? What is God teaching the individual in the passages, and how are they reacting against the teachings of God? Once we have done this, it is time to truly reflect upon how we measure and examine the true nature of our hearts and response to others and, to be honest, how we react to and believe the passages.

Confessional Devotional Response: The Search for Godliness

Taking our honest responses to the passage—the events themselves as well as the behavior of the characters therein—we hold these up against Christ's standards and "confessionally" admit where we fail and ask the Holy Spirit to continue to mold and shape us to conform us to the image of Christ. Positionally, though, we always remember that there is no condemnation for those in Christ.

The exposure of our failings in the light of Christ's standards are confessed as sin as we seek conformation and restoration of fellowship with God. The Positional Devotionist knows that while we continually fail in our standards, we are assured of forgiveness as we privately confess these failings. Confessional devotion, therefore, is following the flow and pattern of the sacrificial system as our devotion becomes a form of living sacrifice to God. The flow of the sacrificial system proceeded in three steps:

1. Repentance and acknowledgement of sin: the sin offering
2. Total commitment back to God: the burnt offering
3. Restoration of fellowship with God: the peace offering

But given our Positional Identity, it is essential that we always remember that if we are already forgiven and assured of our position in the household of God, confession therefore is restoration of fellowship and acknowledgement that we know that God is just and pure and His mercies endure forever. Such consideration of our reactions to any particular passage will also bring to mind other factors pertaining to our personalities that will become exposed as the Holy Spirit searches the inward parts—we must be attuned to this and not hesitate to confess and address as necessary.

Reflections Using the Precious Gates of Devotion

The final stage as we seek to worship God through our reading is using the Precious Gates of Devotion as a means to explore more deeply our own reflection in the mirror of Scripture and to seek unity and companionship with God through them. By considering each Gate, as we have done before, we seek to dig deeper, spiritually, into the text and our reactions to it. By doing so, we seek to use these not only as entry points into the presence of God but as a means of self-examination to our reaction to the text.

Gate 1: The Gate of the Consideration of the Divine

How we react to what is written, the events retold, and the theology discussed is, in reality, indicative of how we react to the divine itself. When we consider the miracles and the ways of God that are depicted within Scripture, our hearts and minds should be aligned with the heart of God and the mind of Christ. This means that as we enter into this Gate, we meditate on what has been revealed in these passages about the ways of God, His attributes, and how His divinity is revealed. We should consider how all reflects and points to Christ and how His own divinity is revealed through His exercise of His authority as God incarnate. This is the approach to Scripture that is accepted by God, for it reflects His own requisite for reverence, respect, and recognition for who He is.

Consideration of His Works

Reflective consideration of His works, in this instance, is how we react to the text through the inspiration of the Holy Spirit. The smallest revelation in Scripture that points us to Jesus and nurtures our souls is as much a work of God as the parting of the Red Sea. The conviction of sin and the desire to dig deeper and to learn more of His ways than any reading of Scripture produces from us is, again, a work of God. For such as these come from God and from nowhere else. If we, through reading the word, are equipped and edified, then this too is the work of the Lord. If we then edify others by explaining these works, then this fulfills the very purpose of all inspiration: to lead us closer to God and to allow others to see Jesus more through the light that shines from us.

Metanarrative Works: The Way

Our reflection on the passage in question and our reaction to it in terms of its location within the grand plan of God, its consideration and contextual position whether in history, prophecy, or theology, is determined by our appreciation and appropriation of these metanarratives into our own discourse. Meaning that if we do not believe in or doubt these works, then our devotion itself becomes virtually meaningless not only for our own edification but also in how it is perceived and received by God. For these are His attributes and His ways, and to study and consider them is deeply rewarding for us who believe, as they affirm and reaffirm not just our faith but the One in whom we have faith.

Positional Works: The Truth

To reflect and contemplate how God has revealed Himself and His ways in these passages draws us to the point of how we also see and recognize Jesus within them. This is the purpose of all revelation, and without it revelation itself is diminished. We are drawn to the truth of how we see Positional Blessings within these passages, how those who are righteous display them, and how the text is correctly interpreted through them. To see this and to recognize this within the texts is revelatory and deeply satisfying. To do so is to edify our hearts and nurture our souls as we dwell richly on the grace upon grace that God bestows on us.

Transforming Works: The Life

The Precious Gates of Devotion are considered precious for what they mean to every Devotionist as we seek to enter into the glorious presence of God. To reflect upon the transforming works of God through these times of reflective reading causes our devotion to return to how the Lord has assisted us to learn more of Himself through them in order that we can see the good and holy fruit of this through greater understanding, leading to the transforming of minds and aligning of our hearts. As we see and seek out our sanctification, we see in our reactions to these passages how God wishes to conform us to His image and to bless us with the sure and certain knowledge that He will one day absorb us into the complete unity with the Godhead. And thankfully, in the meantime we see more and more how such knowledge of our Positional Blessings is absorbed within us, to His glory, so that our times of reflective reading and personal devotion become ever sweeter and more rewarding.

That such can happen to us is, of course, to the glory and honor of God. As we reflect on these passages and our experience within them during these times of reading, so we realize that without the guidance of God through the Holy Spirit in our lives, we would be utterly lost. It becomes more and more bewildering to the believer how we ever coped prior to having the Spirit within us. Such is what is exposed within these times of reflective reading when we consider our own reactions and look honestly into our hearts; so we see with great humility how short we still fall when we come to God's holiness, grace, and love, but with humility too we accept as true what He says He now thinks of us because of (and only because of) our belief in Jesus.

Gate 2: The Gate of Transcendent Trust

All of Scripture speaks of Jesus, and because of our position in Christ, we can trust what it says to be true and trust the truth of what it says about the Godhead and how we are regarded by God as believers. It is because of Jesus that we can trust in what the word of God says, for He alone is worthy of our trust because He alone will never let us down or leave or forsake us. Hence in our devotion we can trust that whatever is revealed to us in the passages that are read, no matter how convicted we are through them, then we can trust that nothing will separate us from the love of Jesus, that there is no condemnation for us, that God is always willing to forgive when we let Him down, and that we have and will always have peace with Him. And hence because of this, it is His desire that we have the peace of God when we come into His presence during our times of reading devotionally and afterwards as we reflect upon all that has been taught, revealed, and exposed.

Transcendent Trust and Fervent Faith—Hand in Hand

Trust, as we have said before, produces faith and from faith we have hope. But hope for those who are grounded and grasp the reality of God in their lives, and the true reality of the Holy Spirit within them with all that implies, is not hope but certainty, as we have said before. Our devotional considerations should always make this singular fact more and more obvious to us: none of this would be possible without Jesus. He is the reason for, and He is the author of, our trust, faith, hope, and certainty. All reflection and devotion must ultimately draw to a close with this conclusion.

Gate 3: The Gate of Familial Confidence

We said before that the purpose of the Bible is not the Bible itself but the revelation of God—who He is, what He does, and how He chooses to engage with His creation. When we read to learn more of Him from the position of the understanding of our Positional Blessings, so we can read with the confidence of the familial. When a child speaks of his parents, it comes from a knowledge of and experience of those whom no one else sees as they do. And such is the manner that the believer is able through the guidance of the Holy Spirit to read of the ways of God—without fear or recrimination, and with the complete and certain knowledge and experience of unconditional love. This is the confidence with which we are able to approach Scripture, to reflect upon it, and to learn from it. And perhaps, above all, this is the position from which we are to take comfort from it. As we read of our God and what He is like, so our hearts swell with admiration and love; and as we reflect on His ways and His attributes, so we are assured ever more of our own eternal assurance of being forever in His care and considered by God Himself to be a beloved child within His household. If we spend eternity just reflecting on this alone, then that would be enough. And yet the closer we get, the more we know that for God it is indeed enough for us in this life but that He has (as is so reflective of His abundant nature) prepared for us so much more. For beyond this He has ordained that He will, in His own timing, receive us to Himself, and our glorified bodies will be ever with the Lord. But He does not stop there, for even beyond that He will go even further in that ultimately our destination in our identity in Jesus will be completed by God as we are unified with Him so that we are forever one with Father and Son and Holy Spirt. This should ever be for our contemplation and gives us the entitlement to be confident in the Scriptures, for it is not them but God that we have confidence in. Our confidence is given to us as an end product of our acceptance of the glorious gifts of Positional Blessings that adorn the Precious Gates of Devotion with divine beauty.

For all that God has done, for all that He has blessed us with, this is how He wants us to read and engage with Scripture. For to read it this way is to learn to love Him more and more, to align our hearts with His, and to transform our minds to that of Christ's. To read it this way is to nurture our souls and to comfort and to edify. To read it this way is one component in our journey of being what He has already made us—His people. And this devotion is the only form of reverence that is becoming for the righteous believer.

Post-Reading

Waiting in the Outer Courts of His Presence

DEVOTIONAL READING OF SCRIPTURE, as we have discussed, has a purpose which is different from other forms of Scripture reading, such as for study. This purpose is to draw us closer to God, help us to learn and assimilate His ways into our lives, so we can personally, privately, individually learn not only to live in accordance with His strictures but most importantly to love Him more deeply. Without this end in mind, all our efforts are not exactly in vain, but perhaps not as fruitful as they could be—which is why sometimes we come away from times of reading less satisfied than others.

The feeding of the soul through these times also means that they should be followed by a period of digestion before we embark on the other activities necessary in our daily lives. This "digestive period" is important if we are to absorb it all and to "take it with us" so that we can continue the contemplation of what we have learned not just about God but, more importantly, about His relationship with us and ours with Him through these periods of immersive reading. We need, in other words, a period of waiting: waiting to enter into His presence as we consider the passages, but also a period of consideration or contemplation once the readings have been completed. This is where we engage with the Spirit to show us more and to illuminate more to us. This is especially in relation to what the Lord wishes us to learn from the passages in question, to help us draw closer to Him and to keep us in His ways on the path of righteousness.

Once we have finished our times of devotional reading of Scripture, time needs to be taken to absorb within ourselves all that we have read, considered, and encountered concerning its meaning and application to us. We need to learn to appropriate in this way so that what we read and what we learn, especially regarding ourselves, does not fall by the wayside or become quickly forgotten. This practice can take many forms, from the writing of such recollections in the form of journaling or in the form of notes, or just through times of quiet contemplation and cogitation—what the Bible describes as meditation.

To assist in this—and please be assured that this is in no way meant to be either dogmatic, proscriptive, or restrictive in your own deliberations—we previously looked to the psalmists for themes that could be used to give some structure to these periods of post-reading contemplation. These themes were identified from the psalmists' own deliberations and discourses regarding their souls' needs and affects, and they can be used not only immediately after reading but perhaps even as measures to concentrate upon during times of personal devotional ruminations on Scripture and the ways of God in general.

Consequently, these themes can be used constructively and applied to each of the methods of personal devotional reading that we have discussed, as the Precious Gates are opened and we wait upon the Lord. These themes and their application to devotional reading then can be expounded upon as follows:

- Awe and Wonder at God: Psalm 8:3–4

All of Scripture is inspired by God, and we are to learn of His ways through it. Therefore, we should seek Him through each passage, to see how His attributes are reflected in it and to be enriched as we consider just how beautiful He is in His majesty and grace. How intricate, intense, and utterly consistent He is, as shown through the word. And as we consider these in relation to each passage, therefore we gain greater and greater understanding of Him as we stand in awe of Him, and yet marvel at our privilege of knowing Him and being considered part of His household.

- Praise, Thanksgiving, and Gratitude: Psalm 95:2

The only reasonable response to awe and wonder is praise. Our reaction to each passage and each time of immersive reading must be to praise God for who He is, His word, what He has revealed of Himself through it, and importantly what He has revealed about ourselves. Thanksgiving for this is expected from God. He expects gratitude from us for who He is and what He does. This again needs to be our reasonable response to the revelation given in His mercy and needs to be framed in the light of the fact that this has only been feasible because of the Holy Spirit within us, leading and guiding and ever moving us closer to Christ and Christlikeness—which, in itself, should only ever produce awe, wonder, and eternal gratitude.

- Received Peace: Psalm 23:1–3

The reading and digestion of Scripture can be challenging and difficult at times, especially as we hold it up as a mirror and let God's light expose our inner hearts and minds through it. This can be challenging not only as we consider ourselves but also when we read passages that sit uncomfortably, perhaps seemingly condemning our status and state. We must therefore firstly approach our devotional reading on the basis of the "received peace" that we have as part of our position in Christ, and knowing that there is no condemnation for those in Christ Jesus.

- Love and Loving-Kindness

The attributes of God that reveal most of His character to us are love and loving-kindness. This is what He gives to us, expects in return, and expects us to give others. These then become the yard sticks on how we reflect upon these passages or texts that expose our hearts and help us marvel at His own love for us.

- Longing for His Presence: Psalm 42:1–2

The consideration of love always produces longing to be in the presence of the one who is loved. This is the way with Scripture immersion; it should produce always this longing as the Holy Spirit within us yearns for us to be more like Christ so that we want His presence in our lives. This produces feelings always of knowing that our citizenship is now in heaven and that we are to be continually looking into the heavenly realm for our comfort of eternity. But Jesus is also ever present, and the Lord is always with us, so each Scripture immersion should produce the response of longing for His presence with us not just while reading or contemplation, but ever-present with us in all that we do. And hence we must live in this light, which produces greater character as we take responsibility for ourselves in the light of His presence.

Personal Study for Great Gain

WITHIN A DISCUSSION ON devotion, it is important to address at times some "gray areas" around what is and what isn't devotion—or rather the acts of devotion that are to be considered as such. Just as there are ways of reading Scripture that are not technically "devotion," and indeed there are ways of praying that are not strictly speaking "devotional," so the same is perhaps even more true when it comes to studying the Bible.

To be clear, to study the Bible is a good and profitable exercise for the believer. The Devotionist will even approach the studying of the Bible with a heart aligned and mind devoted to God, but even so this does not make this activity devotion per se, for it is not directed at God. However, to study Scripture through using good commentaries, books, and other study tools—even watching teachings and sermons—is all beneficial but needs to be tempered with caution regarding false teaching, doctrinal error, and deception, at worst, or distraction and overemphasis, at best, even when the materials are correct and edifying in themselves. While such study can be deeply satisfying and enriching, it can also be distracting. It can become obsessive, and many a time it can cause one to go down "blind alleys" where faith can become intellectualized and distorted from what matters to God.

Of course, study can improve our understanding of God and His ways, which is a very good thing, but this practice is not, in itself, devotion. This is my point, for we return again to what does matter to our

God: that we love Him with all of our hearts and that we are a people unto Him. Thus, when studying the Bible and seeking to go further and deeper with studies by using commentaries alongside the general reading of the Bible, or reading books about discernment, prophecy, and theology, the Devotionist should certainly do so in a spirit of dedication to God. And this is laudable, of course, if—and only if—such study draws us closer to a deeper appreciation of God and His ways. We must, in all things, be wise as serpents and gentle as doves, for while our understandings can be hugely enhanced and enriched by the knowledge imparted, at the end of the day it is fallible; it comes not from God but from the minds of men and women—no matter how qualified they are, whether academically or in terms of service, all have biases, and everything comes from a particular mindset or theological framework. The problem is exacerbated in our times and in the nature of our culture as we become fixated on specific teachers or pastors or upon specific subjects, even as godly as some may seem, such as the gifts of the Spirit or the timelines and events surrounding eschatology and the second coming. The Bible of course warns us against such obsessions and how we too easily err when it comes to technicalities and minor issues, such as timelines and genealogies, and our instructions regarding this have always been simple and couldn't be clearer: "But avoid foolish disputes, genealogies, contentions, and strivings about the law; for they are unprofitable and useless" (Titus 3:9).[1] Such directness from Paul comes from the heart that knows the dangers and pitfalls that such can have on the normal, everyday believer. There is a tendency of some to be too easily swayed by clever teachings that seem so holy and inspirational but are not actually from God. We should always be conscious that it is the will of the Holy Spirit to guide us and teach us in order

> that we should no longer be children, tossed to and fro and carried about with every wind of doctrine, by the trickery of men, in the cunning craftiness of deceitful plotting, but, speaking the truth in love, may grow up in all things into Him who is the head—Christ—from whom the whole body, joined and knit together by what every joint supplies, according to the effective working by which every part does its share, causes growth of the body for the edifying of itself in love. (Eph 4:14–16)

---

1. See also 1 Tim 1:4.

We have, though, an immense treasure trove of Christian works to draw upon. God has blessed us with being the beneficiaries of such a vast storage of experiences of Him that have been given to many men and women over the centuries whose writings, teachings, sermons, poetry, music, and fine art have served to create a huge well of knowledge that can be drawn upon in abundance—and so easily in our current day. Yet herein lies the problem: for all this availability of knowledge at our fingertips, many seem further from God than those we read of in times past, who had only a miniscule fraction available to them compared with what we have now. When I consider the writings of the Cistercian monks, or those of others like Brother Lawrence, Walter Hilton, Thomas à Kempis, and other Devotionists from times past, it shows that not only does the spirit of devotion not change but that perhaps we do not gain so much from all this knowledge after all—for their love of God and closeness to Him is on a level far deeper and superior to our own, despite all the advantages we have. Thus, while such access can be extremely beneficial in many ways, we must become wary that it does not impact the very desire of God for us, which is Him being in our presence continually.

Of course, there will be some who may immediately point out here that it is God's desire that we mature in our faith, that we move from milk to meat, and that we are to study to show ourselves approved by God (2 Tim 2:15). Putting nuances of translations, the change of meaning of words from the seventeenth century, to one side, this is to miss my point entirely. For I am by no means saying that studying is not beneficial and can be extremely edifying and faith-enhancing as we examine texts in detail, study God's prophetic plan, learn of His ways through teachings on creation, or through learning of the supporting evidence and proofs via the wonderful number of excellent apologetics teachers. Indeed, to learn of church history and to read Christian works of the past, and present, is extremely enriching and important to gain a rounded and more full faith. However, my point in this series is to ask the simple questions: Is this beneficial? Probably. Is this necessary? No. And most importantly, Is this required? The honest answer to give is quite simply no. For God has already laid down to us what He requires from us, and this we have discussed in great detail. While I personally have loved over the years engaging in all the above, my concern has come back to the fact that not every ordinary, everyday Christian either has the time or the inkling to engage in any, let alone all, of these. Does that make them second-rate or inferior in God's eyes? Certainly not! And to think so utterly diminishes the power and purpose of our salvation and the atoning sacrifices of Christ. We can never add to our salvation, thankfully, and so we should never feel in any way less significant in God's eyes simply because, for whatever reason, we do not engage in any of these study practices.

A Recommendation for Personal Study

Having said all the above, there is one form of study that I would highly recommend for anyone wishing to go deeper in their understanding of the ways of God, and that is to undertake the of studying themes and even set words within the text. The purpose of these studies, though, should really be solely to improve your understanding of Christ and to draw you closer to Him. Such themes might include then a study of God's attributes and characteristics, the prophecies pertaining to the first advent of Christ, the fulfillment of the feasts of Israel by Christ, and simply the studying of such words as "sanctification." Such study can often be undertaken by using the concordances in study Bibles, and in some Bible dictionaries—though again, one must be considerate of the theological bias of the editors and contributors of these when undertaking these exercises. Many study Bibles include chain references and subject references, which are again extremely useful for these exercises.

As I said, this is a recommendation that certain people would find rewarding, but it is in no way mandatory and should in no way cause anyone to deviate from experiencing where the real reward lies for us—namely, in the participation of our Living Devotion in everyday life.

Positional Devotional Prayer

For this reason I bow my knees to the Father of our Lord Jesus Christ, from whom the whole family in heaven and earth is named, that He would grant you, according to the riches of His glory, to be strengthened with might through His Spirit in the inner man, that Christ may dwell in your hearts through faith; that you, being rooted and grounded in love, may be able to comprehend with all the saints what is the width and length and depth and height—to know the love of Christ which passes knowledge; that you may be filled with all the fullness of God.

Ephesians 3:14–19

Such is the perfect, biblical summary of why the Devotionist engages in personal, private prayer. Its reason is not for personal gain (if by gain we mean the contemporary materialistic, physical usage of the word) but rather for spiritual enrichment, edification, and sanctification. Private prayer, therefore, corresponds with what we described previously as the whole desire of God to have a people unto Himself who willingly love Him and want to fellowship with Him above all else.

For the Devotionist, private prayer is predicated upon all that we have said of the privileges bestowed to those who believe fully—namely, the unconditional direct access to our loving Heavenly Father. The Devotionist knows that this privilege is only because of our Lord and is in effect a Positional Blessing for those who through faith in Jesus are part of the household of God. This position presents to the believer unheard of, and utterly unmerited, privileges of not only having direct access to God but having Jesus Himself acting as mediator between us and God the Father (1 Tim 2:5). One could spend a lifetime just dwelling on the awesomeness of these two concepts that we take too quickly for granted or never fully digest and dwell upon. Imagine that we can come boldly before the very Creator of the universe. Imagine that: He who is the embodiment of divinity actually intercedes on our behalf. And this is only because it is believers alone who are indwelled by God Himself—and hence, it is the Spirit within us, crying out to the Father, who yearns for us to communicate with the Father through the Son. This picture is perhaps too awesome to hold onto, and yet scripturally this is true.

Understanding Personal Prayer—A Biblical Analysis

Expectation of Being Heard

First of all, there is a difference in what we can describe as "personal devotional prayer" and "prayers of need" or "personal circumstantial prayer," both of which are absolutely valid and indeed vital for our honesty with God. We see the difference played out continually in the psalms themselves (frequently within the same psalm) where the psalmist calls upon God regarding particular issues and circumstances while also speaking with/to God in deeply emotional and spiritual ways reflecting the absolute concerns of His heart. By definition, personal circumstances are just that—private and particular to the individual praying. God, of course, is interested and concerned with all that goes on in our lives, and we are called to pray about all things and to pray continually. However, I would contend that private devotionist prayer can be defined as being where the individual believer engages with God directly and personally to enrich our spiritual growth and nurture our own souls through direct, intimate, and familial communication with our beloved Savior and holy Heavenly Father.

The starting point in addressing the question "Why pray?" is that we are called to pray. If our God was an impersonal God who simply calls on us to pray with little or no expectation that our prayers will be answered, then the passages in the Bible that instruct us to pray would become meaningless at best and deceptive at worst. Conversely, thankfully throughout the entire Bible, our God is presented as a personable God who indeed interacts positively and actively with and on behalf of His people. For example, using integrated theology, it would be impossible to make such statements as "God is love" without Him interacting with His people. Prayer, in a nutshell, is human communication with the divine. That the divine Creator of the universe wants us to interact with Him in such an expectant and personal manner should be a matter of complete awe and wonder for all who are privileged to engage in such an activity. Sadly, though, this sense of privilege is too often diminished through our own apathy and indifference. Our attitude to prayer becomes then a reflection on how we view ourselves, our relationship with God, and how much we need and trust Him. Our God is not capricious, and He always has our best interests at heart. Even when we go through trials and tribulations, He is there for us and always will be.

It seems utterly obvious to state that one of the reasons that we engage in private prayer is that we do so with the expectation that God will hear us and answer in a manner to His choosing. To obtain a proper perspective on this subject, we must consider the total teaching of Scripture, not just one or two verses. Occasionally we may discover a promise in the Bible that appears to guarantee unconditionally that God will answer any prayer we may offer:

> Ask, and it will be given to you; seek, and you will find; knock, and it will be opened to you. For everyone who asks receives, and he who seeks finds, and to him who knocks it will be opened. Or what man is there among you who, if his son asks for bread, will give him a stone? Or if he asks for a fish, will he give him a serpent? If you then, being evil, know how to give good gifts to your children, how much more will your Father who is in heaven give good things to those who ask Him! (Matt 7:7–11)

> And whatever you ask in My name, that I will do, that the Father may be glorified in the Son. If you ask anything in My name, I will do it. (John 14:13–14)

Invariably these promises have stated or assumed conditions that become clear when we understand the whole teaching of Scripture on the subject, and indeed such statements should never be taken out of their context, for to do so leads to many and dangerous errors of teaching and doctrine—frequently culminating in hemorrhaged hope and fractured faith.

Nevertheless, it is still too easy to dismiss them in such a way. They are biblical promises and are to be treated as such; and yet, at the same time, they must be understood in the context of the whole of biblical teaching.

Asking in the Will of God

The point, though, is whether what we are asking for is within the will of God for us. That God will give us what we ask for is clearly stated, and it is clearly in His nature never to withhold blessings from us when we ask—see Matt 7:7–11 and Luke 11:5–13. But the point for the Devotionist here is whether we are firstly able to identify what it is we are to ask for, and secondly, do we actually take responsibility for this and actually ask for them? For as the apostle James says, "Yet you do not have because you do not ask" (Jas 4:2b).

Identifying what it is that God really wants to bless us with is probably a suitable starting point in the consideration of private prayer. We do not have many of God's blessings simply because we fail to ask Him for them. Our spiritual welfare and condition are important to God, but Scripture is clear that it is our own responsibility to nurture our souls, to draw close to God, and to ask in faith for receipt in abundance of the spiritual blessings that are already in fact ours in heavenly places (Eph 1:3). And yet, at the same time, we need to be watchful of the manner in which we ask Him:

> You ask and do not receive, because you ask amiss, that you may spend it on your pleasures. (Jas 4:3)

Clearly, then, asking for what is "amiss" would include prayers for self-gain rather than that which would be important to God—namely, our spiritual growth. As we have said earlier, though, this does not mean that God is not interested in our personal circumstances (and those for whom we pray also), but as He has full and complete omniscience, He knows that frequently the core of our need is a spiritual one that manifests in our limited understanding as a physical or circumstantial one. So, what is it then that would not constitute being "amiss" in God's eyes? The answer, as always, is consistent throughout Scripture:

> For this reason we also, since the day we heard it, do not cease to pray for you, and to ask that you may be filled with the knowledge of His will in all wisdom and spiritual understanding; that

> you may walk worthy of the Lord, fully pleasing Him, being fruitful in every good work and increasing in the knowledge of God; strengthened with all might, according to His glorious power, for all patience and longsuffering with joy; giving thanks to the Father who has qualified us to be partakers of the inheritance of the saints in the light. (Col 1:9–14)

It is God's will that we should appropriate these spiritual blessings both for ourselves and for other believers—that is, we are to pray for each other that we should appropriate them to the utmost, both as individuals and corporately.

> If any of you lacks wisdom, let him ask of God, who gives to all liberally and without reproach, and it will be given to him. But let him ask in faith, with no doubting, for he who doubts is like a wave of the sea driven and tossed by the wind. For let not that man suppose that he will receive anything from the Lord; He is a double-minded man, unstable in all his ways. (Jas 1:5–8)

Praying for the Will, and in the Will, of God

The basic principle of private devotional prayer is praying for the will of God to be perfected in ourselves. The will of God is, as we have said multiple times already, quite simply our sanctification (1 Thess 4:3).

Like all doctrine, we must approach prayer from God's perspective, not just our own. Hence, one of the fundamental and more difficult issues to contend with in prayer is God's will. He is sovereign and He will not give His glory to another—that we know. Prayer, then, is always to be viewed in this context, for God will never contravene these two principles, and so our method, manner, and expectations of prayer must be conditioned by this correct biblical understanding of the nature of God.

Praying in God's will means praying in harmony with the promises, plans, and prophecies that God has given. When we pray for God to fulfill His promises, we can be confident that we are praying in God's will. The will of God for us believers which the Holy Spirit describes through Paul is set out in Rom 12:1–21. This passage is a perfect example of the Christian "walk" with God—a walk that is utterly unachievable without the guidance and help of the Holy Spirit. That we are unable to even remotely attain these requirements without the Holy Spirit should inspire us all the more to pray for them both for ourselves and for others. If there were ever one thing that we would do well to pray for—whether for ourselves or for others—it would be that the Lord should grant us the ability to understand and do His will.

> Epaphras, who is one of you, a bondservant of Christ, greets you, always laboring fervently for you in prayers, that you may stand perfect and complete in all the will of God. (Col 4:12)

The will of God must be strived for by all believers, but we are only given this desire and the ability to strive on account of having the Holy Spirit within us. Paul's prayer for believers was that they be filled with a knowledge of God's will (Col 1:9, 4:12). And he admonished foolish believers who made gaining an understanding of God's will their chief aim. And in these passages, we see a glimpse of that will. It might seem a tautology, but it is true to say that it is God's will that we know and understand His will. Thus, the only way that we can undertake this is to actually pray that God would do this for us—this is where we know that He would never hold back His good gifts. It is His will that we ask for them for they have already been made available to us as a by-product of the bestowment of our Positional Identity and the Positional Blessings. In addition, as we who believe are indwelled by the Holy Spirit, who is the Counselor and Guide, so He will always point us to Jesus, who alone is wise (Jude 25). It is clearly God's responsibility to carry this out to its logical completion (if it were otherwise, it would give us the glory and not God, who as we know will not give His glory to another):

> Now may the God of peace who brought up our Lord Jesus from the dead, that great Shepherd of the sheep, through the blood of the everlasting covenant, make you complete in every good work to do His will, working in you what is well pleasing in His sight, through Jesus Christ, to whom be glory forever and ever. Amen. (Heb 13:20-21)

So as regards the individual and the corporate church, we know that when we pray in God's will, we are pushing on open doors, so to speak. We know that it is God's will that all come to a knowledge of Him. We know that it is God who will teach us His ways. We know that only through the help of the Holy Spirit can we truly acquire the fruit of the Spirit, but it is our responsibility to ask for them and to keep asking for them. We know that God hears our prayers, as it is His will that we have this fruit. By extension one can apply this to the whole church. It is a sad fact that most of the errors ever taught are as a direct result of people not knowing or appreciating the will of God and having a knowledge of Him and His purposes. Our prayers, therefore, should be for all believers, both individually and corporately, to cry out for discernment (which is nothing less than an appreciation of the knowledge of God). Consider these words:

> Yes, if you cry out for discernment,
> And lift up your voice for understanding,
> If you seek her as silver,
> And search for her as for hidden treasures;
> Then you will understand the fear of the Lord,
> And find the knowledge of God.
> (Prov 2:3–5)

Along with discernment comes an appreciation of the plans and purposes of God. God has set a plan, and He will not deviate from it—such is the certainty of the word of God. Thus, in terms of prayer this frequently is where confusion arises as to what is the will of God for our personal and private prayers—our devotional prayers, in other words. Certainly, there is a time and place for intercessory prayer on behalf of nation and people, but this should not form part of what is considered as devotional prayer, which has an entirely different purpose than intercession. Intercession is an extremely valid form of petitioning the Lord about specific sets of circumstances, which one can, of course, undertake personally and privately, but as I said, devotional prayer is different for it is private dialogue between the child of God and God about matters which are personal and relational, rather than abstract or interventionist.

Personal Circumstantial Prayer

It would be a strange kind of loving relationship if we were told that God is not interested in our personal lives, in our struggles and infirmities. Somehow, we seem to swing from not believing in His interest to only praying about these personal issues. God would be a poor role model for us if He was utterly uninterested in our very human lives, our concerns, health issues, financial issues, family issues, and the like. But the truth of it is that He is interested and very concerned—and He wants us to come to Him with these issues and concerns personally, privately, and as children, no matter our age. Not to do so is, in fact, an affront to His divine characteristics and the reality of God in our lives.

It is in this area that we are most likely to feel frustrated before God as we seek solace for seemingly unanswered prayer. While we think mainly and naturally in terms of circumstantial prayer when we think of unanswered prayer (health, financial issues, concern for loved ones, and the like), the same is also true of aspects of devotional prayer. This might include aspects of faith, doubt, characteristics contrary to the fruit of the Spirit, and other areas where we need to confess and implore the Lord to deal with our failings.

Before we talk about personal devotionist prayer, I think we should openly discuss what for many is this thorny issue of unanswered prayer. Quite simply, why does God grant some prayers and not others? Sometimes it seems that God is completely silent and uninterested. If this is true of the everyday Christian, we can take comfort perhaps from the fact that it has ever been thus, and every believer has always struggled with this issue, even the greatest of prophets such as Jeremiah:

> Even when I cry and shout,
> He shuts out my prayer.
> (Lam 3:8)

Many people share Job's frustration of crying to God, day and night, but receiving no reply:

> Oh, that I had one to hear me!
> Here is my mark.
> Oh, that the Almighty would answer me,
> That my Prosecutor had written a book!
> (Job 31:35)

However, as Christians we know that we now have just what Job was asking for—Jesus emphatically is our intercessor (Heb 7:25)! And even more than that, we have the Holy Spirit who is able to express our prayers even when we are not. Without wanting to seem trite or insensitive, biblically we are shown that there are numerous things that God will wish to teach us as we ponder the paradox of seemingly unanswered prayer and His promises to give us what we ask for. The strength that is available to us through our Positional Identity means that we can draw deeply from the well of His unwavering love for us as we seek greater patience and understanding of His ways, and take comfort in the certainty that we will be shown and given the grace to learn from what His purposes are during these times of waiting. These are the character-strengthening actions that conform us to Him; they are perhaps the lessons we all need to learn, especially in this age of expected immediate gratification.

Personal Devotional Prayer—The Way of the Devotionist

> And when you pray, you shall not be like the hypocrites. For they love to pray standing in the synagogues and on the corners of the streets, that they may be seen by men. Assuredly, I say to you, they have their reward. But you, when you pray, go into your room, and when you have shut your door, pray to your Father who is in the secret place; and your Father who sees in secret will reward you openly. And when you pray, do not use vain repetitions as the heathen do. For they think that they will be heard for their many words. (Matt 6:5–7)

The Private Room

The context of what Jesus says in Matt 6:6 above is one of countering the false claims of the religious elite, the Pharisees, who were known for their outward and public displays of piety—or what we can describe as "performed piety" and "self-holiness"—that is, projected rather than genuine. We would describe them today as being legalistic: preferring form over substance, display over private practice. But note the references to the word "you" in the passage. Jesus is of course referring to those who were in the crowd during the Sermon on the Mount. This was His first public appearance and was most likely attended by very ordinary people: the poor, the downtrodden, the sick, and the needy. Note then how He doesn't differentiate and how He doesn't segregate according to religious piety or understanding—it is a ubiquitous "you" to all who were there: men, women, and children. Note, too, how He speaks with them not only with absolute authority but also with absolute confidence in, and expectation of, the people there. He expects them to pray, and He expects of them that they will heed His words and act on them. His confidence also rests in the results of their prayer in the private room. These words must have been regarded as totally unprecedented and were undoubtedly seen to be as hugely liberating and revolutionary as they were. Note that His directive is not to go to synagogue or temple to pray (even on one's own), but He is directing the audience toward taking responsibility for their personal relationship with God, thereby instigating even the start of a deeper, more private, and more honest means of devotion than had been previously spoken of. Bear in mind, at the time whole families would have lived together in the same house; it would have been cramped and completely non-private. Therefore, the call of Jesus here is to make the effort, to find the place, and to make the time to be alone with God in a place where there are no distractions and no peer pressure to perform, as is true of most corporate or even family settings. This is not just a call to private prayer but to genuine private prayer that produces real spiritual fruit and a soul that is nurtured. It's a love expression, not a performance.

In our contemporary world that is all so busy, crowded, and pressured, how do we accommodate such times of prayer into our schedule, whether in terms of timing or physical, practical location? Obviously, everyone's situation is different, and we will speak of the concept of the "private place of the heart" in a later section, but for now the private place of prayer for all has to be sought—even if it is simply one's bedroom, or occurring at times when others are not around. Is there a perfect time for this? The answer is of course no, as God is no more attentive at one particular time of day or night than another. How regular does it have to be? I think that this is a genuine case of quality over quantity. All Jesus said was "when you pray," not how frequently. Private prayer needs to be genuine, non-legalistic, and should be entered into with a feeling of eagerness and warmth, and so should be something that we learn to want to create space and time for. In other words, it should become precious to us and valued by us enough to make it a valued and precious experience to be repeated frequently.

There are, though, ramifications for the believer if we spend too long away from private prayer—I would say even more so than if we just spend time away from reading Scripture, for we need the personal and intimate contact with our God for our souls to become nourished. As we have discussed in detail earlier, our souls can become downcast, and we need to find our way back into direct fellowship with God to restore this. This, when combined with the fact that God's concern is always for our spiritual growth and health and that Jesus's expectation is that we would and should have times of private prayer, means that we must conclude that private prayer is essential to both this growth and our soul's nourishment.

Preparing to Approach God Through Prayer

How do we prepare to approach God through prayer in a Positional Devotionist way? Perhaps the best way to discuss this is in terms of what we can describe as "reverential intimacy." The mind and heart of the Devotionist are attuned to the attributes of God, encompassed in His holiness and sovereignty, and this particularly applies to how we approach the Lord in prayer. While it is true that we who believe can enter boldly before Him, this has to be tempered with an understanding of whom it is we are approaching and how He is to be approached. We need to garner and foster a true perspective on with whom it is we are dealing, to whom it is we are talking, and of whom it is we are perhaps questioning, enquiring, or resting in the presence of:

> Moreover the LORD answered Job, and said:
> "Shall the one who contends with the Almighty correct Him?
> He who rebukes God, let him answer it."
> Then Job answered the LORD and said:
> "Behold, I am vile;
> What shall I answer You?
> I lay my hand over my mouth.
> Once I have spoken, but I will not answer;
> Yes, twice, but I will proceed no further."
> (Job 40:1–5)

But it is also, as we have said numerous times but needs always to be stressed, because of Jesus that we are able to come boldly to the throne of grace, and it is because of Jesus that we are able to enjoy this full access for we who believe are already fully forgiven, fully indwelled by the Holy Spirit, fully at peace with God, and fully members of the household of God. This is the difference between the believer now and the righteous in the Old Testament, like Job in the passage above. For Job, while he was most definitely righteous in the eyes of God, he was not indwelled by the Holy Spirit as believers are now. Believers now do not need to consider themselves to be "vile" as Job did because the Lord does not see us that way any longer. Now our righteousness is based on our belief in Jesus, and through that the indwelling of the Holy Spirit—meaning that when God looks upon us now, He sees our belief in His Son and the Holy Spirit within us. This is why we are already clothed in righteousness and already have every spiritual blessing in heavenly places. It is important that we as believers acknowledge and really appropriate this, for to do otherwise is an affront to God's gracious provision to us and to the efficacious power of Jesus's sacrifice for us.

The Lord is our Father, and it because of this that our spirits as children of God call out to Him "Abba, Father," which means that we are entitled to this sense of familial intimacy with Him—in the way children are with their parents:

> For you did not receive the spirit of bondage again to fear, but you received the Spirit of adoption by whom we cry out, "Abba, Father." (Rom 8:15)

> And because you are sons, God has sent forth the Spirit of His Son into your hearts, crying out, "Abba, Father." (Gal 4:6)

This sense of familial intimacy ascribes to the relationship trust, confidence, and comfort. This does not mean, however, that we are not to see our sin as repugnant in God's eyes and in need of addressing if we are to be restored to full fellowship with Him. This again makes us lean toward regular periods of private prayer, as we need to be continually cleaned for the dust of sin to be washed away. But as with actual dust, this sin does not penetrate but needs to be brushed away and off of our righteous clothes so that the Lord will once again see us as He wishes to. This means that we are to continually come before Him to ask for forgiveness for our sins, while always thanking Him for having dealt with sin and death at the cross.

The clear implication of Scripture, and this is as true for the believer as for the Old Testament righteous, is that the longer we leave off addressing our sins, the more weighted down by them we become—our light dulls, so to speak, and we open ourselves up to guilt and self-condemnation, which only leads to further distancing from God. This is why sins need to be dealt with regularly and quickly, simply as part of our pattern of relationship and devotion to the Lord; and as we said before, the Lord has always been faithful to forgive:

> When I kept silent, my bones grew old
> Through my groaning all the day long.
> For day and night Your hand was heavy upon me;
> My vitality was turned into the drought of summer. Selah.
> I acknowledged my sin to You,
> And my iniquity I have not hidden.
> I said, "I will confess my transgressions to the LORD,"
> And You forgave the iniquity of my sin. Selah.
> (Ps 32:3–5)

This brings us fully then to how we approach the Lord in private prayer—or rather how we prepare ourselves for what is a very serious and precious exercise. Reverentially speaking, as we said, while we have full unlimited access to God, times of specific private prayer with our divine Lord should involve a sense of what can be described as "formal informality." Are there processes we need to go through as we seek to come before the Lord in private prayer? And if there are, then doesn't this preclude such activity becoming regular for normal Christians leading and juggling busy lives, which is the very point we started with at the very beginning of this book?

It is perhaps, then, at this point that I will start to edge carefully into what some might see as being slightly controversial, but in my defense, I think many of the Devotionists of old would stand alongside me. I would suggest that given the importance given to times of private prayer by Jesus Himself and to continual prayer by the apostle Paul, this should take precedence over even times of personal reading of Scripture. This in no way invalidates anything that we said before about the private reading, but all I would say is that if the will of God is our sanctification and if the objective of devotion is to become the people of God that He wants us to be, then times of private prayer should be sought and planned for above all else. As we said before, the Devotionist will actually go beyond this, but whether it's a few minutes grabbed at either end of the day or times set aside for quality sessions, the heart of the Devotionist should be to seek these times and create them. Again, we come back as always to the will of God, for as such times of intimacy are part and parcel of what He's looking for, then if we do not, in and of ourselves, feel the need to seek them and do not feel we have this heart, then all we need to do is ask. To ask God for a heart of personal and private prayer is the very starting point in this journey. That we have to ask is true, but the act of asking is in itself prompted by the Holy Spirit. One could argue that it has to be, in fact, for as with all things with God, our private prayer must be to His glory, and so the very desire for it must come from Him.

Returning to the point of access and preparation, while it is perfectly true for the believer that we are able to come boldly before the throne of grace to approach God in prayer with confidence, we are perhaps guilty of not paying attention to the manner in which we begin the approach, as it were. This is of course implicit in the very reason for the steps approaching the temple in Jerusalem—the steps signifying a transition from the worldly to the divine presence and enabling a period of reflection as the faithful ascended them, to transition the mind and heart in both anticipation and preparation. This is of course why Jesus said what He did in Matt 5:23–24 about how when we bring our gift to the alter, if we have something that we need to address with another, we are to seek reconciliation first and then return. This, of course, is a picture of both the requirement for self-examination prior to entering into God's presence and representative of what we termed previously as the single interconnected commandment; for to Jesus it is as doxologically and theologically erroneous to seek to enter the presence of God while in conflict with our brethren as it is to seek restoration with others without addressing one's own standing, status, and heart-attitude with God first. To come to this realization requires a time of reflection on behalf of the believer in preparation of entering into the presence of God. It is true that we might frequently think that we do not know what to pray about or how to pray, and hence this period of reflection (however brief) is quite simply the place to start and, if need be, to finish. To offer this much to God can be sufficient and is immensely restorative to our spiritual health.

As we prepare our hearts to enter into His presence, we do so in like manner to entering into the temple, where the holy of holies was. We are entering into a space where we are expecting to meet with the divine, and therefore there are matters of spiritual health and attitude that we need to address within ourselves in consideration of this:

- The Washing of Feet

The Devotionist knows that while we have been forgiven and have been washed and cleansed by the Holy Spirit, yet we do pick up the dust of sin that needs to be brushed away. We know that as we confess our sin, God is faithful to forgive us (1 John 1:9), but this does not mean that we can afford to be complacent about it and about God how views sin. Thus we need, as part of our preparation process, to reflect upon our attitudes and actions, to examine ourselves honestly so that we can come before Him humbly to confess our sins as our failings before Him alone (Ps 51:4).

- Peace with God

By definition, all believers are indwelled by the Holy Spirit (Rom 8:9) and therefore have peace with God (Rom 5:1). The preparation of attitude then for the believer when entering into a time of private prayer is that our hearts must reflect that we not only have peace with God, but through our time of preparation for prayer, we must "let the peace of God rule in our hearts" (Col 3:15). The emphasis here, as we said before, is not only on the word "let" but in this case the word "rule." For this peace must dictate our attitudes and approach to prayer and communication with God. But to appropriate this we need to fully absorb the implications of not only whom it is that we have peace with but also why we are able to have peace with Him. Among all humanity, we alone as believers are able to enjoy the peace of God because we have peace with God, which is only ours because of the sacrifice of Christ and because it is God's sovereign desire and will that we let the Holy Spirit conform us ever more to the image of his Son, Jesus Christ. Hence, we must be prepared to fully accept this and to settle once and for all in our hearts that it is only because of our belief in Jesus that there is no condemnation for us, and that therefore we can approach God in full acceptance of His grace and mercy toward us. The only reasonable response to which, as we draw into His presence, is of course praise and thanksgiving.

The Precious Gates of Devotion in Private Prayer

The function of what we have been terming the Precious Gates of Devotion is merely to endeavor to encapsulate the heart attitude of the Devotionist as the believer prepares to enter into the presence of God through various acts of private devotional practice, whether in reading Scripture or through private prayer. As we have said before, they are considered precious both by God and by the believer on account of the very fact that they lead us into His presence and prepare the believer for the beauty that is set before us.

How do we apply the Gates of Devotion to our times of private prayer? We can use them as a means of entry into the presence of God as we examine ourselves through them and ask the Holy Spirit to help us and to guide us in our efforts to become more Christlike. We have many barometers in Scripture that we have been given against which we can measure and examine ourselves—the fruit of the Spirit, the mind of Christ, our walk with God—but while it is true that we are called to ever improve upon these, our position in Christ means that we are not to look upon these in a self-recriminatory way. This is vital to comprehend and is perhaps one of the most radical aspects of truly grasping not only our position but our identity in Christ. Our spiritual improvement will in no way make us more loved by God than we already are, it will in no way cause Him to set us apart from others in His estimation of us, and it will in no way affect our eternal salvation or make it conditional in anyway. No, we are to examine ourselves and to want to better ourselves so that our love for God increases and so that we can represent Him better to those around us. In other words, we engage in all devotion because we love Him and because we want to love Him more—and because we love Him, we want to be in the beauty of His presence.

Gate 1: The Gate of the Consideration of the Divine

To enter the presence of God through the consideration of the divine in prayer is a fundamental prerequisite in biblical terms. We see this in the psalms, the prayers of the Old Testament saints, and of course in the Lord's Prayer. One only needs to look at such magisterial passages as 1 Chr 16, 1 Chr 29:10–13, and Dan 2:20–23 to appreciate this. Of course, in prayer such passages could simply be repeated, verbally, back to God as a starting point in prayer that sets the heart and mind into a position of meekness and humility before Him. As we have discussed previously, the heart and mind of the Devotionist is already attuned to the Lord's complete majesty; indeed, it is essential in private prayer that even though we can be intimate and familiar, we should also be humble and reverential.

Consideration of His Works

The Devotionist is, or becomes, acutely aware that to dwell upon and give thanks for the works of God is an intrinsic part of entering into the presence of God through private prayer. His works of salvation, Positional Blessings, and sanctification are those that are most directly relevant, of course, to the individual's personal relationship with God and therefore in the nurturing function of private prayer. In addition, it is through the very nature of the privacy of this engagement that believers can display directly to God their deepest understanding of the privileges that have been bestowed upon them and express through prayer the most gratitude for them. It is, of course, also through prayer that we as believers can focus on these blessings to enhance our relationship with God, to seek greater understanding and appropriation of them so that we

> may walk worthy of the Lord, fully pleasing Him, being fruitful in every good work and increasing in the knowledge of God;

strengthened with all might, according to His glorious power, for all patience and longsuffering with joy; giving thanks to the Father who has qualified us to be partakers of the inheritance of the saints in the light. (Col 1:12–14)

Metanarrative Works: The Way

The fact that God sent Himself in the form of His only Son to die for us should never be forgotten or become secondary in our thoughts. For to God, this is the most important thing, and our belief, appreciation, and eternal gratitude to Him for this should reflect every aspect of our relationship with Him, particularly so in our prayer life. It is only because of Jesus's perfect, once only, sacrifice that we are allowed and entitled to enter into the Father's presence so freely. This fact and this miracle that God has chosen to bless us all with is cause for endless praise, adoration, and wonder at the magnitude of love that our God not only has but is. This is what and who our God is, and He is to be greatly praised and resolutely adored by all of us who believe in Him—this then is now our function, our responsibility, and our privilege.

Positional Works: The Truth

Through His perfect work on the cross and His subsequent resurrection and ascension, Jesus demonstrated for all time His authority over all creation, including all the laws of science, time, matter, and energy. Through the exercise of such authority, He demonstrated that as the Creator, He has the authority to work outside of creation's physical constraints—such demonstration of course means that He has the authority and ability to undertake acts of re-creation too, whether that's in the rebirth of every believer or the future reconfiguration of the resurrection of each believer in the form of their glorified bodies, and indeed ultimately the authority to draw all things unto Himself and to recreate the literal new heavens and new earth. What this authority demonstrates for us in our private prayer is that as the Author and Finisher of our faith, He has the right and the power to decide what is truth and what is true for those for whom He died. Thus, this is the way we must—not should, but must—regard the Positional Blessings that came at such a price and have been bestowed by the Father upon us, not because of anything we have done but because of

His infinite love that He has for His Son. Our blessings in this life are a mere trifle compared to that love—mere crumbs on the altar of holiness compared with that which the Father has for the Son—and to that with which we will partake of once we are eventually joined to them in unity (1 Cor 2:9).

Transforming Works: The Life

When we fully comprehend what it is that God wants from us as believers and truly realize that all that is required of us is to love Him completely, then this transforms our private prayer life into one of taking responsibility to engage with God directly through the Holy Spirit, to appropriate more of what has been given to us already, and to seek His assistance in that which He wants from us—namely, the transformation of our minds and the further alignment of our hearts, summarized in the term "sanctification."

It is through and within our times of private prayer, therefore, that we can seek to thank the Lord for what we already have and to implore Him to teach us His ways and to transform our minds so that we can abide with Him. In humility, meekness before God, and through private prayer, we can search for this sanctification by asking the Holy Spirit to help us with the growth of His fruit in our lives and characters and to direct us ever closer to Jesus.

Reflective Moments Between Gates

Reverence with God is the requisite of all prayer—we must be mindful and respectful of whom it is we approach in prayer. He is God, after all, and our approach to Him must be based on this sense of holiness and awe. But this is not the end point either, for we are able to appropriate all else He has for us purely because He is able and precisely because He is God, and as such the knowledge of the efficacious attributes produces trust, comfort, and love, for when we pray we know that it is His lovingkindness that sustains us.

> The Lord will command His lovingkindness in the daytime,
> And in the night His song shall be with me—
> A prayer to the God of my life.
> (Ps 42:8)

Gate 2: The Gate of Transcendent Trust

> Now to Him who is able to do exceedingly abundantly above all that we ask or think, according to the power that works in us, to Him be glory in the church by Christ Jesus to all generations, forever and ever. Amen. (Eph 3:20–21)

If God were not able to hear or answer our prayers, then to paraphrase the words of the apostle Paul in a different context, we of all people should be most pitied. But He is and He does. And it is because of this, when combined with His absolute sovereignty over all things past, present, and future, that we are able to trust Him in our times of personal engagement with Him. We can trust Him with our most intimate challenges, concerns, and fears, as well as sharing our joys and our need for comfort. Intimacy in prayer can only come from this position of trust—a trust founded upon the very traits and characteristics of God: there is no darkness in Him; He will never let us down; and He alone is the only true constant for He alone has the power and the authority over all things and knows all things and yet loves us with a fervor that defies all understanding and reason.

Reflective Moments Between Gates

> My mouth shall tell of Your righteousness
> And Your salvation all the day,
> For I do not know their limits.
> (Ps 71:15)

Through private prayer, we transform our trust into fervent faith in God as we both absorb what the Scriptures say and also experience the reality of trust in His loving-kindness. As we take the words of the Devotionists in the psalms and elsewhere and pray through them, we immerse ourselves within them in prayer for ourselves and others. When we read them, we can speak and pray them over ourselves and pray that we can appropriate the heart that lies behind them—the heart of the Devotionist who knows that these are not merely true, but can be almost seen as divine ordinations for the believer to hold onto and live life abundantly through, in peace with God:

- Trust in His loving-kindness (Pss 25:6, 20; 26:3; 36:7; 40:11)
- Trust in His ability to see us through in times of trouble (Pss 57:1, 77:2)
- Trust Him in times of affliction (Pss 77:2, 116:4)
- Trust Him to comfort us in all our anxieties (Pss 17:19, 94:19)

Gate 3: The Gate of Familial Confidence

Intimacy, tempered with respectful reverence, should be at the very core of private prayer. Confidence in private prayer is never shouted or overdramatic. While our certainty in both God's abilities and our own blessings means that we are able to implore and petition the Lord within our private prayers, with fervor as befitting our heart and soul's need, this need not ever be a performance. Hence, of course, the instruction to do so in a private, secluded place where one is literally not seen so that performance is unnecessary, but also where one can be open, frank, and intimate with God without feeling inhibited by onlookers. Familial confidence is based on God, of course, but in prayer it is also based on our own inhibitions and reticence to be exposed as wanting, needing, insecure, and uncertain. The honest display of these traits is countercultural in some ways, but at the same time private prayer must not become the Christian version of therapy sessions. Overfamiliarity and being "pally-pally" when it comes to engaging with God is not biblical, but the confidence that comes from understanding our position in Christ and the Positional Blessings that have been bestowed certainly is. The confidence we have as His beloved children comes from the sure and certain knowledge that we will not be condemned for our shortfalls, that we have peace with God, and that there is nothing that can separate us from His love. From these rocks are hewn the foundations of our intimacy and familial confidence that entitle us to be in His presence and regarded by Him as being sanctified, forgiven, washed, and cleansed of all our iniquities by the precious blood of Jesus.

Thus, in prayer we can reflect and remember His greatness toward us whom He blesses with such intimacy and familiarity that is ours by entitlement through the blood of Christ alone. This is our monument to Him in prayer.

> This I recall to my mind,
> Therefore I have hope.
> Through the Lord's mercies we are not consumed,
> Because His compassions fail not.
> They are new every morning;
> Great is Your faithfulness.
> "The Lord is my portion," says my soul,
> "Therefore I hope in Him!"
> The Lord is good to those who wait for Him,
> To the soul who seeks Him.
> (Lam 3:21–25)

Waiting in the Outer Courts of His Presence

Through our times of private prayer, God searches us, refines us, and shapes us. This can be a wonderful, joyful experience that is often accompanied by discomfort as the divine meets the mortal, as Spirit meets the flesh, and as perfection meets imperfection. When looked at like this, of course, at times it may prove uncomfortable—and yet, He is always gentle and kind with believers. If admonished and disciplined, it is always in love for He only does so with those whom He loves (Prov 3:11–12).

More often than not, though, we experience times of waiting and seeming delay in our prayers. So-called bolts of lightning are extremely rare, and more likely are the lessons that God wishes us to learn through patience and delay. This is in no way meant to seem trite, for the delay in answered prayer can be extremely saddening and even faith depleting. I, myself, have been writing this whole book during one of the most stressful periods of my entire life, when everything in every direction seems to be imploding with no visible letup in sight. If I am to be honest, unanswered prayers regarding so many things have undoubtedly been debilitating at times, for the solutions would be so easy for God to implement at the drop of a hat, so to speak. And yet, here I am reflecting on what God is, or might be, teaching me through this—and waiting, nevertheless.

For the Christian it should come as no surprise that one of the fruits of the Holy Spirit is patience. These fruits are personal and behavioral fruits. Thus, when praying we should do so in such a way that demonstrates that not only have we appropriated our Positional Blessings but that we also understand that we need to exercise the fruit of the Spirit in all circumstances, let alone specifically when we are addressing God

Himself. As always, part of appropriating our Positional Blessings means that we also know that when we feel deficient in these fruits, then when we ask for them from the Father, He will in no way hold them back. But when we pray for them, we know we must pray in faith without doubt:

> Therefore I will look to the LORD;
> I will wait for the God of my salvation;
> My God will hear me.
> (Mic 7:7)

> Wait on the LORD;
> Be of good courage,
> And He shall strengthen your heart;
> Wait, I say, on the LORD!
> (Ps 27:14)

> Then He spoke a parable to them, that men always ought to pray and not lose heart. (Luke 18:1)

Biblically speaking, along with patience must come perseverance, but our patience must also be rooted in the confidence that God will hear and will act. Our response is one rooted and grounded upon our understanding of the nature of God, who is to be blessed for such mercy and grace that has always been shown to those whose hearts are aligned with his:

> For I said in my haste,
> "I am cut off from before Your eyes";
> Nevertheless You heard the voice of my supplications
> When I cried out to You.
> (Ps 31:22)

> I love the Lord, because He has heard
> My voice and my supplications.
> (Ps 116:1)

Will God answer our prayers if we pray with more urgency? Don't such actions seem contrary to His nature in that our behavior is seen to compel Him into action? The answer is in what God sees within us being manifested openly. Fervency can come from a genuine heart that is aligned with God's will in a particular circumstance, such as the desire for God to heal the believer of a certain sin or characteristic that keeps occurring. This fervency then comes from a heart that genuinely wants to change in accordance with God's desires. It is an anguish that is definitely prompted by the Holy Spirit within the believer and hence is an acceptable form of offering to God.

> Lord, You have heard the desire of the humble;
> You will prepare their heart;
> You will cause Your ear to hear.
> (Ps 10:17–18)

Where we come into the realm of personal circumstances, the genuineness might still be there, but the alignment of God's will might not, in which case we potentially fall foul of James's point about praying "amiss," mentioned earlier in Jas 4:3. As members of His household, we have the right, as it were, to be bold in our prayers and petitions. This is part of our familial standing with God and the confidence we have in our salvation and the Positional Blessings gifted to us.

> As for me, I will call upon God,
> And the Lord shall save me.
> Evening and morning and at noon I will pray, and cry aloud,
> And He shall hear my voice.
> (Ps 55:16–17)

> Give ear to my words, O Lord,
> Consider my meditation.
> Give heed to the voice of my cry,
> My King and my God,
> For to You I will pray.
> My voice You shall hear in the morning, O Lord;
> In the morning I will direct it to You,
> And I will look up.
> (Ps 5:1–4)

This "right" even comes down to how we are able to implore God fervently and boldly, without fear of reprisal or reprimand as we make our petitions known in the strongest terms:

> Hear the voice of my supplications
> When I cry to You,
> When I lift up my hands toward Your holy sanctuary.
> (Ps 28:2)

> Hear, O Lord, when I cry with my voice!
> Have mercy also upon me, and answer me.
> When You said, "Seek My face,"

My heart said to You, "Your face, Lord, I will seek."
Do not hide Your face from me;
Do not turn Your servant away in anger;
You have been my help;
Do not leave me nor forsake me,
O God of my salvation.
(Ps 27:7–11)

Therefore I will not restrain my mouth;
I will speak in the anguish of my spirit;
I will complain in the bitterness of my soul.
(Job 7:11)

In short, we must recognize our own helplessness and therefore pray persistently, humbly, fervently, and with boldness—consider, for example, the anguish that Job expresses in Job 7:11–21, and reflect where such honesty with God comes from. We must trust in God's ability to provide our needs, obey Him by understanding His will, and sincerely entreat Him in faith. Then when He does grant the request, we appreciate the answer all the more.

Blessed be the Lord,
Because He has heard the voice of my supplications!
The Lord is my strength and my shield;
My heart trusted in Him, and I am helped;
Therefore my heart greatly rejoices,
And with my song I will praise Him.
(Ps 28:6–7)

I waited patiently for the Lord;
And He inclined to me,
And heard my cry.
(Ps 40:1)

I love the Lord, because He has heard
My voice and my supplications.
Because He has inclined His ear to me,
Therefore I will call upon Him as long as I live.
(Ps 116:1–2)

How Then Shall We Pray?

This question has probably been asked of every single Christian since the time of Christ, and by the righteous long before that. As is so frequently the case with God, unless the answer comes from Him, it is no answer at all. Even prior to the resurrection, the disciples recognized that the answer is simply the petition: "Lord teach us to pray, as John also taught his disciples" (Luke 11:1). The recognition that this reveals is that personal prayer was not something that was generally taught within the confines of their normal religious experience of the Torah and synagogue. For us believers today the matter is as true as it was then. Thankfully, we now have the ultimate guide and comforter dwelling within us to teach us directly the ways of the Lord and the way into His presence.

Private Prayer: "That Which Concerns Us"

As I said before, many people don't have times of private prayer because they say that they do not know what to pray or how to pray. I would venture that such sometimes comes from a position of feeling that we ought only to be bothering God with the big things and that He is not really interested in our day-to-day concerns. In fact, the opposite is true—while it is good to have godly anguish and concern over many big-picture things going on around us, our aligned heart should also recognize that God is sovereign over all things, and all is under His control. The other side of this is that they feel that all they end up praying about is everyday concerns and think that it sounds like a shopping list of requests and petitions that make us more like petulant, demanding children than "serious Christians." Either way, we seem to become convinced that we are not serious in our faith unless we become known as "real intercessors" or "prayer warriors" and other such unbiblical, man-made concepts. Ultimately, we are the individuals of the people of God, and the times we have with the Lord should be times of comfort and peace that confirm our status and identity in Him.

Most everyday Christians thus become caught in this dilemma of knowing that times of private prayer are to be sought but owing to a confusion of what to pray about and how to pray, they end up being perplexed and frustrated, which ultimately leads to lack of motivation and even abandonment of private prayer. So where is the answer? The answer is actually in a realignment and adjustment as to how private prayer is not only conceived, as we have been saying, but also in a revision of understanding of what is actually to be prayed for and about. This is not about putting in strictures and confining measures leading to legalism and "vain repetition," but a freeing of the spirit to engage with the Lord in a manner that opens up our hearts in accordance with His will and His purposes.

In Ps 138:8, the Devotionist King David simply states, "The Lord will perfect that which concerns me." This simple phrase is manifested from such a profound acknowledgement of the sovereignty and purposes of God and how they must materialize in our lives. Indeed, its implications are of such import for our purposes regarding private prayer that we need to elaborate on them. It is clear from this statement that there are matters according to God that we need not be concerned with and matters that we should be concerned with. Amazingly, those matters that we should be concerned with, the Lord Himself will perfect. So, what are these matters? Quite simply, we return to the very start of this entire dialogue for the answer. What matters to God is that we, as His people, love Him with all our heart, mind, and strength and love our neighbors as ourselves, and as Jesus loves us. This is what God is concerned about perfecting within us—and this then is the focus of our attention in private prayer. This is summarized in the New Testament as our sanctification and our conforming to the image of Christ. The Lord then will perfect this within us. Thus, it is to private prayer that we turn to engage with God regarding these matters, both for ourselves and for those who also "concern" us—namely, those in our immediate sphere of influence, defined as our "neighbors" only through proximity, whether physical (family, friends, colleagues) or spiritual (Christian friends, church members, and other believers).

Immersion in Private Prayer

Devotional private prayer consists of times of focus on the Lord and immersing oneself through prayer in the beauty of His presence.

While what follows might seem to some to be programmatic and therefore almost legalistic in its approach, it is merely suggestive of a framework that I hope will help engender a closer, more precious relationship with God through private prayer. One of the great problems with any time of personal prayer is wandering thoughts—where we start to pray and quickly our thoughts go elsewhere and we become so easily distracted. These pointers, then, I hope may give some form of structure that might be useful. It may also be useful to pray out loud, much as we said about reading Scripture out loud, for it helps to focus the mind by joining our thoughts with the physical action of speaking (clearly one should do this as loudly or quietly as you feel comfortable in doing).

Awe and Wonder at God

God is One and the only true God. God is only good and there is no darkness in Him at all. Personal acknowledgement of Him and His ways in our lives comes from an understanding of His Providence and omnipresence. Our private prayers encompass His attributes as we show awe and wonder at God in expectation of the miraculous to come and the miracles already performed. It is always to be recommended to read, aloud or inwardly, passages of great praise to God in order to set our hearts and minds in their right place—suggestions might include the Lord's Prayer (Matt 6:9–13), Job 38, Ps 45, or David's magnificent declaration of praise voiced in 1 Chr 29:10–15.

Praise, Thanksgiving, and Gratitude

God is worthy. As we consider the magnificence of the who our God is, we can give Him the glory for all that He has done. This should be in the generic or the specifically circumstantial as we give Him the glory for answered prayers and also for His Providence in prayers yet to be answered. By generic, we mean such miracles (for this is what they are) as our salvation, being born again, being indwelled by the Holy Spirit, being part of the household of God, the gift of our position in Christ—to name but a few. By specifically circumstantial, we of course mean events that are miraculous that are specific to ourselves and to events in our personal lives—giving God the glory in all matters.

Received Peace

God is peace. Having peace with God opens our private prayer life completely, as there is no condemnation for those in Christ Jesus. Therefore, when we ask for more from God, it is from this perspective: that it is His whole desire to conform us to the image of His Son. With received peace and assurance of our salvation, we can ask for help in our abilities to show more of the fruit of the Holy Spirit in our lives. We can focus on these as a means to improve our walk with Him—asking in full assurance that our prayers will be heard as we struggle with any particular aspect of the fruit, or when wanting to experience more of the mind of Christ, or when we want to learn to love and live in accordance with His instructions and guidance. All of this comes from the position of received peace.

So, when we need to stand on the rock of Christ in our spiritual battles with the enemy and with our sinful selves, we can stand and withstand because we know our identity is irrevocable. Hence, when we need the armor of God, we can ask for it. When we need protection of our souls and nurturing of our souls, it is there for the asking. Received peace also means that we are not to be concerned with the buffeting of the turmoil of the world around us. Received peace therefore leads to hope, and hope to received peace. For we have living hope in Christ and our eternal position. This then affects our private prayers as we feel comfortable and secure enough to focus on what matters to God in the here and now—and what matters to God is our sanctification.

Love and Loving-Kindness

God is Love, and He loves to love us. God not only loves us unconditionally, but He also shows this through His loving-kindness toward us. In return, we perhaps do not pray enough to love Him more—not only to love, but to adore and to honor in our adoration. As we learn to love Him more, so we learn all the more to love what He loves. And as we do so, we learn that who He loves above all else is His Son and those who believe in Him too. Hence our prayers to love Him more become prayers to love each other more and to show loving-kindness to others, as He has shown to us. And as we learn to love Him more, we become ever more appreciative of all that He is doing and has done—and so we love the world as His creation, and we learn to see the world in its beauty through His eyes. When we ask in prayer to be able to see more of the world through His eyes, so certain parts become dimmer and others are drawn more into focus—the ultimate focal point being Jesus Himself. And hence when we learn in prayer to focus on the good, so in prayer we learn to focus irrepressibly upon that which God sees and will always revert to the ultimate point of God's attention and concern:

> Now to Him who is able to keep you from stumbling,
> And to present you faultless
> Before the presence of His glory with exceeding joy,
> To God our Savior,
> Who alone is wise,
> Be glory and majesty,
> Dominion and power,
> Both now and forever.
> Amen.
> (Jude 24–25)

Longing for His Presence

As we draw closer to God, so we know that He's drawing closer to us (Jas 4:8). The Spirit within us calls out, "Abba, Father," as we long to be in His presence both in the here and now. But also, as we focus on the Lord in prayer, so we long for the time when we will be with Him fully. Our heart sings, "Maranatha, Lord"—come, Lord Jesus, come—not just eschatologically but all the time. "Maranatha, Lord" should be our perpetual and continual prayer for more of the Lord in our lives, all the time. And this is a presence to be sought perpetually, at all times. This is the heart that the Lord is seeking from us—this is the longing He deserves.

Taking Personal Responsibility

Private prayer edifies and enriches our souls not just for our own benefit but also to strengthen our characters in our own relationship with God and how we engage with the world around us, specifically how we represent Christ and how we engage with those in our immediate sphere of influence. Here we seek in prayer for the Lord to assist us as we take on the responsibility of representing Him, for our walk with Him, and for how we are with others. It is our responsibility to ask for His help and guidance so that we can glorify Him and not just focus on ourselves.

Lectio Divina and Praying for Ourselves

Of course, devotionally, we can take many of the passages quoted above and use them to steer and guide our considerations of the Lord's blessings through our times of prayer. We can use them to locate and center our appreciation of Him, since to trust in the truth of the word of God is essential to the furthering of our faith and our prayer life. They can, therefore, not only form part of what we described earlier as Lectio Divina (along with the passages we sited as pertaining to our Positional Blessings) but can be used as passages to pray and declare out loud to the Lord in our times of private prayer. Clearly, the connection between Lectio Divina and private prayer is a strong one, and in fact elements are interchangeable—if such activities assist the believer in achieving focus and clarity of attention on the Lord in these moments of privacy, then they are useful indeed and approved of by the Holy Spirit.

Praying for Others

Praying for others is a peculiar privilege that we take too lightly. While we are clearly able to pray for others regarding their specific needs and our specific concerns for them, we frequently neglect to pray on their behalf for that which really matters to God. Thus, the most beneficial prayers that we can seek to offer others concern their understanding and appreciation of the works of God in their lives and appropriation of their identity in the household of God. In essence, therefore, what we pray for ourselves, so we should pray for those who concern us. We pray that they grasp and appropriate each Positional Blessing. We pray that the fruit of the Holy Spirit grows within them and that they learn to let their light so shine that the world sees their fruit and glorifies the Lord for them (Matt 5:16). We pray for their own faith and continuance to walk steadfastly in it, despite the turmoil of the world around them and the distractions of contemporary life. We pray that they grasp the fullness of the beauty of Christ and enjoy the richness of the abundance of life in Him.

It is here that the apostle Paul becomes so exemplary in our consideration of others. Note in his Epistles how he identifies in the church members what is good and godly and commends them for it. One surmises that these commendations might actually have come as a surprise to the recipients but are indicative of how not only others can see the godly where we cannot, but also of where God identifies to others that which within us is from Him. Having identified this, we give God the glory and the thanks for the work He is doing in others, and hope they do the same for ourselves (see 1 Thess 1:2–4, 2 Thess 1:3, Col 1:3–4). We note from Paul, too, that this is the primary stance he takes even when it would be so easy for criticism and condemnation to be the first and initial reaction. Look how he starts, for example, this letter to the Corinthians:

> I thank my God always concerning you for the grace of God which was given to you by Christ Jesus, that you were enriched in everything by Him in all utterance and all knowledge, even as the testimony of Christ was confirmed in you, so that you come short in no gift, eagerly waiting for the revelation of our Lord Jesus Christ, who will also confirm you to the end, that you may be blameless in the day of our Lord Jesus Christ. God is faithful, by whom you were called into the fellowship of His Son, Jesus Christ our Lord. (1 Cor 1:4–9)

It is good and holy to identify these traits in those whom we love and to pray that the Lord nurtures them and protects them within them, and that He also adds to them more and more blessings. This is easy to do for those whom we love and are close to. But we are called by Christ to go beyond that, as we are called to love as He did. And hence this is perhaps a good way to break through that barrier where we find it hard to pray for those whom we are less close to, at best, or find "difficult," at worst. This identification of that which is good within these people and our prayer for them, accordingly, is then an excellent first step and will open our hearts for those in ways that only God can instigate. I can speak from experience in that the same is true in a non-Christian context as well—whether at work or other situations. God can perform mighty transformations through this simple practice of identifying the good and the positive in others and commending them for it in prayer.

It is to the prayers of Paul for others that we can turn to again for the perspective that what is important to God is the development of our knowledge of God and our understanding of His ways. When we are ever unsure or stuck concerning what to pray for others or indeed ourselves, we can take texts such as Eph 1:17–21 and apply them to ourselves in prayer by inserting ourselves into the text and personalizing it; or indeed by replacing the pronouns with the name of someone else, thereby literally inserting them into the blessing of the prayer. Here then we finish where we started, for private prayer achieves parity and compatibility with personal reading of Scripture, where we can either insert ourselves or others into the text or simply use the text itself as a prompt for prayer. Consider, for example, the following:

> He has delivered us from the power of darkness and conveyed us into the kingdom of the Son of His love, in whom we have redemption through His blood, the forgiveness of sins. (Col 1:13–14)

To pray that we or our loved ones truly understand and appropriate this glorious and magnificent truth is to embark on the heart of the Devotionist. Let us consider its implications and who has done this for us—meditate on it, ruminate on it, and pray that the Lord so shines this light into our very being that its beauty goes to the core of our being.

PART 4

Living Devotion

The Exit Gate

The Precious Gate of Received Peace

Peace and Righteousness

TO LEARN TO ENJOY the peace we have as believers with God is part of the purpose of devotion, but to participate *with* the peace of God is the very essence of Living Devotion. As Jesus said, "Let not your heart be troubled" (John 14:1)—for if you do not have peace then our souls suffer, and we cannot honestly engage in devotion. Lack of peace is lack of trust in the Lord and in His promises, in all our Positional Blessings, and in His sovereignty. Peace is a very under-considered doctrine, and yet it is one mentioned by Christ and the apostles a great deal. It also happens to be the one which is probably of most daily significance for the life of the ordinary Christian: without peace, we cannot enjoy the presence of the Prince of Peace.

As we leave our times of devotional acts (immersive reading and private prayer included), so we leave in a spirit of peace with, and a confidence in, the Lord. This is part of our status and yet we value it so little. Spiritual, Christian peace has become circumspect and diminished, as the overall concept of peace has become sullied through various worldly connotations and limitations. The peace of God, though, has no such limits. We think we have to strive and "do," whereas the doctrine of peace says, "just be" and "let the peace of God rule in your hearts" (Col 3:16). And if it rules then it must do so all the time, otherwise it would not be ruling but would be only a momentary, ephemeral assertion of dominance that quickly fades to give way to something else—in this case, more likely doubt, apprehension, uncertainty, and anxiousness, all the very opposite of peace with God, rather a direct result of lack of peace. When we have peace, we can enjoy and live and love God to the best of our abilities. Without peace, we cannot love God with our whole heart. It is simply impossible to do so, for lack of peace is lack of trust in His attributes. Peace, then, is the opposite of the strife which was ordained as the punishment of rebellion imposed on Adam and Eve—and hence we can see peace ultimately as our new covenant reward in Christ. To have "rest" and to be free from labor and strife is part of the divine plan of God. The believer's destiny of having peace with God has always been part of what can be termed the whole plan and desire of having a people unto Himself. Ultimately, peace with God is peace in God. As He embodies peace and we will be joined with Him in unity, then this is part of the will of God for all believers. But just as eternal life starts the moment of salvation, so does having peace with God, and hence it's enjoyment also starts at this point. This is to be applied in the here and now and not just occasionally but always, perpetually, for (and note the verb tenses here) "having been justified by faith we have peace with God" (Rom 5:1). This peace—both present and future, positional and eschatological—can only be brought about by God Himself, for only God can instigate both present and future together simultaneously. Just as Jesus is the Prince of Peace, so His peace will come to full fruition in His kingdom to come but is available within each believer now through the indwelling of the Holy Spirit. And as Jesus is the Prince, so we are heirs of peace—so through this we have peace in our hearts and souls. Our true peace is both now and also ultimately assured with the eternal kingdom of the Prince of Peace, where there will be no more tears, pain, struggle, or enmity, and all will be perfected by our perfect Lord and King of Peace.

We perhaps see now why every apostolic letter in the New Testament mentioned peace as a blessing upon the readers of their epistles. Not only is this a factor of it being a typical Jewish blessing that they have coopted into a Christian context, but it had clearly already become an important factor that the recipients were to consider in their lives and as part and parcel of their walk with Christ. Again this "blessing" now is completely lost for us today, and I wonder if we are the poorer for it. For today we are taught that peace is both nebulous and man-made and considered achievable only by those who are naive, childish, deluded even. But to the apostles, it is a favorite concept and consequence of our faith in Christ—most definitely a product of their understanding of the culmination of the sacrificial system and an appreciation of what it really means within our hearts, and to our souls, to finally have peace with God, permanently. This is what is being imparted to the gentiles, that whereas once we were at enmity with God, now there is finally peace, the true Sabbath rest. And rest is the ultimate divinely instigated human condition, for the Hebrew mind, that was imparted to us through this. It is the ultimate destination that the Sabbath points to: a period of toil followed by rest. All of creation speaks of this. Death, though, is not the ultimate end of toil for those of us who believe, but rather it is peace with God in all eternity. We cannot enjoy full peace until we in effect *become* peace as we are joined with God in unification. And in this life, peace in the believer leads to confidence in our walk and our relationships with God, as is described in Acts 9:31: "The churches throughout all Judea, Galilee and Samaria had peace and were edified. And walking in the fear of the Lord and in the comfort of the Holy Spirit, they were multiplied."

Here we see the clear link between peace that leads to edification and the "comfort" that comes from the Holy Spirit, as the Comforter. It is important to note that these churches mentioned were within predominately Jewish and Judaic areas, but there was at that time great hostility in normal circumstances between Jews and Samarians who for centuries had been enemies in both faith and culture. We see, therefore, that peace comes from God alone through Christ. We see that the dividing wall of separation between Jew and gentile is already being bridged as Eph 2:14 says, and we see the beginnings of the most marvelous doctrine of equality in Christ being outworked so early on in the expansion of the church and expounded on in Rom 10:12, Gal 3:26–28, and Col 3:9–11. What, you might ask, is the relevance of this in a discussion on devotion? For the ordinary, everyday believer, I would answer, "A great deal." For to us as ordinary Christians in our times of devotion, it is essential that we know that we are no less loved or cared for by God than anyone else. We are all partakers and recipients of exactly the same blessings in equal and utterly non-preferential measure. For our devotional purposes, both for ourselves or when praying for others, this enables us to focus more on God and our own relationship with Him rather than paying attention to the opinions or agendas of others or even being distracted by comparisons with peers or other believers as a whole. For as equal members of God's household, we can have peace with ourselves, others, and with our

God. Quite simply, peace is the cornerstone of our personal relationship with Him and is our privilege, as believers, to behold.

Truly we see that the Comforter brings peace in our hearts—not just with God but with other believers—for if there is no peace then there is no comfort. Too often and too sadly, we see this in too many believers today who still struggle with the weight of their past and of past sins or of future peril, of being uncertain in their salvation, and who do not have peace as they continually feel that they must strive perpetually to gain and retain God's favor. This, as we discussed before, is contrary to the foundational doctrinal premise that God will not give His glory to another (Isa 42:8): if you can lose your salvation that means (by definition) that you have done something to do so, which means that others are not doing those things and thereby they are retaining their salvation. This logically means that there are some who are retaining their salvation by doing or not doing something that others are or aren't—in other words, this is retention by works. And if you can work to retain, then logically this effort is to your credit and not to God's. Therefore, you would be able to claim the "glory" for not having undertaken the thing that leads to loss of salvation or for having achieved the thing that leads to retention, and therefore one can boast in these works. This is so clearly contrary to Eph 2:8–9 and Isa 42:8 that to think otherwise is purely fallacious. Therefore, the concept of the loss of salvation is contrary to one of the very foundation premises of the nature of God and how He considers His own attributes. It reflects, in addition, a complete lack of appreciation as to who it was, as God, who died on the cross and what His death and resurrection achieved. This especially includes the impact of the work of God the Holy Spirit, for it implies that His work is deficient and lacking in power, whereas the Bible says that the exact opposite is true in that we "are kept by the power of God through faith for salvation" (1 Pet 1:5). As such, it is also an affront to God in relation to the unilateral bestowing of His Positional Blessings, for, in effect, these blessings are the divinely distributed products of that which is promised within the new covenant in Jer 31:31–34 and Ezek 36:26–27. It is also—and this is important as we consider this in relation to its impact on our devotion—absolutely contrary to what and how the Holy Spirit operates and the very purpose of sanctification, which is the taking of a formerly sullied enemy of God that has been recreated and reborn and reshaping them to conform to the image and auspices of Jesus Christ. This is a process that cannot fail, for God has said as such. Thus, the impact of this on the believer's devotion is not to be underestimated and dismissed, for it means that the believer can focus on being what God requires without hindrance and apprehension, in the sure and certain knowledge that what God has decreed can never be annulled by human hands or even by the wiles of the Devil (Rom 8:38–39).

The Precious Gate of Received Peace

This is the Gate that embodies the received peace that our devotionist souls know only too well:

> The Lord is my shepherd;
> I shall not want.
> He makes me to lie down in green pastures;
> He leads me beside the still waters.
> He restores my soul;
> He leads me in the paths of righteousness
> For His name's sake.
> (Ps 23:1–3)

What is received peace? It is the peace we have within our hearts when we know where we stand with God, that we know His blessings and His love, and, above all, that we are at peace with Him. That King David displayed such understanding is shown in references like Ps 23, for such sentiment can only come from a heart that is not only aligned with God but is also deeply at peace with God. David shows assurance in God's love and care, he shows acceptance of this love and tenderness, and he shows complete surrender to His sovereignty for he gratefully appreciates that all these blessings are bestowed upon him by God alone, at His sole discretion. He knows that these blessings are completely in accordance with, and completed by, God's nature and heart to bless those who love Him, whose hearts are aligned, and who heed and love His voice. Peace is received, therefore, for it is bestowed by and because of God. But it is also gifted, and as a gift needs to be accepted and appreciated for its value not only for what it is but because of the One who gave it. This is therefore the key here, the value that is ascribed to this peace by the recipient. This is, as it were, the individual's appropriation of the blessings of God toward the people of Israel as described in Deut 28 if they would heed the Lord's voice and obey His commandments, and hence this is its application to the individual as we, too, heed His voice and obey His commandment to love Him with all our heart.

As we pass through this Gate, it brings forth both reflective and anticipatory emotions and spiritual blessings that prepare us for life within the "real world."

Reflective Emotions: "Because of God"

As we reflect on God through and within our times of devotion, we understand that the blessings that have been gifted to us are solely and exclusively because of God alone. As we reflect on God through and within our times of devotion, we understand that the blessings that have been gifted to us are solely and exclusively because of God alone. And so, as we contemplate what has been achieved by God through these times of devotion—the calming and quietening of our souls (Ps 131:2)—we come to see and behold that it is only God and being in His presence that can revive and strengthen our souls, which is the ultimate plea and yearning of all Devotionists (Ps 119:25):

> Return to your rest, O my soul,
> For the Lord has dealt bountifully with you.
> (Ps 116:7)

> In the day when I cried out, You answered me,
> And made me bold with strength in my soul.
> (Ps 138:3)

And our souls, as we pass through the Precious Gates, go from this state to that of knowing the peace and joy that comes from our Lord:

> And my soul shall be joyful in the Lord;
> It shall rejoice in His salvation.
> (Ps 35:9)

> For He satisfies the longing soul,
> And fills the hungry soul with goodness.
> (Ps 107:9)

> My lips shall greatly rejoice when I sing to You,
> And my soul, which You have redeemed.
> (Ps 71:23)

Praise for His Works

The reviving and restoring of our souls through the presence of God is a work of God and should be considered as such. To move from being downcast and even despondent at times through to the experience of love, joy, and hope that is available to us through the presence of God, is a blessed work of the Holy Spirit within us and should be acknowledged as such—for alongside acknowledgement comes gratitude, which is, to be fair, the only reasonable response our wonderful God deserves (Pss 105:1–5, 107:21–22). This gratitude takes the form of blessing the Lord in return for what He has done for us—it is giving Him the credit and praise for what He alone can achieve for our souls, hearts, and minds:

> Bless the Lord, O my soul;
> And all that is within me, bless His Holy name!
> Bless the Lord, O my soul,
> And forget not all His benefits. . . .
> Bless the Lord, all His works,
> In all places of His dominion.
> Bless the Lord, O my soul!
> (Ps 103:1–2; 22)

> I will bless the Lord at all times;
> His praise shall continually be in my mouth.
> My soul shall make its boast in the Lord;
> The humble shall hear of it and be glad.
> Oh, magnify the Lord with me,
> And let us exalt His name together.
> (Ps 34:1–2)

We bless Him because He alone is worthy, because of who He is and what He has done. That alone is enough. The Lord loves for us just to declare back to Him all He has done and all that He is. He loves to be blessed for His attributes and how they work in our lives. And when we truly appreciate this, then the most natural thing is to declare this to others, and by doing so, we honor God. He wants His works to be known so that they point to Him and give Him the glory for what He has done in a believer's life, not least of which is just the blessings He delivers through our times of devotion and through our experiences of Him while being devoted to Him.

> Come and hear, all you who fear God,
> And I will declare what He has done for my soul.
> I cried to Him with my mouth,
> And He was extolled with my tongue.
> If I regard iniquity in my heart,
> The Lord will not hear.
> But certainly God has heard me;
> He has attended to the voice of my prayer.
> Blessed be God,
> Who has not turned away my prayer,
> Nor His mercy from me!
> (Ps 66:16–20)

The heart of one who has experienced the goodness of God is also one who cannot help but tell others of His works. This is the way of God: He blesses so the blessings can become a testimony of His goodness and hence, while enjoyed individually, must be declared and spoken of as a witness to others (Ps 145:1–7, 10–13). Consequently, the extolling of His works to ourselves and among others is not only symptomatic of truly grasping the plans and purposes that God has revealed through our times of devotion, but also, perhaps more crucially, can greatly edify and enrich others as focus is given away from ourselves to the wonder and awe due to God. Consider for example the words of King David in 1 Chr 29:10–13, and see how his praise is totally focused on God alone, coming as it does from his aligned heart. The following excerpts expertly demonstrate this point—namely, that the product of devotion is the impact on the personal responsibility of the believer to declare and act upon the blessings of God:

> But I will hope continually,
> And will praise You yet more and more.
> My mouth shall tell of Your righteousness
> And Your salvation all the day,
> For I do not know their limits.
> I will go in the strength of the Lord GOD;
> I will make mention of Your righteousness, of Yours only.
> (Ps 71:14–16)
>
> I will extol You, my God, O King;
> And I will bless Your name forever and ever.
> Every day I will bless You,
> And I will praise Your name forever and ever.
> Great is the LORD, and greatly to be praised;

And His greatness is unsearchable.
One generation shall praise Your works to another,
And shall declare Your mighty acts.
I will meditate on the glorious splendor of Your majesty,
And on Your wondrous works.
(Ps 145:1–5)

Anticipatory Emotions and Applied Peace

Oh, give thanks to the LORD! Call upon His name;
Make known His deeds among the peoples!
Sing to Him, sing psalms to Him;
Talk of all His wondrous works!
Glory in His holy name;
Let the hearts of those rejoice who seek the LORD!
Seek the LORD and His strength;
Seek His face evermore!
Remember His marvelous works which He has done,
His wonders, and the judgments of His mouth.
(Ps 105:1–5)

Oh, that men would give thanks to the LORD for His goodness,
And for His wonderful works to the children of men!
Let them sacrifice the sacrifices of thanksgiving,
And declare His works with rejoicing.
(Ps 107:21–22)

The apostle James calls upon believers to be doers as well as hearers of the word (Jas 1:22). All of Scripture is very clear that the expectation of God is that we act upon hearing His voice, that we take responsibility for our faith and for our devotion to Him. This, of course, is in itself a response to the love we have for Him. It was always the case that we "do" because we "love" first; and all that we do for Him comes from this love, otherwise it is a waste of effort, no matter how spiritual we may think we are being (1 Cor 13:1). In other words, all is circular and all points back to Jesus for He alone is the center and the Author of our faith. Being doers of the word is therefore just participation with the Spirit as He sanctifies us and conforms us to the image of Christ. All else is dross to be blown away in the wind. And so as we pass through the Precious Gate of Received Peace, we do so with fortified faith based on trust in His attributes and in the appropriation of the Positional Blessings that have been so freely gifted to us. Through this we truly become "doers of His word" when we adopt the principles and precepts of applied peace that encompass Living Devotion.

Living Devotion

The Reality of God and the Monday Morning Syndrome Revisited

As we edge toward the end of our deliberations, let's return to the Monday Morning Syndrome and the experiences as described at the beginning of this work—experiences of frustration with what is taught, or not taught, concerning how we are to live as believers and what it is that God really requires of us. This frustration frequently develops into feelings of inadequacy and failing faith, as we struggle with juggling everyday life with what we have been told our Christian life should entail.

As we have meandered through Scripture and identified the glorious golden thread of devotion, we discussed the requirements of God and concluded that the Lord is only interested in how our whole hearts are dedicated to Him, and then discussed what this means in the context of our lives now as Devotionists. We explored the fundamental aspect of taking responsibility to engage in and enjoy the times of nurturing our souls, and that this nurturing can take various forms of activity and acts through devotional reading and private prayer. We explored also how by using the metaphorical Precious Gates of Devotion, we can learn to enter into the presence of God through these times of private devotion encompassed within Positional Devotion. Through this we can see how as Devotionists we can learn to live to enjoy and embrace the Positional

Blessings of our Positional Identity. This leads to confidence in Christ, through our Living Devotion.

Externalism: The Difference Between Being Devout and Being Devoted

The religious are devout; the Devotionist is devoted. Being "devout," while not in itself anything to be concerned about, can easily become the mindset of legalism and function over freedom and form, of display and performance over participation and privacy. To be devoted is about "being"; it is obsession and dedication to the object of devotion—namely, God. To be devoted is literally "living" for the object of devotion, being dedicated and wholehearted in that dedication. To be devoted, then, is going beyond the normal, the expected—it is ongoing, all-absorbing, and participatory. Living devotion is not just undertaking the acts of devotion, but it is always, all the time, being devoted. It is a description that once attained can never be removed for it reflects the position of the believer in the household of God. It is part of our identity and is available to all. "I am devoted," says the believer, "because He is devoted." "I am devoted because that is who I am in Christ. I am obsessive because that is how God is about me and because that is how the members of the Trinity are about each other." Being devoted, then, is not something that the believer attains through extra-diligence or super-insight into the mysteries of God in some kind of gnostic, superior way—it is the response available to all believers in appreciation and application of the gifted Positional Blessings. To be devoted is to be a believer; it is both a privilege and a right, a gift that is freely available and applicable to all. If you do not feel this, then be assured that as a believer there is no condemnation from Christ; and if you want it, then all you have to do is ask, for it is a gift that is available to all.

The Internalization of the Devotionist

The Devotionist's devotion to being devoted to God requires dedication and discipline. This dedication, though, is not perfunctory and is not undertaken as a performance or under legalistic obligation but from an internalized absorption of the Positional Blessings and identification with the privileges that have been gifted to us.

But is devotion merely the acts of devotion? Or is it deeper? We would, of course, suggest that acts of devotion, so to speak, come from a heart that is aligned, dedicated, and devoted to the Lord. This is true, but does devotion then only materialize through these acts? We would argue otherwise that actually the acts are merely part of the picture. Just as the going to the temple and the offering of sacrifices did not in itself make one "right with God," so these acts (while being sacrificial in the sense of being an offering to the Lord) are only acceptable to God when they themselves come from a heart that is dedicated and devoted to the Lord. These acts are material manifestation and practices that the Devotionist might choose to perform to enjoy times in the presence of God and out of loyalty to Him. But we would argue that this is not the complete picture. For these acts must come from a devotionist heart, rather than from a performance as a means of gaining favor or even just knowledge. God does not see devotion as a performance—devotional acts are mere acts of sacrifice to the Lord and are only acceptable if they themselves are performed out of love, and because of love. This is why they can become as "clanging cymbals" (1 Cor 13:1) and even an abomination if they are undertaken by those in whom God does not dwell.

Acts of Devotion: Externalism, Internalism, and the External Expressions of the Devotionist

Engaging in the acts of devotion, as important to nurturing our souls as they are, does not detract from the fact that they are, by definition, temporary, ephemeral, and momentary by nature. And while they can be hugely edifying and beneficial in shaping and molding who we are and our Christian characters, we need to look further, into how devotion becomes not just "for the moment" but "permanent."

> And these words which I command you today shall be in your heart. You shall teach them diligently to your children, and shall talk of them when you sit in your house, when you walk by the way, when you lie down, and when you rise up. You shall bind them as a sign on your hand, and they shall be as frontlets between your eyes. You shall write them on the doorposts of your house and on your gates. (Deut 6:6–9)

How does the injunction of the wearing of tassels, marking the house, and speaking of the Lord as described in Deut 6:6–9 possibly translate and apply to our own daily lives now within the devotionist mindset?

Education and Speaking of the Lord Spontaneously

Part of the mindset of the Devotionist, as we discussed at the beginning of this entire discourse, is learning to think about the Lord in terms of how His attributes are displayed both through Scripture and in the world around us. As we are part of this world, clearly, then this mindset also encompasses how the attributes of God manifest in our own lives and even through us as the Holy Spirit's work within us becomes visible to others, both believers and nonbelievers. This is nowhere more true than in our understanding of what we described as being the reality of God in our lives—He is real and so are His attributes of omniscience, omnipotence, and most important in this regard, His Providence.

As Devotionists we see God's work in our lives and through the world around us all the time. We see His beauty manifested in creation, we see His orchestration of history, prophetic fulfillment (both past and present), and the providential outworking of His divine plans. But the imperative of the Devotionist is not only to see, contemplate, and give glory to God for these things but also to edify others by sharing about the works of God to others, no matter their age—friends, family, and everyday contacts where possible. To speak of the wonder and glory of God both in the abstract but also in the precise is an important factor not only for the augmenting of our own faith but also for the strengthening of the faith of those around us. The speaking of the works and blessings of God in our lives brings God, as the Living God, into the living realities of our lives, which are vitally important lessons for all believers, especially the young in age and faith. Our God is living and involved, and He is there for us. It is clear, also, that God likes to be spoken of—whether spontaneously, as described in Deut 6:6–9, or also more formally in group or family settings. To speak of Him in such ways brings glory to Him, as God wants to be included and to be seen as being involved in our lives. He is not remote and distant but ever-present and all-involved, so to speak. Unlike fake gods, He cares, is interested, and is able and willing to act. This to Him is the vital message that needs to be imparted both to the young and to those who are lost and "heavy laden." For through us, they see that there is "hope" and that there is "light."

Speaking of Him and educating others about Him (young and old) is also vital for our own edification and devotion as we recognize His work in our own lives and see Him at work in the lives of others. Helping them to see Him as such serves to give Him the due recognition that He deserves. So, whether through the admiration of creation directly, or through how He has created the concept of beauty that we can appreciate in art, music, and through our own ability to create, which comes from God as creator and is part of the fabric of humankind formed in the image of God, these are the things that as we think about and speak about, so they become part of the reality of God in our lives. Hence, we see this as part of what the apostle Paul means in Phil 4:8–9 as he sought to edify the church there by reminding them that the way of the believer is to focus on that which is of God, not that which destroys faith and distresses our souls:

> Finally, brethren, whatever things are true, whatever things are noble, whatever things are just, whatever things are pure, whatever things are lovely, whatever things are of good report, if there is any virtue and if there is anything praiseworthy—meditate on these things. The things which you learned and received and heard and saw in me, these do, and the God of peace will be with you. (Phil 4:8–9)

Visual Memorials

The biblical case for memorials, or external expressions, is clear—from the setting up of a memorial after crossing the river Jordan to the wearing of prayer shawls, and into the new covenant through the Eucharist and even baptism. These are both reflective of the heart of the believer and also a means of self-identification, celebration, and community collaboration. They are, in addition, educational and cultural motifs, for their purpose is to ask the questions of what they represent and why: Why do we perform these rights and what do they express? The same is obviously true for Christian art and music and has been so for hundreds of years and was, of course, vital to the spiritual promulgation of the faith during periods of mass illiteracy, such as during the Middle Ages. How can we see this implemented today in our personal lives, and should we express ourselves in such a way? Clearly this has been a debate that has continued since Christianity began and certainly since the Reformation, as Christianity divided into camps of those for and against visual representations of faith. If we take clothing for example, is there a form of clothing that is acceptable to the Lord? Certainly the Puritans and their successors thought so; but didn't their austerity in clothing actually come to represent an idol and uniform in itself, when it came to what was/is acceptable or not, in exactly the same way as they would point to the priestly garments of the established churches?

While modesty for both men and women in their clothing, especially during times of worship (whether private or corporate) is undoubtedly a good thing, it should be so out of respect for whom is being worshiped, rather than any fear of looking compromised in our faith. And so, what of other contemporary artifacts that we adorn, such as wearing crosses around our necks? Is this acceptable or idolatry? Certainly in the early years of the Reformation in England, the wearing of crosses was considered to be idolatry and was a means of identifying those who still held to Catholic belief systems. As we said earlier, memorials are biblical and to think otherwise is not so: to wear a symbol such as a cross is a means of identifying oneself to those around us, as a symbol of one's belief system or a motif that is associated with being Christian. It is a "monument" that may lead to discussion and opportunities for sharing faith and incorporating Jesus into our daily lives. It is, of course, not to be worn as a means of gaining favor with God, but if as a means of devotion and dedication (and even faith enhancement), then again to do so reflects the heart of the believer in wishing to express their honoring of God in a visual way.

The same can be true of adorning one's home with Christian artifacts, be they paintings of Christian scenes, crosses, embroidered or printed Bible verses, and the like. Does doing so make us any more approved of by God? Of course not. Might it help in reminding us of the Lord and bringing Him to remembrance in our daily lives more often? Very possibly. And if it were to do so, then surely this would be a good thing—for didn't God instigate the placement of mezuzahs on doorposts for just such a reason (Deut 6:9)? But technically, and in God's eyes, what is the difference between this and the adorning of churches with beautiful imagery depicting biblical scenes? None whatsoever. Indeed, the very austerity of churches and places of worship that is designed to remove all forms of so-called idolatry from being present is in itself an act that idolizes the visual by making a statement on what is not there and on the vain philosophies of man in deciding on God's behalf what He should approve of.

Blandness and austerity reflect harshness and remoteness, not warmth, compassion, and above all love—and so "Whither beauty?" becomes "What love is this?" By imagining that God would approve of such acts of anti-creation and deconstruction goes against His desired purposes for us to acknowledge that beauty can only come from Him and to consider what it is meant to declare to His creation about Himself. To communicate the things of God in a manner that the illiterate and ill-informed can understand and enquire of is part of the very reason for giving us "creative" abilities in the first place. Why are we able to create beautiful art, music, poetry, and literature (even the beauty of the spoken word through sermons and the Bible itself) if that ability has not been imparted to us from the Creator Himself? Beauty within the spoken word, whether through sermons or preaching, is wonderful but insufficient for it is transitory, ephemeral, momentary, does not linger, and cannot be revisited (or could not until modern day recordings). But art and music are not, for they can be revisited and can speak to the soul at a different more personal level where interpretation, application, and appreciation is more private and personal—and hence becomes deeper and more meaningful to the individual.

The appreciation of both that which is external and internalized is, as I said, part of us and placed within us from the moment we were formed by God. Our innate ability to recognize beauty in all its forms—whether in landscapes or on canvas—so clearly demonstrates this fact. Only humankind reflects God in this capacity—no other animals or mammals, or any other created thing, shares this capacity to appreciate beauty or even to think it exists. It is unique to us, through God, and we deny God one of His most wonderful attributes by not using this ability to create and/or appreciate it in order to further His glory and point people to Him. For we would not have any concept of what beauty is if it were not part of the creation mindset of God—for when He created, He created it beautifully because to do so is reflective of His own internal and external divine beauty. More importantly, and more fundamental to our whole understanding of beauty, is the fact that God created all things not out of some arbitrary whim but for a very specific reason: creation was undertaken both through and, even more wonderfully, for His Son, Jesus Christ (Col 1:16). Beauty then emanates from within the Godhead, is manifested physically and spiritually through the Godhead, and only exists because of the Godhead. Hence our appreciation of beauty comes from being made in His image, for no other created being appreciates beauty and is also able to create beautifully—whether artistically or through music and even through language, written or spoken—and hence to diminish or deprive believers of access to beauty that reflects our beautiful Creator is plainly wrong and very possibly soul destroying in its demeaning of God's attributes. It is here, therefore, that we see how beauty and devotion intermingle—for when our appreciation of beauty points to the Author of beauty, so our hearts and souls connect with Him through it. Beauty, though, is never static, rigid, exhaustive, restricted, or confined. It can, though, mysteriously also include both the mundane and the enigmatic in equal measure—it is, in other words, entirely similar to, and absorbent of, devotion that is living.

Giving Preference to Other Believers

This is an aspect of externalism that is again too little considered in relation to our lives as Devotionists and manifests in our attitudes to the world around us in a way that is of considerable relevance to the normal Christian. Of course, any discussion on Living Devotion in relation to how we reflect our devotion in the real world must at some stage address how we engage, and are seen to engage, with the world in all its contexts. This is, of course, an extremely relevant and complex subject for the ordinary Christian as it applies to literally every aspect of our lives—and of course there are many books that have been written about having a Christian mindset and being "in the world and not of it," and the like. My own experience of such books is that they seem to always leave me with mixed emotions and end up finding them both unhelpful and unedifying. To me, somehow whatever their intentions or motives, they inevitably always seem to promote what amounts to legalism, leaving me feeling condemned for my own "inadequate" and "not-committed-enough" Christian lifestyle—while also completely missing how complex, frustrating, and quite simply hard it can be to live as an everyday Christian in the "real world." Most of us have no aspirations to become missionaries or evangelists or pastors or to enter into any form of ministry, for the very reason that we are not all called to do so, are not all interested in doing so, and (most likely of all) it is just not practical for most Christians to contemplate doing so. What is more, this has been the case for the vast majority of believers since time began. As we have said, we have normal, everyday lives to lead with normal, everyday commitments and responsibilities which cannot be ignored and nor should they be—biblically and according to God's instructions, anyway. These are, I must stress, my own personal feelings and experiences of such books and teachings, and I am sure that there have been multitudes who have been blessed by them, so I will not detract from that. Having experienced through writing this book the time and effort that it takes to write at all, then I cannot criticize entirely the effort and commitment that such writers have undertaken, one assumes, with the heart-felt intention of encouraging and benefitting others. And, of course, all this is not to say that part of our times of private prayer will not include addressing the need for wisdom in handling matters in the world and for engaging in with the mind of Christ, and I would also hope that we ask the Lord to guard our hearts from that which could harm us spiritually and emotionally—as Devotionists this is precisely what we should be doing, for sure.

There is one aspect of how we engage in the external world, though, that is little commented upon, as far as I am aware, and yet, in my experience within working in a secular environment, that I have always considered to be a practical and easily followed piece of scriptural advice—which, in itself, can prove to be an example to family, believers, and nonbelievers alike. This piece of advice is quite simply to be found in the phrase "giving preference to one another" (Rom 12:10)—meaning, in context, to other believers. This is not passive but active and deliberate. It can manifest in such actions as simply preferring to be with other believers over being with nonbelievers. In the workplace, this can mean avoiding after-work drinks in preference to simply going home to be with one's family, or to activities with other believers. But mostly it is about where our heart is: it is preferring to be with other Christians because that is where the soul is nurtured and edified, while deliberately avoiding situations where we can become sullied through mere association, not even participation. We should be conscious that the Holy Spirit within us is not comfortable in all situations and will make us feel uncomfortable in various ways. This should be considered not as a hindrance but as a means of helping us to resist entering into such situations where our faith can be compromised and our identity in Christ to others around us can also be compromised in the world's eyes. We need to be careful and astute, but if undertaken also in a clear, uncompromising, and loving manner, it can become a positive witness to both our families and fellow believers and also to nonbelievers, as they see that we are indeed dedicated to whom we believe, not flinching from His life-enriching values. Of course, it can come at a cost too. This does, however, demonstrate what we have discussed as the internalization of the external and the externalization of the internal as we engage with the real world in real world situations that affect the normal Christian in many ways with great frequency. Private devotion is where the preparation is made, though, for the believer to be able to engage and survive in what can often be quite hostile environments as we make these personal stands for what and for whom we believe in. Private devotion is essential in this for it is where we draw on the well of comfort and strength through the Holy Spirit and ask for holy wisdom from the One who alone is wise (Jude 25)—while always remembering, of course, that it is our positional right to ask of God what He has already gifted to us:

> My brethren, count it all joy when you fall into various trials, knowing that the testing of your faith produces patience. But let patience have its perfect work, that you may be perfect and complete, lacking nothing. If any of you lacks wisdom, let him ask of God, who gives to all liberally and without reproach, and it will be given to him. (Jas 1:2–5)

What then are the greatest of acts of devotion we can undertake while we are in the external environment, as we engage in our daily lives? The answer has to be this: guarding our hearts. It is our hearts that God is interested in and as such their protection is very much a form, and expression, of Living Devotion. This effort of guarding, of course, needs to be undertaken from both within and without the Christian environment, for we are to be as gentle as doves and as wise as serpents. To protect our hearts, and those of loved ones, means that we have to become aware that not everything, all the time, is what it might seem—not all is wise and not all is profitable, even within the Christian community, which is why discernment of spirits is called a gift and why we are called to avoid contentions and contentious people for the pure reason that we need to guard our hearts. The easiest way to guard our hearts is simply to recognize danger and avoid engagement—for by engaging we necessarily get entangled into disputes and disputations that can frequently end up having personal and faith implications. Far better, then, for the sheep of His pasture to recognize that our only responsibility is to heed His voice and to follow Him. He is our Master, at the end of the day, and as the

Good Shepherd, He is both the Master and the Good Shepherd of His flock; we are wise to remember that He alone truly has our best interests at heart. Perhaps one can regard, then, this entire discourse as a means of addressing this point of being wise in our faith and looking for what God requires rather than what the expectations and agendas are that others might seek to impose on us. In other words, we are to become privately devoted Devotionists wedded and dedicated to loving God, nurturing our souls, and participating in His beautiful blessings—put simply, being His people and Him being our God.

The natural question that arises when considering what we do as Christians is, "Do works also constitute acts of devotion?"—meaning, whether external activities are also acts of devotion. And if not, then does this mean that they do not technically fit within what is required from us as believers? Or is faith and devotion the only "work" that is truly required of the ordinary believer? The answer to this question is in fact hidden in what is implied in the very question itself. For some reason, devotion is seen as something secondary to other activities that believers are supposed to engage in. This, I believe, is a complete fallacy and is a vital issue to address, for what could be more important than the strength and depth of our personal relationship with God? This is the starting point of all that follows as it is our love of, and devotion to, God that produces the light within us that so shines before others (believers and nonbelievers alike) so that they see our good works and through them glorify God (Matt 5:16). We should never underestimate the personal edification that can be achieved by believers experiencing and being strengthened through the adoption of their position in Christ and the Positional Blessings. Again, my purpose here is to encourage us all to think through what the real heart of God for us is. To ask, and explore, what He really wants from us ordinary, everyday believers is vital for our own faith. We should look at all things and quite simply ask ourselves the only question that ultimately matters both to us and to God: Does this help me love God more?

Personal devotion is undertaken for the sake of not only our own faith and comfort in Christ but also so we can engage with our fellow and encourage them to do the same. It is just too easy to be led and to be diverted—often with the best of intentions and love from others—away from what our souls need and what our relationship with Christ really deserves from us in terms of our own private dedication and devotion to peace and righteousness away from the influence of competing voices and agendas. But even this is always so that we can learn to love God more and to represent Him better to other believers and the outside world. Devotion then must always be a purposeful activity for it to be acceptable and recognizable by God. Herein lies the difference, then, between what many people see as devotion and what the Devotionist does: to many people, devotion is just another form of something that is done or performed, but to the Devotionist, devotion is about being and living in the perpetual presence of God.

Living Devotion—The Golden Thread Woven into Our Daily Lives

The biblical position on all acts is to divide everything into that which is permissible, essential, and profitable. It is for each of us to decide for ourselves, in our own personal relationship with God, which of these is the most important for our relationship with God. To be very clear about this, the only thing that God is interested in receiving from each and every believer is ever increasing amounts of love and devotion. From this all else follows, and only from this is all else acceptable to God. This must be, therefore, where our own focus is as individual private believers—and nothing and no one should distract or detract us from this purpose.

What then, we ask, of the private devotional acts that we have discussed in previous chapters? Are they necessary at all? If so, how often are we to do them and for how long on each occasion? These are always the immediate thoughts that come to mind as we consider devotional acts—and has been the case down the centuries in most denominations. How many times to make confession, how many times to take communion, how many times to pray, for how long and how frequently? These are all natural questions, of course, and the reader is absolutely right to ask them—for they surely fall into the category of sub-questions pertaining to the questions first asked around the feelings of inadequacies felt by many ordinary believers. But we return to the point here that conformity and obligation is the nemesis of spiritual growth and devotion. The Lord requires and deserves a relationship with each of us who believe that is not confined to mere formality of expressions, obligated appearances, and scheduled performances, but intertwined with the perspective of engaging with the divine and the privilege of having permanent access and the joy of personal participation with our glorious God.

Positional Devotion is not momentary or ephemeral. Simply participating in the acts of devotion is categorically not Living Devotion. Living Devotion is empowered by the Holy Spirit and is therefore attainable by all Christians and available to all who ask. It is living because it pertains to, and is empowered by, the Holy Spirit within us. It is living because our God is living, just as water, the word of God, and even hope are "living" when pertaining to the Holy Spirit; so is our position in Christ and hence so is our devotion (John 4:10, 7:38; Heb 4:14; 1 Pet 1:3). Living devotion, then, is not exclusive or even exotic, or only achieved by the select few, and it is certainly not the prerogative of those who deem themselves superior, elite, or select. Devotion is internalizing the external and externalizing that which the Lord is perfecting internally—the transformed inner self, as Paul described it, becomes externalized and visible in order that people can see this transformation and give God the glory for what He is doing within you, even when you cannot see it yourself.

The taking of the golden thread of Living Devotion and weaving it into our hearts so that it literally becomes the very fabric of our lives and is the thread that draws together our faith and our characters has been the very purpose of all that has been discussed in this book. Scriptural history is full of examples of those who have lived before us in accordance (knowingly or otherwise) with the beautiful precepts of Living Devotion—consider Mary the mother of Jesus, King David, and the prophet Daniel, as all were ordinary believers first, living as devoted Devotionists. Consider the likes of the Cistercian monks and ponder that it is not the way that they lived that is necessarily the profitable example, it is the heart that is revealed in their writings—or rather, it is the revelation of the consistency of the Holy Spirit that is revealed in their writings. This is consistency at which we should marvel, for we see in them, from nearly a thousand years ago within people as far removed from our contemporary culture as is feasible to imagine, the same Spirit as is revealing Himself today. This is the miracle and the proof of how God works through His devoted ones.

This is where the point of this discourse really culminates in that while we are told in Scripture and in history of those who exemplify the Devotionist's heart, there are countless others throughout the ages who are just ordinary believers, loving God and being devoted to Him and His ways. These truly are the "people of God," the people that God has proved Himself for, the people whom He has prepared and is preparing as the beautiful bride of Christ whom He will receive unto Himself, perfected by Him to be ever with Him and joined with Him in unshakable unity for eternity.

The Precepts and Process of Living Devotion

What are the precepts of Living Devotion and how can we describe them? Perhaps these can be best condensed into the simple and single word, "pursue"—for we are told that we are, as part of our devotion and dedication to Jesus, to pursue both peace and righteousness.

The Kingdom of God Is Pursuing Peace and Righteousness

> Therefore let us pursue the things which make for peace and the things by which one may edify another. (Rom 14:19)

> But you, O man of God, flee these things and pursue righteousness, godliness, faith, love, patience, gentleness. (1 Tim 6:11)

> Flee also youthful lusts; but pursue righteousness, faith, love, peace with those who call on the Lord out of a pure heart. (2 Tim 2:22)

The pursuit of peace and righteousness is a personal activity that must come from within, for as the Holy Spirit dwells within us, so true peace and righteousness can only come from Him and by Him. For as the psalmist says, "For the Lord is righteous, He loves righteousness; His countenance beholds the upright" (Ps 11:7). And hence the pursuit of peace and righteousness for the believer is integral to our lives as Devotionists. After all, peace with God can only come from the peace of the Holy Spirit, as God, who always points and leads the believer to Jesus: "For He Himself is our peace" (Eph 2:14). And hence this pursuit is integral to our very purpose as believers. We are to hunger and search for peace and righteousness as we hunger to nurture our souls. Indeed, our souls can only be at peace through the Holy Spirit, and righteousness that comes from God must be the goal—for God is the perfection of peace, as much as He is the combination of all His other attributes.

> For the kingdom of God is not eating and drinking, but righteousness and peace and joy in the Holy Spirit. (Rom 14:17)

The pursuit of both righteousness and peace bears good fruit. Fruit in this context is synonymous with the experience and appropriation of our Positional Blessings and are in perfect sympathy with the fruit of the Holy Spirit working within us. They are inseparable, which is why peace and righteousness are often mentioned together—for you cannot, when considering the functions of the Holy Spirit, have one without the other. They are not quite interchangeable, but they are inseparable in a Christian context. So, the pursuit of righteousness and peace becomes the pursuit of aspects of our lives which are already there for the asking and increasing. For they are freely given as part of our position in the household of God and freely endowed to the believer as part of the gift of our Positional Identity—all we need to do is ask, with the certain knowledge that, as always, there is no condemnation for not having done so already. Indeed, not to ask and not to apply is not exactly detrimental to our walk with God, but to do so makes it so much richer, which is after all what He wants for us (Col 3:15–16).

> Being filled with the fruits of righteousness which are by Jesus Christ, to the glory and praise of God. (Phil 1:11)

> (For the fruit of the Spirit is in all goodness, righteousness, and truth). (Eph 5:9)

> Now the fruit of righteousness is sown in peace by those who make peace. (Jas 3:18)

Living Devotion is learning, therefore, to "live" peace and appropriate righteousness—in other words, yet again to be doers, as well as hearers, and to let the light of righteousness shine from within us, to the glory of God:

> If you know that He is righteous, you know that everyone who practices righteousness is born of Him. (1 John 2:29)

> Little children, let no one deceive you. He who practices righteousness is righteous, just as He is righteous. (1 John 3:7)

> In this the children of God and the children of the devil are manifest: Whoever does not practice righteousness is not of God, nor is he who does not love his brother. (1 John 3:10)

Living Devotion is both external and internal—the declaring and speaking of the works of God is at the very core of the reaction we as His children are to have to His greatness and all His ways. This is meant to be spontaneous and impossible to contain and keep to ourselves so that others are blessed, convinced, edified, and convicted by such declarations of wonder at the genuine impact living this devotion has on the Devotionist:

> I have proclaimed the good news of righteousness
> In the great assembly;
> Indeed, I do not restrain my lips,
> O Lord, You Yourself know.
> I have not hidden Your righteousness within my heart;
> I have declared Your faithfulness and Your salvation;
> I have not concealed Your lovingkindness and Your truth
> From the great assembly.
> (Ps 40:9–10)

> My mouth shall tell of Your righteousness
> And Your salvation all the day,
> For I do not know their limits.
> (Ps 71:15)

To summarize therefore, righteousness is not just something that we do, as most probably think, but is something that we are—as is implicit within the words of the Devotionist King David (who would know): "Offer the sacrifices of righteousness, And put your trust in the Lord" (Ps 4:5). In our context, these sacrifices are the acts and being of devotion; they are the actions of the Devotionists in dedicating our lives and hearts to the Lord. And this not through actions, but through transformed minds, realigned hearts, and devoted devotion, dedicated and determined to distinguish ourselves from the inside outwards to His glory and our sanctification and onwards to the time of our own transitioning and translation into His likeness. Remarkably, this has always been the conclusion for the Devotionist as we consider the culmination of all the graces and mercies of God:

> As for me, I will see Your face in righteousness;
> I shall be satisfied when I awake in Your likeness.
> (Ps 17:15)

> Mercy and truth have met together;
> Righteousness and peace have kissed.
> (Ps 85:10)

> Nevertheless we, according to His promise, look for new heavens and a new earth in which righteousness dwells. (2 Pet 3:13)

Pursuing Contentment in Christ

> Now godliness with contentment is great gain. (1 Tim 6:6)

Contentment is one of the most powerfully countercultural concepts in the Western world. It is in direct contravention to all that we are told is of value to us as individuals. To be content is to seem to be static, unworldly, unambitious, and quite simply unconformist to our consumerist conditioning. But to the believer, contentment—when combined with godliness, righteousness, and our spiritual Positional Identity—is great gain precisely because from contentment comes peace, security, and the stability of standing immersed in our immovable identity in Christ. Simply put, our contentment is again available to us by entitlement, because we believe and have been gifted such exceptionalism through the appropriation of our Positional Blessings. With contentment, therefore, we can concentrate on that which is our *calling* (Eph 4:1), which is to be the people of God and to behave accordingly. Contentment comes from transforming our minds and hearts towards God and can be seen as the final expression and emotional experience brought about through the full immersion of the devoted—baptized, as it were, into Living Devotion.

The Process of Living Devotion: The Deliberate Acts of Putting On . . . and Being

> And that you put on the new man which was created according to God, in true righteousness and holiness. (Eph 4:24)

The process of Living Devotion is one of taking responsibility and acting on the blessings of God. It is what the apostle Paul describes above as "putting on"—namely, clothing ourselves in—the righteous robes that have been so freely given to us. It is the acknowledgement and acceptance with no resistance of our beloved status in God's household; this, though, needs to be put on, literally each day as we awake to consider the wonder of God in all His grace and truth. Just as we are to put on the whole armor of God (Eph 6:11), so we are to do so with our Positional Blessings. And we put these on through and as part of our Living Devotion to God. But as Paul indicates here, this is a deliberate act that requires attention and diligence. This becomes imperative in both our eyes and the Lord's when we consider that the act of the re-creation of ourselves, the "new man," itself emanates from God's "true righteousness and holiness." To think otherwise, is to think in a manner that is contrary to God's own way of thinking. This style of thinking is referred to in Scripture as being carnally minded and is the opposite of the mind of Christ, for "to be carnally minded is death, but to be spiritually minded is life and peace" (Rom 8:6)—for Jesus Christ is life and the Author of life and the Prince of Peace.

To be spiritually minded is life and peace—who would not want this? It is means to enjoy the fruit of our Positional Blessings, to live and have peace; to live as if we have been saved and have peace with God is to be spiritually minded. This is to focus on that which is above and upon that which concerns God in order that we can have comfort as we trust in God in our lives—so that we do not need to be anxious, for anxiousness is the opposite of being spiritually minded. And this spiritual mind is the fruit of devotion, in both its acts and its being. For it becomes full immersion into Christ, since to live with the sure and certain knowledge that there is nothing that can separate us from the love of God means that we can enjoy life with all its abundance for we have this mindset of belonging to God, being indwelled, and sealed for redemption. Indeed, our re-created selves have become so already in righteousness and holiness (see Eph 4:24 above)—we are already holy, as God is holy, and as such we are already separated out and are made righteous by Him through our faith in Christ. Our righteousness is therefore our right-standing with God through faith in Christ. Our practice and possession of righteousness, then, is our living within the covenant of God and benefitting from the privileges held within the new covenant in the form of its present and future bestowed blessings.

This changes everything, including what we regard as devotion. For to be spiritually minded is living with a mind that has been transformed by the Holy Spirit dwelling within us—our entire body, mind, and soul becoming a temple for the Holy Spirit to dwell in (Rom 12:1). For we are no longer ourselves but Christ who dwells in us, and when this is so, then we can say "to live is Christ" (Phil 1:21). The natural struggle, though, for all ordinary Christians with this concept is that it always leads to feelings of guilt and shame that we are never doing enough for Christ, or that our need to be in the workplace rather than, say, "on the mission field" makes us feel inferior and uncommitted, if we are being honest. What we have tried to explain is that this is not the way that Jesus sees it, for the fruit of righteousness is not guilt and condemnation, but peace, joy, and hope in the Holy Spirit. And as we are all "in the Holy Spirit" for He is in us, then the fruit of peace and righteous belongs to all believers. It is the fruit that grows on our position in Christ; it is the fruit of our salvation and is a part of our Positional Identity. To practice righteousness is to practice the life available to us within and through the Positional Blessings. And we are to pursue these blessings; in other words we are to go after them, to secure them, and capture them in our hearts so that we can stand on them and the truth that they have for us when we need to nurture our souls or to embattle the world against us when need be. The pursuit, then, of peace and righteousness is the pursuit of these blessings with the help of the Holy Spirit within us—a pursuit that will only be completed when God Himself makes us like Him and when all things are perfected by Him. This then directly affects our entire being and perspective on everything in relation to our lives and devotion, for as Paul said to His beloved fellow believers in the Colossian church:

> If then you were raised with Christ, seek those things which are above, where Christ is, sitting at the right hand of God. Set your mind on things above, not on things on the earth. For you died, and your life is hidden with Christ in God. When Christ who is our life appears, then you also will appear with Him in glory. (Col 3:1–4)

What we have seemed to have lost in our modern world and our modern understanding of what it means to be Christian is that our relationship with God is based around joint encounters with shared sense of commonality and purpose. Modern Christianity has lost its direction because it no longer knows what it is for and for whom. We somehow have decided that God was created for us and our wellbeing rather than God so loving that world that He gave His only Son to save it and us. This is a complete vault farce of relationships. Somehow, we seem to have come to the conclusion that we, and our own lives, are not individually included in the plans and purposes of God, even if we think we know or care what they are. And even those that do know, or care, seem only to be concerned with the minutiae of theological deliberations, eschatological interpretations, or squabble about their "callings," commitment, and which so-called gifts they may or may not have. But in reality, all of that is just the means obscuring the goal. But the goal and the whole desire of God, as ever, remains the same—to have a people unto Himself. It is for us to discover this and for us to live as such: fully and undeservingly blessed by His riches of unlimited love and generosity through the life and work of Jesus Christ.

"Yes, but How?"

After all this, we are back at this question again. The question though, as always, is the one that all really seem to avoid, and by the grace of God I shall try not to. The question we all ask is, "Yes, but how?" We should never leave a discussion on devotion at the conceptual level for, to the everyday believer, this is totally unsatisfactory and unsatisfying at the same time; unless we do so, we are in fact no further forward as far as most people are concerned. It is true that we have through our discussion on the Precious Gates of Devotion tried to articulate methods and measures that can be used and undertaken to assist us in our devotional lives, but to be clear this is not Devotional Living. The clue to the answer to the question *how* is actually held within the word that has been chosen to describe the life of the Devotionist, *living*.

To ask *how* then is in fact the premature question that we all jump to in our haste and laziness. The real question that the Bible addresses is *why*; and this must be answered before we can even discuss the question *how*. So *how* is actually framed in answer to the question *who*: To whom are we devoted? And therefore our answer to *how* has to be contained within the question itself. If we are devoted to God who is living, and as such so must be all His attributes, then our devotion must be living too. It must encompass all things because everything was made through Jesus and for Him. When we see our devotion though this lens, or prism, then our devotion is living in a way that it is both alive and is life itself. And so, as we look upon that which concerns us, then it becomes what God is—God is living, and He is also beauty, love, and life. All these things are from God, and hence to absorb them, appropriate, and participate in them becomes the focus of our souls. Why? Because Living Devotion is appropriating the life in all its abundance that Jesus promised; Living Devotion is abiding with Christ and Living Devotion is oneness unbounded and unrestricted with the Father, Son, and Holy Spirit. All these Positional Blessings, as well as our very Positional Identity itself of course, are bequeathed to us by God Himself; hence absorbing them, participating in them, and coopting them produces devotion that is living, all-encompassing, and ultimately synonymous with life itself—as it was breathed into Adam at the first, so it is within us, living and breathing and calling out, "Abba, Father!" Living Devotion, then, is peace and oneness with God—it is living life in the full context and within the full enjoyment of boundless blessings. It is the full enjoyment of the incorruptible beauty of our intimacy and identity with Christ. In His words, if this were not true, He would have told us so—but it is true; and He, through the Holy Spirit, has laid it all before us within His Scriptures and through the teachings of the Holy Spirit in nature, history, Providence, and the displays of His sovereignty and power.

The answer to *how* is not in the specifics of the *what* and *when*, but in the heart and mind. It is in the continuous and permanent realignment of our hearts so that we do not just draw near to God but are already near, close, and in His presence continually. There is no longer any separation, no times of distance even in the midst of the everyday grind and worldly hostilities to our faith that we all endure, for God is with us always, everywhere. There is nowhere where He is not, for He is within us, all the time. Living Devotion is simply living and embracing this fact. He has said that He will never leave us nor forsake us and so this living becomes so comforted as we are ever present with the Lord who is our redeemer, our Savior, our constant help, our intercessor, our forgiver, and the Author and Finisher of our faith. Our devotion is living with the fact that He alone is wise and that He has authority over all things. It is truly living life as we truly know, believe, and understand that God Himself chose in His infinite generosity not only to die for us so that we can have eternal life but that through Him this eternal life already started the moment of our salvation. No one can remove it, no one can steal it from us for it was His alone to give to us—all we have to do is embrace this generosity and live life in accordance with these wonderful, bountiful, remarkable, and utterly undeserved Positional Blessings. This is our God and He is our Father, Son, and Holy Spirit. And all He wants is for us to be His people: forever living devotedly in our devotion to our most majestic God.

Full Identification Through Complete Immersion

> And whatever you do in word or deed, do all in the name of the Lord Jesus, giving thanks to God the Father through Him. . . . And whatever you do, do it heartily, as to the Lord and not to men, knowing that from the Lord you will receive the reward of the inheritance; for you serve the Lord Christ. (Col 3:17, 23–24)

> Finally, brethren, whatever things are true, whatever things are noble, whatever things are just, whatever things are pure, whatever things are lovely, whatever things are of good report, if

> there is any virtue and if there is anything praiseworthy—meditate on these things. The things which you learned and received and saw in me, these do, and the God of peace will be with you. (Phil 4:8–9)

This is full immersion, then, when our identity becomes fully in Christ. When all that we do becomes always unto the Lord (Col 3:17, 23–24), then we begin to absorb what true identification with God means. This does not mean, however, that we are all to give up our day jobs and normal lives to throw ourselves into ministry or missionary work—as loftily as these ideals are promoted and presented to us—but means that in all humility, we are to dedicate and devote our thoughts and actions to Him and to live according to our position in Christ as best we can, always looking for His soon return and longing to be in His presence ever more. And yet, in the meantime, our role as His people is simply to live and to enjoy the abundant life He has given us through Him, to immerse ourselves in our faith and be obsessively dedicated to our devotion of Him and for Him. For then we learn to know, accept, and embrace that all we are required to do, every day, is to heed the advice of Jude 21 and keep ourselves "in the love of God, looking for the mercy of our Lord Jesus Christ unto eternal life": becoming and being the people of God that He longs for and deserves.

When the dreaded Monday morning comes, then, we instead look in the mirror and (inspired by the words of the Angel Gabriel to Joseph in Luke 1:21) look back at ourselves and say, "Through the grace of God and belief in perfect sacrifice of Jesus, I am a member of the household of the Almighty; I am a child of God and citizen of heaven; I am indwelled and sealed by the Holy Spirt and already have the eternal life that can never, and will never be, removed. Of this I am certain because of Jesus, and because of Jesus there is nothing and no one under heaven and earth that can separate me from the love of God; and because of this I am certain that I have peace with God and am able to now live abundantly with and connected to Him. When I fail, there will be no condemnation, for He knows my frailties but will love me nonetheless and will restore both me and my soul, to give us rest and comfort when all around us seems so frail and broken, for I know that He is always with me and will never leave me or forsake me, not because of anything I do or have done but because of who He is and what He has said and what He does. I am beautifully considered to be part of the bride of Christ whom He will one day receive unto Himself, and thus I will be ever with Him. And in the meantime, I dedicate myself to Him who alone is worthy of all honor and praise, love and gratitude." And then carry on with the rest of our days in peace and with the confidence in Christ that can only come from fully embracing the beautiful gifts of our Positional Identity, always looking to the Lord for comfort and always aware of His presence and Providence in our lives. Thereby we will be living in the Reality of God as Devotionists, without compulsion and unnecessary complications but with hope and certainty in our future and in His never-ending and never-failing love: a love that is secured through His power and embedded within each and every one of us who believe—no caveats, no hidden conditions, no extras that need to be attained and worked for, just unfailing grace, unmitigated mercy, undeserved favor, and incomprehensible generosity.

> Now may the God of hope fill you with all joy and peace in believing, that you may abound in hope by the power of the Holy Spirit. (Rom 15:13)

Conclusion
The Glorious Tapestry of Living Devotion

POSITIONAL DEVOTION CAN BE likened to a gift from God that He has preprepared for every single believer to receive and own upon their salvation. It is up to the believer to accept this gift and to enjoy to the full its contents—for they bring life, peace, comfort, and confidence in our status in God. Sadly, though, too few unwrap the gift of our Positional Blessings, let alone unravel the tapestry to appreciate its depth and vividness. Too few are even aware of the existence of these blessings in the first place and hence are hampered in their growth in devotion, knowledge, and understanding of the ways of God that are so crucial to our lives as Christians. We hope that this discourse will go partway there to help us all take ourselves and others in hand and genuinely encourage ourselves, and provoke others, to discover that the psalmist was telling the truth when he implores us to "taste and see that the Lord is good" (Ps 34:8). For He is and we should.

This gift can be likened to an intricate tapestry depicting the beauty of divine love, grace, and the magnificence of unparalleled generosity. The metaphor of likening devotion to a tapestry is even more vivid when one considers the talent, the time, the creativity, and the dedication it takes to create such an object of beauty. Indeed, the metaphor extends even further when one thinks that the purpose of a tapestry is not beauty for its own sake, but it has function too; it has durability and strength and is to provide warmth, as well as being a means to portray in intricate detail a message or depiction of something that has value and meaning to its creator, that are conveyed to those who look upon it and who are involved in its formulation. This tapestry is unique, though, for it is divinely made, for within it every believer can interweave their own golden thread of devotion; hence, the tapestry itself becomes ever expanding, ever more beautiful, as each believer's thread is added—and so it becomes alive and is thus called the "Beautiful Tapestry of Living Devotion."

Within this tapestry is depicted in its fullness the splendor of all that God has achieved for the believer by the death and resurrection of Jesus—it shows what is available to every believer to be gazed upon in awe, gratitude, and above all love. Hence, this is all the more poignant when we consider Living Devotion as a tapestry not just because of who wove it and how each thread is so expertly interwoven or for whom it was given, but because of its function as a means to draw the beholder closer to God so that they, too, become part of the picture, part of the very fabric of what is being portrayed in and through the tapestry: the people of God.

The tapestry depicts the fullness of blessed Positional Blessings that have been granted to every believer. The picture is multilayered and multidimensional—it has to be, for each element is integrated and dependent upon the other. And at the same time, each element builds in layers of beauty as it portrays something of such great worth that only a divine mind could have conceived it. When we look upon it as a whole, in its entirety, its utter magnificence is beyond compare and beyond what is conceivable to our finite minds. And when we do try to describe it, to view it as a whole and to define it, we fumble for lack of sufficient celestial vocabulary to do so; instead, our souls step in for us and simply respond in the perfect, heavenly language of love: *Abba, Father!*

Perhaps we can also envisage the tapestry depicting the people of God entering through the Precious Gates of Devotion into the presence of God and a life of Living Devotion. Above these Precious Gates, the tapestry shows that these words are written in ruby-red thread, the color of the deepest wine from the vineyard of God in remembrance of the priceless cup of Christ, from which He drank so deeply that all might believe and that those who do, have eternal life:

> Behold, the tabernacle of God is with men, and He will dwell with them, and they shall be His people. God Himself will be with them and be their God. And God will wipe away every tear from their eyes; there shall be no more death, nor sorrow, nor

crying. There shall be no more pain, for the former things have passed away. (Rev 21:3–4)

Perhaps this portion of the tapestry might have multiple layers and sections that portray how the Lord has taken His beloved children by the hand and is revealing to them what they mean to Him as He welcomes them into His household, permanently. As He does so, He's pictured bestowing upon them His unconditional blessings in the form of their new Positional Identity. Perhaps there is one layer that is threaded to reveal their translated status from being once His enemies living in darkness and beholden to their sinful natures, to now newly recreated, born again, and beloved citizens of heaven. Perhaps another layer would reveal the believer's renewed condition of having peace, hope, and full security in and with God. And yet another layer would show to the awe and wonder of the believers, and to the awestruck angels looking on, how through the perfect sacrifice of God Himself, the believer has been given eternal life and will one day become one with the Father and the Son. The final portion of this section would show the believer bowing in abject adoration and gratitude before the Lord as the Positional Blessings are being so generously bestowed in such divine abundance. As these blessings are being gifted, the tapestry depicts the astonished believer exclaiming in such incredulity words that are embroidered in the most exquisite lettering made from the Golden Threads of Devotion—and what these words declare is the believer's only reasonable response to the gift of such blessings:

> *Behold what manner of love the Father has bestowed on us,*
> *that we should be called children of God!* (1 John 3:1)

Appendix

The Blessed Positional Blessings

Passages for Reflective Reading, Lectio Divina, and Private Prayer

Comfort, yes, comfort My people!
ISAIAH 40:1

Let not your heart be troubled, neither be afraid.
JOHN 14:27

ONE OF THE MOST amazing aspects of Christianity are the Positional Blessings that have been gifted to us by God, upon the very instance of salvation. An understanding of these blessings is essential, vital even, for the Christian, for in order to be effective in our witness and in our walk with God, we must be sure of the foundation upon which we stand. It is essential for us to realize and yet so easy for us to forget and to return to struggling in our way and in our own strength—this book has sought to address this.

We would refer you back to the section in part 1 titled "Positional Identity and Positional Blessings" for the exposition and explanation of these Positional Blessings, and to the sections in part 3 on Lectio Divina and private prayer, for the texts that we have set forth below are meant to serve as a guide to assist you in your considerations of the enormity of

God's grace, mercy, and generosity to us as believers. They can be used as a means of contemplation as individual texts, in subject groups, and of course as a whole—my hope is that by doing so, you will "let the peace of God rule in your hearts" in order that you will also "let the word of Christ dwell in you richly in all wisdom" (Col 3:15–16).

The following passages can be used for study and further consideration, as well as for Lectio Divina and private prayer, and are by no means exhaustive. I am sure there will be many others that you'll come across that you will wish to personalize and different categories that you will wish to add—or at least I hope you do. In the meantime, as you use this book and these passages and share them with others, my prayer is that you and they first come before the Lord in your times of devotion to seek Him and to "ask that you may be filled with the knowledge of His will in all wisdom and spiritual understanding; that you may walk worthy of the Lord, fully pleasing Him, being fruitful in every good work and increasing in the knowledge of God; strengthened with all might, according to His glorious power, for all patience and longsuffering with joy; giving thanks to the Father who has qualified us to be partakers of the inheritance of the saints in the light" (Col 1:9–12).

The Transfigurative and Transformative Positional Blessings

Read, contemplate, and digest with awe and wonder at the mercy, grace, and loving-kindness of our God—for you know that as you "draw near to God and He *will* draw near to you" (Jas 4:8, emphasis mine). Notice the tenses of the verbs and the unconditional status of the statements, and through this, our hope, trust, and confidence in Christ will grow ever greater and more assured.

- John 15:11

    These things I have spoken to you, that My joy may remain in you, and that your joy may be full.

- Romans 14:17

    For the kingdom of God is not eating and drinking, but righteousness and peace and joy in the Holy Spirit.

The Transfigurative Positional Blessings

You Are Saved by God Alone, According to His Purposes and by His Ordained Means

- Titus 3:4–7

    When the kindness and the love of God our Savior toward man appeared, not by works of righteousness which we have done, but according to His mercy He saved us, through the washing of regeneration and renewing of the Holy Spirit, whom He poured out on us abundantly through Jesus Christ our Savior, that having been justified by His grace we should become heirs according to the hope of eternal life.

- Ephesians 2:8–10

    For by grace you have been saved through faith, and that not of yourselves; it is the gift of God, not of works, lest anyone should boast. For we are His workmanship, created in Christ Jesus for good works, which God prepared beforehand that we should walk in them.

Because of Your Faith in Jesus, You Are Declared to Be Righteous in the Eyes of God

- Romans 3:24

    Being justified freely by His grace through the redemption that is in Christ Jesus . . .

- Romans 5:18–19

    Therefore, as through one man's offense judgment came to all men, resulting in condemnation, even so through one Man's righteous act the free gift came to all men, resulting in justification of life. For as by one man's disobedience many were made sinners, so also by one Man's obedience many will be made righteous.

- Philippians 3:8–11

    Yet indeed I also count all things loss for the excellence of the knowledge of Christ Jesus my Lord, for whom I have suffered the loss of all things, and count them as rubbish, that I may gain Christ and be found in Him, not having my own righteousness, which is from the law, but that which is through faith in Christ, the righteousness which is from God by faith; that I may know Him and the power of His resurrection, and the fellowship of His sufferings, being conformed to His death, if, by any means, I may attain to the resurrection from the dead.

Recreated Upon Salvation—Being Born Again

- John 3:3

    Jesus answered and said to him, "Most assuredly, I say to you, unless one is born again, he cannot see the kingdom of God."

- 1 Peter 1:3–5

    Blessed be the God and Father of our Lord Jesus Christ, who according to His abundant mercy has begotten us again to a living hope through the resurrection of Jesus Christ from the dead, to an inheritance incorruptible and undefiled and that does not fade away, reserved in heaven for you, who are kept by the power of God through faith for salvation ready to be revealed in the last time.

- 1 Peter 1:22–23

    Since you have purified your souls in obeying the truth through the Spirit in sincere love of the brethren, love one another fervently with a pure heart, having been born again, not of corruptible seed but incorruptible, through the word of God which lives and abides forever.

- 2 Corinthians 5:17

    Therefore, if anyone is in Christ, he is a new creation; old things have passed away; behold, all things have become new.

Indwelled by the Holy Spirit

- John 14:16–17

    And I will pray the Father, and He will give you another Helper, that He may abide with you forever—the Spirit of truth, whom the world cannot receive, because it neither sees Him nor knows Him; but you know Him, for He dwells with you and will be in you.

- Romans 8:9

    But you are not in the flesh but in the Spirit, if indeed the Spirit of God dwells in you. Now if anyone does not have the Spirit of Christ, he is not His.

- 1 Corinthians 3:16

    Do you not know that you are the temple of God and that the Spirit of God dwells in you?

Sealed by the Holy Spirit

- Ephesians 4:30

    And do not grieve the Holy Spirit of God, by whom you were sealed for the day of redemption.

- Ephesians 1:13–14

    In Him you also trusted, after you heard the word of truth, the gospel of your salvation; in whom also, having believed, you were sealed with the Holy Spirit of promise, who is the guarantee of our inheritance until the redemption of the purchased possession, to the praise of His glory.

Familial Repositioning

You Are a Child of God

- John 1:12–13

    But as many as received Him, to them He gave the right to become children of God, to those who believe in His name: who were born, not of blood, nor of the will of the flesh, nor of the will of man, but of God.

- 1 John 3:1

    Behold what manner of love the Father has bestowed on us, that we should be called children of God!

You Are a Member of the Household of God

- Ephesians 2:19–22

    Now, therefore, you are no longer strangers and foreigners, but fellow citizens with the saints and members of the household of God, having been built on the foundation of the apostles and prophets, Jesus Christ Himself being the chief cornerstone, in whom the whole building, being fitted together, grows into a holy temple in the Lord, in whom you also are being built together for a dwelling place of God in the Spirit.

We Are Heirs

- Romans 8:16–17

    The Spirit Himself bears witness with our spirit that we are children of God, and if children, then heirs—heirs of God and joint heirs with Christ, if indeed we suffer with Him, that we may also be glorified together.

- Galatians 4:7

    Therefore you are no longer a slave but a son, and if a son, then an heir of God through Christ.

- Titus 3:4–7

    But when the kindness and the love of God our Savior toward man appeared, not by works of righteousness which we have done, but according to His mercy He saved us, through the washing of regeneration and renewing of the Holy Spirit, whom He poured out on us abundantly through Jesus Christ our Savior, that having been justified by His grace we should become heirs according to the hope of eternal life.

- 1 Peter 1:3–5

    Blessed be the God and Father of our Lord Jesus Christ, who according to His abundant mercy has begotten us again to a living hope through the resurrection of Jesus Christ from the dead, to an inheritance incorruptible and undefiled and that does not fade away, reserved in heaven for you, who are kept by the power of God through faith for salvation ready to be revealed in the last time.

All Believers Are Equal in the Eyes of God

- 1 Corinthians 12:27

    Now you are the body of Christ, and members individually.

- Romans 10:12

    For there is no distinction between Jew and Greek, for the same Lord over all is rich to all who call upon Him.

- Galatians 3:26–28

    For you are all sons of God through faith in Christ Jesus. For as many of you as were baptized into Christ have put on Christ. There is neither Jew nor Greek, there is neither slave nor free, there is neither male nor female; for you are all one in Christ Jesus.

- Colossians 3:9–11

    Do not lie to one another, since you have put off the old man with his deeds, and have put on the new man who is renewed in knowledge according to the image of Him who created him, where there is neither Greek nor Jew, circumcised nor uncircumcised, barbarian, Scythian, slave nor free, but Christ is all and in all.

- Romans 12:3–5

    For I say, through the grace given to me, to everyone who is among you, not to think of himself more highly than he ought to think, but to think soberly, as God has dealt to each one a measure of faith. For as we have many members in one body, but all the members do not have the same function, so we, being many, are one body in Christ, and individually members of one another.

You Are a Citizen of Heaven

- Philippians 3:20

    For our citizenship is in heaven, from which we also eagerly wait for the Savior, the Lord Jesus Christ.

- Luke 10:20

    Nevertheless do not rejoice in this, that the spirits are subject to you, but rather rejoice because your names are written in heaven.

- 2 Corinthians 5:1–2

    For we know that if our earthly house, this tent, is destroyed, we have a building from God, a house not made with hands, eternal in the heavens. For in this we groan, earnestly desiring to be clothed with our habitation which is from heaven.

The Transformative Positional Blessings

Upon salvation the Scriptures declare our position with God as having been transformed so that all who believe should know that they now have these blessings:

Eternal Life

- John 3:14–16

    And as Moses lifted up the serpent in the wilderness, even so must the Son of Man be lifted up, that whoever believes in Him should [a]not perish but have eternal life. For God so loved the world that He gave His only begotten Son, that whoever believes in Him should not perish but have everlasting life.

- John 3:36

    He who believes in the Son has everlasting life; and he who does not believe the Son shall not see life, but the wrath of God abides on him.

- John 5:24

    Most assuredly, I say to you, he who hears My word and believes in Him who sent Me has everlasting life, and shall not come into judgment, but has passed from death into life.

- 1 John 2:25

    And this is the promise that He has promised us—eternal life.

- 1 John 5:11–13, 20

    And this is the testimony: that God has given us eternal life, and this life is in His Son. He who has the Son has life; he who does not have the Son of God does not have life. These things I have written to you who believe in the name of the Son of God, that you may know that you have eternal life, and that you may continue to believe in the name of the Son of God. . . .

    And we know that the Son of God has come and has given us an understanding, that we may know Him who is true; and we are in Him who is true, in His Son Jesus Christ. This is the true God and eternal life.

- John 10:28

    And I give them eternal life, and they shall never perish; neither shall anyone snatch them out of My hand.

- John 17:3

    And this is eternal life, that they may know You, the only true God, and Jesus Christ whom You have sent.

Reconciliation to God and Being Above Reproach in His Sight

- Romans 5:10–11

    For if when we were enemies we were reconciled to God through the death of His Son, much more, having been reconciled, we shall be saved by His life. And not only that, but we also rejoice in God through our Lord Jesus Christ, through whom we have now received the reconciliation.

- Colossians 1:21–22

    And you, who once were alienated and enemies in your mind by wicked works, yet now He has reconciled in the body of His flesh through death, to present you holy, and blameless, and above reproach in His sight.

Having Been Redeemed and Purchased by God

- 1 Corinthians 6:19–20

    Or do you not know that your body is the temple of the Holy Spirit who is in you, whom you have from God, and you are not your own? For you were bought at a price; therefore glorify God in your body and in your spirit, which are God's.

- 1 Peter 1:17–19

    And if you call on the Father, who without partiality judges according to each one's work, conduct yourselves throughout the time of your stay here in fear; knowing that you were not redeemed with corruptible things, like silver or gold, from your aimless conduct received by tradition from your fathers, but with the precious blood of Christ, as of a lamb without blemish and without spot.

Redemption Through His Blood and Forgiveness

- Colossians 2:13

  And you, being dead in your trespasses and the uncircumcision of your flesh, He has made alive together with Him, having forgiven you all trespasses.

Having Been Washed and Cleansed

- 1 Corinthians 6:11

  And such were some of you. But you were washed, but you were sanctified, but you were justified in the name of the Lord Jesus and by the Spirit of our God.

Peace with and Access to God

- Romans 5:1–2

  Therefore, having been justified by faith, we have peace with God through our Lord Jesus Christ, through whom also we have access by faith into this grace in which we stand, and rejoice in hope of the glory of God.

No Condemnation from God

- Romans 8:1

  There is therefore now no condemnation to those who are in Christ Jesus, who do not walk according to the flesh, but according to the Spirit.

The Privileges of Access

We Are Able to Come Boldly into the Presence of God

- Hebrews 4:16

    Let us therefore come boldly to the throne of grace, that we may obtain mercy and find grace to help in time of need.

- Ephesians 2:18

    For through Him we both have access by one Spirit to the Father.

- Ephesians 3:11–12

    According to the eternal purpose which He accomplished in Christ Jesus our Lord, in whom we have boldness and access with confidence through faith in Him.

We Have Been Given Every Spiritual Blessing

- Ephesians 1:3

    Blessed be the God and Father of our Lord Jesus Christ, who has blessed us with every spiritual blessing in the heavenly places in Christ.

- 1 Corinthians 3:21–23

    Therefore let no one boast in men. For all things are yours: whether Paul or Apollos or Cephas, or the world or life or death, or things present or things to come—all are yours. And you are Christ's, and Christ is God's.

We Are Now Able to Walk Worthy and to Lay Hold of That Which Jesus Has Done

- Ephesians 4:1–6

    I, therefore, the prisoner of the Lord, beseech you to walk worthy of the calling with which you were called, with all lowliness and gentleness, with longsuffering, bearing with one another in love, endeavoring to keep the unity of the Spirit in the bond of peace. There is one body and one Spirit, just as you were called in one hope of your calling; one Lord, one faith, one baptism; one God and Father of all, who is above all, and through all, and in you all.

- Philippians 3:12–14

    Not that I have already attained, or am already perfected; but I press on, that I may lay hold of that for which Christ Jesus has also laid hold of me. Brethren, I do not count myself to have apprehended; but one thing I do, forgetting those things which are behind and reaching forward to those things which are ahead, I press toward the goal for the prize of the upward call of God in Christ Jesus.

We Have No Need to Be Anxious of the Future That Prevents Our Times of Devotion and Removes Our Peace

- Philippians 4:6–7

    Be anxious for nothing, but in everything by prayer and supplication, with thanksgiving, let your requests be made known to God; and the peace of God, which surpasses all understanding, will guard your hearts and minds through Christ Jesus.

We Can Finally Focus on What Matters to God

- Romans 12:1–2

    I beseech you therefore, brethren, by the mercies of God, that you present your bodies a living sacrifice, holy, acceptable to God, which is your reasonable service. And do not be conformed to this world, but be transformed by the renewing of your mind, that you may prove what is that good and acceptable and perfect will of God.

- Colossians 3:1–4

    If then you were raised with Christ, seek those things which are above, where Christ is, sitting at the right hand of God. Set your mind on things above, not on things on the earth. For you died, and your life is hidden with Christ in God. When Christ who is our life appears, then you also will appear with Him in glory.

- Philippians 4:8

    Finally, brethren, whatever things are true, whatever things are noble, whatever things are just, whatever things are pure, whatever things are lovely, whatever things are of good report, if there is any virtue and if there is anything praiseworthy—meditate on these things.

And We Know That Our Future Is Assured and That We Are Eternally Secure in Jesus Christ

- Romans 8:37–39

    Yet in all these things we are more than conquerors through Him who loved us. For I am persuaded that neither death nor life, nor angels nor principalities nor powers, nor things present nor things to come, nor height nor depth, nor any other created thing, shall be able to separate us from the love of God which is in Christ Jesus our Lord.

Bibliography

Balla, George E. *The Four Centuries Between the Testaments: A Survey of Israel and the Diaspora 336 BC to 94 AD*. Vallejo, CA: BIBAL, 1993.

Bowsher, Clive. *Life in the Son: Exploring Participation and Union with Christ in John's Gospel and Letters*. London: Apollos, 2023.

Brother Lawrence. *The Practice of the Presence of God with Spiritual Maxims*. Grand Rapids: Spire, 1967.

Callahan, James Patrick. *Primitivist Piety: The Ecclesiology of the Early Plymouth Brethren*. Lanhan, MD: Scarecrow, 1996.

Constable, Thomas L. *Talking to God: What the Bible Teaches About Prayer*. Grand Rapids: Baker, 1995.

Edersheim, Alfred. *The Life and Times of Jesus the Messiah*. Peabody, MA: Hendrickson, 2009.

Elwell, Walter A., ed. *Evangelical Dictionary of Biblical Theology*. Grand Rapids: Baker, 1996.

Fruchtenbaum, Arnold. *The Messianic Jewish Epistles: Hebrews, James, First Peter, Second Peter, Jude*. San Antonio, TX: Ariel Ministries, 2005.

———. *Thirty-Three Things: A Study on Positional Truth*. San Antonio, TX: Ariel Ministries, 1985. https://arielcontent.org/dcs/pdf/mbs110m.pdf.

———. *The Three Messianic Miracles*. Tustin, CA: Ariel Ministries, 1993.

Gorman, Michael J. *Inhabiting the Cruciform God: Kenosis, Justification and Theosis in Paul's Narrative Soteriology*. Grand Rapids: Eerdmans, 2009.

Hilton, Walter. *The Ladder of Perfection*. New York: Penguin, 1988.

Kaiser, Walter C. *The Majesty of God in the Old Testament*. Grand Rapids: Baker Academic, 2007.

———. *Toward an Exegetical Theology*. Grand Rapids: Baker Academic, 1981.

Law, William. *A Serious Call to a Devout and Holy Life*. Peabody, MA: Hendrickson, 2009.

Matarasso, Pauline, ed. *The Cistercian World: Monastic Writings of the Twelfth Century*. New York: Penguin, 1993.

McLaughlin, Rebecca. *Jesus Through the Eyes of Women: How the First Female Disciples Help Us Know and Love the Lord*. Austin, TX: Gospel Coalition, 2022.

Metaxas, Eric. *Bonhoeffer: Pastor, Martyr, Prophet, Spy*. Nashville: Nelson, 2010.

Murray, Iain H. *J. C. Ryle: Prepared to Stand Alone*. Edinburgh: Banner of Truth Trust, 2016.

———. *Wesley and the Men Who Followed*. Edinburgh: Banner of Truth Trust, 2003.

Nee, Watchman. *The Normal Christian Life*. Colorado Springs, CO: Cook, 2003.

Newman, John Henry. *Apologie Pro Vita Sua*. New York: Penguin, 1994.

Newton, John. *Collected Letters*. Edited by Halcyon Backhouse. London: Hodder & Stoughton, 1989.

Rolle, Richard. *Richard Rolle Collection: 2 Books*. London: Aeterna, 2016.

Ross, Allen P. *Holiness to the Lord: A Guide to the Exposition of the Book of Leviticus*. Grand Rapids: Baker Academic, 2002.

Ryle, John Charles. *Holiness*. Darlington, UK: Evangelical Press, 1979.

Ryrie, Charles C. *A Survey of Bible Doctrine*. Chicago: Moody, 1972.

Shakespeare, William. *William Shakespeare: The Complete Works*. Edited by Alfred Harbage. New York: Viking, 1977.

Spurgeon, C. H. *According to Promise: God's Promises to Every Christian*. Fearn, UK: Christian Focus, 2001.

Strong, James. *The Strongest Strong's: Exhaustive Concordance of the Bible*. Revised and corrected by John R. Kohlenberger III and James A. Swanson. Grand Rapids: Zondervan, 2001.

Thomas à Kempis. *The Imitation of Christ*. New York: Random House, 1984.

Thornton, John F., and Susan B. Varennem, eds. *Honey and Salt: Selected Spiritual Writings of Saint Bernard of Clairvaux*. New York: Vintage, 2007.

Tozer, A. W. *The Crucified Life: How to Live Out a Deeper Christian Experience*. Bloomington, MN: Bethany House, 2014.

Vauchez, André. *Francis of Assisi: The Life and Afterlife of a Medieval Saint*. Translated by Michael F. Cusato. London: Yale University Press, 2012.

Virkler, Henry A., and Karelynne Gerber Ayayo. *Hermeneutics: Principles and Processes of Biblical Interpretation*. Grand Rapids: Baker, 1981.

Walvoord, John F. *The Holy Spirit: A Comprehensive Study of the Person and Work of the Holy Spirit*. Grand Rapids: Zondervan, 1991.

Walvoord, John F., and Roy B. Zuck, eds. *The Bible Knowledge Commentary*. 2 vols. Colorado Springs, CO: Cook Communications Ministries, 2004.

Wilberforce, William. *Real Christianity: Contrasted with the Prevailing Religious System*. Glasgow, UK: Pickering & Inglis, 1983.

Wilken, Robert Louis. *The Spirit of Early Christian Thought*. London: Yale University Press, 2003.

Wilson, Marvin R. *Our Father Abraham: Jewish Roots of the Christian Faith*. Grand Rapids: Eerdmans, 1989.

www.ingramcontent.com/pod-product-compliance
Lightning Source LLC
Chambersburg PA
CBHW070233230426
43664CB00014B/2283